Moral Issues

Chicago Studies in American Politics

A SERIES EDITED BY SUSAN HERBST, LAWRENCE R. JACOBS, ADAM J. BERINSKY, AND FRANCES LEE; BENJAMIN I. PAGE, EDITOR EMERITUS

Also in the series:

THE ROOTS OF POLARIZATION: FROM THE RACIAL REALIGNMENT TO THE CULTURE WARS *by Neil A. O'Brian*

SOME WHITE FOLKS: THE INTERRACIAL POLITICS OF SYMPATHY, SUFFERING, AND SOLIDARITY *by Jennifer Chudy*

THROUGH THE GRAPEVINE: SOCIALLY TRANSMITTED INFORMATION AND DISTORTED DEMOCRACY *by Taylor N. Carlson*

AMERICA'S NEW RACIAL BATTLE LINES: PROTECT VERSUS REPAIR *by Rogers M. Smith and Desmond King*

PARTISAN HOSTILITY AND AMERICAN DEMOCRACY *by James N. Druckman, Samara Klar, Yanna Krupnikov, Matthew Levendusky, and John Barry Ryan*

RESPECT AND LOATHING IN AMERICAN DEMOCRACY: POLARIZATION, MORALIZATION, AND THE UNDERMINING OF EQUALITY *by Jeff Spinner-Halev and Elizabeth Theiss-Morse*

COUNTERMOBILIZATION: POLICY FEEDBACK AND BACKLASH IN A POLARIZED AGE *by Eric M. Patashnik*

RACE, RIGHTS, AND RIFLES: THE ORIGINS OF THE NRA AND CONTEMPORARY GUN CULTURE *by Alexandra Filindra*

ACCOUNTABILITY IN STATE LEGISLATURES *by Steven Rogers*

OUR COMMON BONDS: USING WHAT AMERICANS SHARE TO HELP BRIDGE THE PARTISAN DIVIDE *by Matthew Levendusky*

DYNAMIC DEMOCRACY: PUBLIC OPINION, ELECTIONS, AND POLICYMAKING IN THE AMERICAN STATES *by Devin Caughey and Christopher Warshaw*

PERSUASION IN PARALLEL: HOW INFORMATION CHANGES MINDS ABOUT POLITICS *by Alexander Coppock*

Additional series titles follow index.

Moral Issues

How Public Opinion on Abortion and Gay Rights Affects American Religion and Politics

PAUL GOREN AND
CHRISTOPHER CHAPP

THE UNIVERSITY OF CHICAGO PRESS   CHICAGO AND LONDON

The University of Chicago Press, Chicago 60637
The University of Chicago Press, Ltd., London
© 2024 by The University of Chicago
All rights reserved. No part of this book may be used or reproduced in any manner whatsoever without written permission, except in the case of brief quotations in critical articles and reviews. For more information, contact the University of Chicago Press, 1427 E. 60th St., Chicago, IL 60637.
Published 2024
Printed in the United States of America

33 32 31 30 29 28 27 26 25 24   1 2 3 4 5

ISBN-13: 978-0-226-83665-2 (cloth)
ISBN-13: 978-0-226-83667-6 (paper)
ISBN-13: 978-0-226-83666-9 (e-book)
DOI: https://doi.org/10.7208/chicago/9780226836669.001.0001

Library of Congress Cataloging-in-Publication Data

Names: Goren, Paul, author. | Chapp, Christopher B., 1979– author.
Title: Moral issues : how public opinion on abortion and gay rights affects American religion and politics / Paul Goren and Christopher Chapp.
Other titles: Chicago studies in American politics.
Description: Chicago ; London : The University of Chicago Press, 2024. |
Series: Chicago studies in American politics | Includes bibliographical references and index.
Identifiers: LCCN 2024020865 | ISBN 9780226836652 (cloth) | ISBN 9780226836676 (paperback) | ISBN 9780226836669 (e-book)
Subjects: LCSH: Abortion—United States—Public opinion. | Gay rights—United States—Public opinion. | Values—Political aspects—United States. | Culture conflict—Political aspects—United States. | Public opinion—United States. | Mass media and public opinion—United States. | Religion and politics—United States. | United States—Politics and government—1989–
Classification: LCC HQ767.5.U5 G67 2024 | DDC 362.1988/800973—dc23/eng/20240514
LC record available at https://lccn.loc.gov/2024020865

♾ This paper meets the requirements of ANSI/NISO Z39.48-1992 (Permanence of Paper).

Contents

List of Figures   vii

List of Tables   ix

CHAPTER 1.   Moral Hunches   1

CHAPTER 2.   The Theory of Moral Power   16

CHAPTER 3.   Moral Messaging   39

CHAPTER 4.   Moral Emotions and Attitude Stability   70

CHAPTER 5.   Stand Patters, Switchers, and Collective Opinion   85

CHAPTER 6.   Moral Issues and Religious Disaffiliation   99

CHAPTER 7.   Moral Issues and Party Change   125

CHAPTER 8.   Abortion, Gay Rights, and American Politics   152

Acknowledgments   167

Appendixes   171

Notes   187

Bibliography   197

Index   217

Figures

Figure 3.1 Moral issues in party platforms, 1972–2020 / 50

Figure 3.2 News content by story type, 1980–2022 / 52

Figure 3.3 Moral issues on television, 1980–2022 / 55

Figure 3.4 Moral issues on congressional campaign websites, 2008–2022 / 58

Figure 3.5 Moral issue billboards in three states, 2014–2018 / 60

Figure 3.6 Political sermons by issue type, 2000–2020 / 61

Figure 3.7 Moral emotions in the news, 1980–2022 / 63

Figure 3.8 Moral emotions on campaign websites, 2008–2022 / 64

Figure 3.9 Moral emotions in party platforms, 1972–2020 / 65

Figure 3.10 Moral emotions in congressional speeches, 1989–2014 / 66

Figure 3.11 Moral emotions in Christian sermons, by issue type, 2000–2020 / 67

Figure 4.1 Public opinion on moral issues, NES data / 73

Figure 4.2 Public opinion on moral issues, GSS and PALS data / 74

Figure 4.3 Disgust sensitivity predicts moral issue conservatism, 2012 and 2016 CCES data / 77

Figure 4.4 Continuity correlations in seven panel studies / 82

Figure 5.1 Public opinion on abortion, same-sex relationships, and gay marriage over time / 88

Figure 5.2 Decomposing change in collective opinion on gay rights / 90

Figure 5.3 Support for gay rights, by birth cohort and year / 91

Figure 5.4 Support for abortion rights, by birth cohort and year / 92

VIII   LIST OF FIGURES

Figure 5.5   Stand patters and switchers on moral issues / 94

Figure 5.6   Mismatched and consistent moral issue opinions across
             panel waves / 97

Figure 6.1   The rise of the nones, 1972–2021 / 100

Figure 6.2   Forest plot summarizing the effects of religious ID and
             moral issues on each other / 115

Figure 6.3   Public opinion on moral issues predicts religious exit,
             2010–2014 / 117

Figure 6.4   Forest plot summarizing the effects of religious ID strength
             and moral issues on each other / 120

Figure 6.5   The relationship between religious ID strength and moral
             issues, 2008–2012 / 121

Figure 7.1   Strong Democrats and strong Republicans became polarized
             on moral issues, 1984–2018 / 126

Figure 7.2   Headlines with political signals / 133

Figure 7.3   Forest plot summarizing the effects of party ID and moral
             issues on each other / 141

Figure 7.4   The relationship between party ID and moral issues,
             1992–1996 / 143

Figure 7.5   The relationship between party ID and moral issues,
             2016–2020 / 145

Figure 8.1   The rise of the nones within different moral camps,
             1977–2021 / 158

Figure 8.2   Moral camps in the parties, 1977–2021 / 160

Tables

Table 7.1   Partisan stand patters and switchers / 139

Table 7.2   Movement from moral progressivism to moral conservatism predicts change in categorical party ID / 146

Table A4.3 Disgust sensitivity predicts moral issues, 2012 and 2016 CCES data / 174

Table A5.1 Linear decomposition of intracohort change and cohort succession / 175

Table A6.1 The impact of religious ID_{t-1} on moral $issues_t$, OLS estimates / 175

Table A6.2 The impact of moral $issues_{t-1}$ on religious ID_t, logistic regression estimates / 176

Table A6.3 The impact of moral $issues_{t-1}$ on religious ID_t with controls for party ID_{t-1} and liberal-conservative ID_{t-1}, logistic regression estimates / 177

Table A6.4 The impact of moral $issues_{t-1}$ on religious ID_t with additional controls, 2010–2014 GSS, logistic regression estimates / 178

Table A6.5 The impact of moral $issues_{t-1}$ on religious ID_t with additional controls, 2006-2012 PALS data, logistic regression estimates / 179

Table A6.6 The impact of strength of religious ID_{t-1} on moral $issues_t$, OLS estimates / 179

Table A6.7 The impact of moral $issues_{t-1}$ on strength of religious ID_t, OLS estimates / 180

Table A6.8 Two-period fixed-effects model of within-person change in religious ID strength / 181

LIST OF TABLES

Table A7.1 The impact of seven-point party ID_{t-1} on moral issues$_t$, OLS estimates / 181

Table A7.2 The impact of moral issues$_{t-1}$ on seven-point party ID_t, OLS estimates / 182

Table A7.3 The impact of moral issues$_{t-1}$ on party ID_t with additional controls, GSS estimates / 182

Table A7.4 The impact of moral issues$_{t-1}$ on party ID_t with additional controls, NES and PALS estimates / 183

Table A7.5 The impact of moral issues$_{t-1}$ on three-point party ID_t, ordered logistic regression estimates / 184

Table A7.6 EIV estimates predicting party-driven/issue-driven change in moral issue positions/party ID / 185

Table A7.7 Two-period fixed-effects model of within-person change in party ID strength / 186

CHAPTER ONE

Moral Hunches

Experts believe the ties that bind people to organized religion and political parties shape public opinion on most issues. In this book, we argue that this depiction does not hold for the key moral issues that define America's long-running culture war. We demonstrate that the feelings people hold about abortion and gay rights possess the power to disrupt their religious and partisan bonds. In big-picture terms, we show that over the past thirty years public opinion on these moral issues has driven the rise of the religious "nones" (or those who claim no religious affiliation) and sorting into political parties.

Let us illustrate this idea by pointing out something that the rarely paired Billy Graham and Donald Trump have in common. The Reverend Billy Graham assumed leadership of his first church in 1946. During his extraordinary career, Reverend Graham preached the Gospel to over 215 million people across six continents.[1] Graham's 1957 crusade in New York City was a shining example. It ran from May 15 to September 1 and drew 2.4 million people, of whom 61,000 formally dedicated—or rededicated—their lives to Christ. Graham's spiritual messages reached millions more via radio, television, books, and magazines. However received, his sermons touched countless lives.

Described as "America's pastor," the "national clergyman," and "America's Greatest Evangelist," Graham landed on Gallup's list of the "Ten Most Admired Men" in the world sixty times from 1955 through 2016, double the number of appearances of runner-up Ronald Reagan. He was a superstar preacher who could seemingly proselytize just about anybody. Consider the impression he made on a young Bob Dylan.

> He was the greatest preacher and evangelist of my time—that guy could save souls and did. I went to two or three of his rallies in the '50s or '60s. This guy was

like rock 'n' roll personified—volatile, explosive. He had the hair, the tone, the elocution—when he spoke, he brought the storm down. Clouds parted. Souls got saved, sometimes 30- or 40,000 of them. If you ever went to a Billy Graham rally back then, you were changed forever. There's never been a preacher like him. (Love 2015)

That said, Reverend Graham had a hunch about the limits of his power to persuade. In a 2004 interview, he declared, "I'm just going to preach the Gospel and not going to get off on all these hot-button issues ... If I get on these other subjects, it divides the audience on an issue that is not the issue I'm promoting. I'm just promoting the Gospel" (New York Times 2005). To be clear, Graham opposed abortion and homosexuality. Privately, he counseled individuals against abortion or same-sex relations. Our point is that he felt constrained from doing so in public. If he defended traditional marriage or denounced abortion, he risked pushing away some followers who held different views. Graham feared that backlash over moral issues might temper some of his followers' enthusiasm toward his religious mission.[2]

Was his intuition right? Would folks cool toward religion based on how they felt about abortion and gay rights? According to many public opinion experts, people do not discard their religion for policy reasons. Instead, the positions people take on moral issues follow from their religious identities. Ted Jelen (2009, 221) summarized the conventional wisdom on public opinion about gay rights: "Virtually all the research on attitudes toward gay rights underscores the importance of religion as a source of opposition." The same holds true for abortion: "Of all the social predictors of abortion attitudes, religion is generally considered to be the strongest" (Jelen and Wilcox 2003, 492). In short, religious identities and orientations shape attitudes toward moral issues. Public opinion on these issues does not shape religious attachments. From this perspective, Reverend Graham had little to fear in speaking out about moral issues. In fact, speaking out may have changed enough hearts and minds to shift the broader political tides in Graham's preferred direction.

Politicians also harbor reservations about the power of moral issues to drive some of their partisan supporters away. Consider Donald Trump in 2015–2016. During his primary and general election campaigns, Trump demonized his Republican rivals, Hillary Clinton, immigrants, Muslims, women, Black communities, and the mainstream media. Here is a sample of quotes from *Politico Magazine* (2016): (1) "When Mexico sends

MORAL HUNCHES

its people, they're not sending their best. They're bringing drugs. They're bringing crime. They're rapists. And some, I assume, are good people" (campaign launch speech, New York City, June 16, 2015). (2) "Donald J. Trump is calling for a total and complete shutdown of Muslims entering the United States until our country's representatives can figure out what the hell is going on" (rally in South Carolina, December 7, 2015). (3) "Our African American communities are absolutely in the worst shape they've ever been in before" (rally in Kenansville, North Carolina, September 20, 2016).

But when it came to gay men and lesbians, Trump held his fire. This uncharacteristic restraint set him apart from some of his GOP rivals. As he steamrolled through the nominating contest, *New York Times* journalist and Trump chronicler Maggie Haberman (2016) reported, "Mr. Trump, who has inflamed tensions with almost every group, from Hispanics to women to African-Americans, has avoided attacking or offending gay men and lesbians during the campaign."

At a campaign event on October 30 in Greely, Colorado, Trump did something that no other GOP presidential candidate had ever done. He unfurled a rainbow flag with "LGBTs for Trump" scrawled across the yellow stripe (Guilford 2016). It is impossible to imagine his chief GOP rival Ted Cruz doing the same thing. It is also inconceivable to think of Trump unfurling a Mexican flag or pressing a copy of the Koran to his breast. Trump's chief campaign strategy was to attack "others." Despite this, he sensed that attacks on gays and lesbians would undercut his support among people otherwise inclined to vote for him. Gay bashing would cost him support from socially moderate and liberal Republicans and independents whose votes he needed in a tough electoral environment.

To many analysts, such worries seem unfounded. The prevailing view is that party identification (party ID) is the bedrock political predisposition in the minds of Americans. In their seminal work, Angus Campbell, Philip Converse, Warren Miller, and Donald Stokes (1960, 128) concluded that "responses to each element of national politics are deeply affected by the individual's enduring party attachments." This view prevails today. Most scholars see party ID as intrinsically sticky, perhaps even an "unmoved mover" (Johnston 2006). Partisans in the electorate take cues from party leaders about what to believe, what to favor, and what to oppose (Zaller 1992; Barber and Pope 2019). Party ID shapes issue attitudes. Issue attitudes do not shape party ID. By this logic, Trump's fears of moral issue backlash were groundless.

Our Argument

The conventional view in political science maintains that powerful leaders of religious and political groups have little to fear by telling their followers what to believe on social and political issues. This is because core identities shape issue attitudes—including attitudes about abortion and gay rights.[3] Issue attitudes do not affect core identities.

Evidently, Billy Graham and Donald Trump were unfamiliar with this research. They instinctively knew to stay away from certain issues. During his long career, Reverend Graham felt far more comfortable trying to save souls than raising emotionally charged social issues. On his presidential quest, Donald Trump gleefully denigrated racial, ethnic, and religious minorities but refrained from attacking gays and lesbians. Both men feared moral issue blowback might damage their respective causes.

Moral Issues advances the claim that feelings about abortion and gay rights shape core group identities. The ties people feel to religious and political groups may be strong, but they are not immune to the power of moral issues to affect identity change. If Reverend Graham preached against the sins of abortion and homosexuality, he would have alienated some potential converts and driven away others who did not share his political sensibilities. If Donald Trump had attacked gays and lesbians as viciously as he attacked racial and ethnic minorities, the backlash would have cost him votes and driven some partisans from the GOP fold. In short, we share Billy Graham and Donald Trump's hunch about the power of moral issues.

This book argues that abortion and gay rights became high-profile issues in American politics and society in the 1980s. In response, Americans began adjusting their religious and partisan identities to reflect their feelings about this pair of bedrock moral issues. We contend the following: (1) When religious identities and feelings about moral issues sit in tension, many people change their religion. Some people leave religion entirely. Others embrace it. And others adjust their level of commitment. (2) When partisan identities and moral issues conflict, large swaths of the public resolve this tension in favor of their issue positions. For some, party ties grow stronger or weaker. Others abandon their party. All told, these individual-level dynamics have sped the decline of religion in American life and altered party coalitions for decades.

Strong Identities, Weak Issue Attitudes

When it comes to the political judgments people make, identities are stronger than issues (Mason 2018). Identities are more stable over time than issue attitudes; they resist the pull of these attitudes, and they shape important political choices more than these attitudes do. For instance, identifying as a member of a labor union will likely outlast and guide views on environmental stewardship rather than the other way around. Put simply, identities are psychologically strong, while issue attitudes are weak (Krosnick and Petty 1995).

For now, we use the property of stability to underscore the difference between strong identities and weak attitudes. By stability, we mean the degree to which psychological orientations persist over time. Research shows that core identities change less than policy positions in the minds of most people (Converse 1964; Converse and Markus 1979; Kinder and Kalmoe 2017; Freeder, Lenz, and Turney 2019). Social scientists deploy a range of techniques to assess response stability. The most intuitive method is to tally up the percentage of the public that stays on the same side of a given divide over time. When analysts use these methods to compare the stability of party ID to that of issues, the former almost always surpasses the latter.

To illustrate, consider data from the 2008–2012 General Social Survey (GSS) panel study. Those who participated in the survey answered a number of identically worded questions in the spring of 2008 and 2012. To gauge the stability of party ID, we turn to a standard question that asks people to place themselves on a seven-point scale ranging from strong Democrat to strong Republican. Comparing responses over time, we find that 78 percent of them stuck with their party. This is a high figure: it tells us that most partisans—nearly eight in ten—remained loyal to their team. Identities endure.

The same can't be said for most issues. Take the basic question of the role of government in American society—arguably the single most important and durable issue on the political agenda going back to the New Deal era. When asked whether "the government in Washington is trying to do too many things that should be left to individuals and private business" or whether "the government should do even more to solve the country's problems," only 50 percent fell on the same side of this issue in 2008 and 2012.[4] If people guessed randomly, the number standing pat would have been 36 percent.

Data like these hammer home the point that core identities endure, and policy attitudes do not; identities are strong, and issue attitudes are weak. People who identified as Democratic (or Republican) in 2008 were very likely to do so again in 2012. This is what stability looks like on surveys. Meanwhile, the lower figure on the role of government indicates that policy positions vacillated unpredictably over time. While some people remain committed to their positions, there is also plenty of churn. Some progovernment types in 2010 took moderate positions in 2014. Some moderates in 2010 drifted into the pro- or antigovernment camp four years later—often for no good reason. Some apostates switched sides entirely. Some even switched sides randomly. This is what response instability looks like.

The conclusion scholars draw from data like these is that few people hold meaningful attitudes on salient political issues. In his seminal works, Philip Converse (1964, 1970) discovered that small fractions of the public—in one case a mere 20 percent—hold real attitudes on issues that divide political elites year over year. In a comprehensive recent investigation, Sean Freeder, Gabriel Lenz, and Shad Turney (2019) estimated that 20 to 40 percent of the public holds stable views on salient economic and social welfare issues. Unimpressive figures, all.

Normatively, these are alarming findings. If people lack real attitudes on key issues, then their policy "preferences" cannot shape their partisan or electoral choices. And elected representatives cannot respond to what does not exist. As Christopher Achen (1975, 1220) has lamented, "Democratic theory loses its starting point—public opinion on policy matters."

The Puzzle of Moral Issues

According to the logic of identity-to-issue models of public opinion, elite discourse on a given issue activates core identities in the minds of citizens. Once activated, these identities guide the positions people take on diverse issues, such as tax cuts, gun control, gay rights, and so on. Identities endure over time and are central to how people see themselves. Issue attitudes wobble erratically and are peripheral to our self-images. This chain of reasoning holds that identities have a causal effect on the policy positions people take (Zaller 1992; Kinder and Dale-Riddle 2012; Achen and Bartels 2016).

Response instability is the norm for most issues. Curiously, it does not apply to the issues that personify America's long-running culture war. A smattering of studies has found that opinions about abortion and same-sex rights outlast opinions on nearly all other issues, including controversial topics like affirmative action, government spending, and health-care reform (Carsey and Layman 2006; Dancey and Goren 2010; Kinder and Kalmoe 2017). To return to the 2008–2012 GSS panel data, 72 percent of

MORAL HUNCHES

the sample stayed on the same side of the gay marriage issue over time—much higher than the 50 percent who did so on the role of government and close to the 78 percent of partisans who remained loyal to their team.

Stable attitudes like these shape political choice. In one notable work, Michael Tesler (2015) found that feelings about gays and lesbians shape presidential evaluation. Specifically, he showed that George W. Bush's "visible opposition to same-sex marriage over the course of the 2004 election year activated attitudes toward gays and lesbians in mass evaluations of his presidency" (813). Notably, Bush didn't change anyone's views about gays and lesbians. His rhetoric simply brought these long-held views to the forefront of voters' minds as they evaluated his candidacy. Tesler found the same process played out when Obama came out in favor of same-sex marriage in 2012.

Findings like these are puzzling. Canonical theories of public opinion maintain that people deduce issue positions from core identities and other enduring predispositions. When public discourse primes an issue, people who receive the message construct policy views that are consonant with the activated predispositions. However, if feelings about abortion and gay rights endure as tenaciously as core identities, one might ask if these feelings influence the groups people affiliate with. Perhaps Billy Graham and Donald Trump were on to something.

We think they were. Our book parses the ways in which visceral feelings about abortion and gay rights drive change in religious and political identities. We show that people revise their religious and partisan ties to accommodate these feelings. Ultimately, we conclude that feelings about abortion and gay rights function as strong attitudes that drive religious and political change in the contemporary United States.

Preview of the Theoretical Argument

Most theories about the origins of public opinion posit that the ties we feel to the groups we belong to condition the positions we take on the issues that matter to our groups (Achen and Bartels 2016). Though differing over some of the theoretical details, these approaches share much common ground. The first point of agreement is that core identities develop earlier in the life cycle and hold steadier later in life than issue attitudes. Parents transmit group attachments to their children during the early and middle-childhood years. These ties crystallize during the impressionable years of adolescence and early adulthood. Young people know which groups they stand with—often, but not always, the groups they stood with during childhood. In adulthood, personal and social networks buttress group ties. As we age, these ties often grow stronger (Sears and Brown 2013). In short, core identities develop early, crystallize quickly, and harden throughout adulthood. This is why they last so long and resist change.

No comparable trajectory exists for the development of issue attitudes. Parents do not pass their policy views on to their offspring. This failure results partly because many parents lack meaningful views of issues. And teens and young adults, preoccupied with personal matters, rarely develop crystallized feelings about issues. Most people do not pay enough attention to politics to develop real policy preferences at any point in the political life cycle. This is why policy attitudes fluctuate erratically and bend in response to stronger predispositions.

All that said, people usually answer policy questions on public opinion surveys—even on obscure topics. Where do these opinions come from? The groups that people belong to shape their views about issues that matter to the group and its leaders. When individuals are part of a group, they go along with what the group favors because the instrumental and emotional pressures to do so are hard to resist (more on this in chapter 2).

Of course, the ability to conform depends on knowing what the group believes. How do people figure out where their group stands on key issues? This is where the information environment comes into play. Opinion leaders and other trusted sources take clear stands on issues, which they communicate through various networks. As this information spreads, in-group and out-group members learn what the groups believe. Group members take cues from both sets of actors to figure out what positions they should adopt. When message intensity for a given issue is high for a long time, political learning is widespread (Carmines and Stimson 1980, 1989; Zaller 1992).

Let us sketch out how the group-based approach applies to public opinion on abortion and gay rights. Starting in the 1980s, the emerging alliance between the religious Right and the Republican Party clarified where key groups stood on both issues. Many Americans ascertained that some religious people and the GOP disliked abortion and homosexuality. They also found out that nonreligious people and Democrats were more supportive of abortion and more tolerant of gays, lesbians, and bisexuals. A large share of the electorate absorbed these lessons. When asked for their opinions in conversation or on a survey, people respond based on

MORAL HUNCHES 9

where their groups come down on both controversies. Religious people and GOP partisans take conservative positions on moral issues. Nonreligious people and Democrats adopt progressive positions. They do so because they face psychological and self-interested motives to conform.

The theory of moral power breaks with the conventional group approach in two crucial respects. First, it contends that attitudes toward moral issues are as stable as religious and political identities. Second, it contends that these attitudes cause people to revise and sometimes change their identities. By identity change, we mean the direction and strength of group attachments. Sometimes feelings about abortion and same-sex rights motivate people to leave their group and even switch sides. Other times, the strength of a given identity waxes or wanes in response to pressure exerted by these feelings.

How can this be? How could moral issue attitudes have become so durable and impactful? Our answer centers on issue messaging in the information environment and the microfoundations of moral issue attitudes. We take up the information environment first. When political elites clash over some matter for a long time, the media and the public take notice. Sustained, intense elite conflict offers people many chances to form impressions about the issue. As we show in chapter 3, messages about abortion, gays and lesbians, and same-sex rights have spread through political media (e.g., news coverage), entertainment forums (e.g., popular TV shows), and campaign communications (e.g., party platforms and congressional websites) since the late 1980s. Given their prominence in everything from TV shows to religious sermons to roadside billboards, even the most inattentive citizens have likely received some messages. This information atmosphere has given Americans lots of opportunities to form enduring attitudes about moral issues. We argue that they have done just that.[5]

Of course, periodic occasions to form impressions carries no guarantee that those impressions will cohere as durable attitudes. Something must nudge people to make consistent evaluations. We theorize that the surfeit of messages in public and private communications repeatedly evoked gut-level emotional responses in the minds of message recipients. Often framed in terms of moral anger and disgust, these messages activated emotions that stabilized the underlying attitudes. As people received such messages, they reacted the same way again and again. For some people, messages about abortion and gays elicited moral disgust against these targets. These automatic emotional responses boosted anti-abortion/anti-gay sentiments (Kam and Estes 2016). We call this "conservative disgust." For other people, anti-abortion and anti-gay messages elicited moral anger and disgust against the perpetrators of these attacks. These emotions rebounded into pro-choice/pro-gay sympathies (Gadarian and van der Vort 2018). We label this "progressive anger and disgust." In short, spontaneous emotional reactions to these messages crystallized moral issue attitudes. The result is that most Americans hold genuine, enduring attitudes toward the defining culture war issues.

It is one thing to claim that attitudes about moral issues are stable, but quite another to claim they are impactful. How could public opinion on abortion and same-sex rights influence bedrock identities like religion and party ID? We offer a two-part answer. First, work in political science and sociology provides evidence that core identities change in response to disparate pressures (Saperstein and Penner 2012; Hout and Fischer 2014; Egan 2020). Some people update their identities for personal reasons. Others do so for political reasons. The degree of change is often small, but it is not negligible.

This leads to our second argument about the impact of moral issue attitudes. Building on work on identity revision (e.g., Fiorina 1981; Franklin and Jackson 1983; Patrikios 2008; Killian and Wilcox 2008; Putnam and Campbell 2010; Hout and Fischer 2014), we theorize that moral issue attitudes shape core religious and political identities. For many years, the information environment has clarified where key religious and political actors stand on abortion and gay rights. Since people hold clear attitudes about these issues, know where the key groups stand, and identities are not fixed, these attitudes can motivate identity change when public discourse is flush with germane messages. Given cognitive dissonance between core identities and moral issues, many people aim to reduce it by bringing their identities in line with their deeply held views on these issues (Campbell, Layman, and Green 2021). All else equal, we theorize that pro-life, anti-gay folks will gravitate toward religion and the GOP. At the same time, pro-choice, pro-gay individuals move away from religion and closer to the Democratic Party.

To recap, group-centric theories hold that religious and political identities outlast attitudes toward abortion and gay rights and shape these attitudes. By contrast, the theory of moral power contends that the psychological strength of moral issues rivals that of religious and party ties. Importantly, core identities, while durable, are not immutable. From time to time, they bend in response to pressure from other psychological forces. When people learn where the relevant groups stand on these issues, some

MORAL HUNCHES

of them adjust their identities to conform to their feelings about abortion and equal rights for gays.

Contributions

Folk theories of democracy hold that ordinary people have genuine views about political issues that influence which parties they identify with and who they vote for. These claims have collapsed in the face of mounting social scientific evidence that people hold weak, ineffectual attitudes on most issues (Achen and Bartels 2016). At the same time, scholars have occasionally noted that attitudes toward abortion and gay rights last longer and waver less than most issues. Abortion and gay rights are "easy" issues that have "moral resonance" that sets them apart from other issues (Converse and Markus 1979; Carmines and Stimson 1980; Kinder and Kalmoe 2017). For the most part, scholars have not pursued the implications these findings have for understanding public opinion and American politics. Instead, the field holds fast to the claim that moral issues, like other issues, are grounded in identities. Attitudes toward abortion and gay rights may be made of sterner stuff than other policy attitudes, but they still reflect deeper social and partisan cleavages. They do not define these cleavages.

Moral Issues breaks sharply with this view. In the pages to come, we aim to convince readers that Americans' feelings about abortion and gay rights affect their ties to organized religion and political parties. We find that these issues have played an important but underappreciated role in American society and politics. In so doing, our efforts advance the study of American politics on several fronts. First, our book shows that politics shapes religion in unexpected ways. To be clear, we are not the first to make this claim. Beachhead studies have demonstrated that political identities shape religious affiliation and experience (Hout and Fisher 2002, 2014; Patrikios 2008; Putnam and Campbell 2010; Margolis 2018). Most relevant to our concerns, some of this work shows that political backlash from liberals and Democrats drove the rise of the "nones" (i.e., the religiously unaffiliated) that began in the 1990s. Our contribution lies in showing that attitudes toward moral issues persist as long as—and sometimes longer than—religious identities; they drive religious sorting; and they sometimes resist the influence of religious ties. Contrary to current understandings, we find that moral issue attitudes—not political identities—motivate religious exit.

Second, our findings complicate the long-standing claim that party ID is the central political orientation in the minds of the American voter. There is no doubt that party ties shape a wide array of political and personal judgments. That party ID shapes political choices is no surprise at this point (Bartels 2002). What is surprising is that party bias now spills over into nonpolitical choices, such as interpersonal attraction and consumption decisions (Gerber and Huber 2010; Nicholson et al. 2016). Our findings do not challenge any of this. They instead suggest that current theories must acknowledge that feelings about abortion and gay rights hold as steadfastly as party loyalties and also structure party ID—indeed, more than party ID structures these attitudes. Party ID is surely a "standing predisposition," but it does move in response to feelings about moral issues.

Third, by documenting the strength of moral issues, our results raise an intriguing possibility about what lies at the heart of mass belief systems. Identity-to-issue theories hold that social and political identities occupy the center of these belief systems, while policy attitudes reside in the psychological hinterlands. But in test after test after test, we find this depiction does not apply to feelings about abortion and gay rights. Americans select into and opt out of religious and political groups based in part on how they feel about abortion and equal rights for gays and lesbians. This suggests that attitudes toward moral issues function as core elements in the religious and political belief systems of ordinary citizens. This centrality emerges, in part, because instinctual moral emotions—moral anger and moral disgust—vest these attitudes with the ability to alter long-standing identities.

Fourth, we find some evidence consistent with group-based theories of opinion formation. Religious and political identities do predict change in public opinion on moral issues. That said, our results show that the effects of issues on identities at least match and more often exceed the effects of identities on issues. This evidence is not consistent with conventional frameworks. Speaking broadly, this suggests that claims advanced by identity-based theories must be tested rather than assumed for some kinds of policies. Our evidence also raises the possibility that other issues rooted in moral anger and/or disgust might engender identity change. Attitudes toward immigration come to mind (e.g., Aarøe, Petersen, and Arceneaux 2017). Indeed, Marisa Abrajano and Zoltan Hajnal (2015) showed that these attitudes predict temporal change in party ID.

What does all of this mean for understanding democracy? At one level, our book pushes back against the argument that people do not hold real attitudes on at least some important issues. The sentiments people harbor about abortion and same-sex rights structure their social and political allegiances as called for by folk theories of democracy. In the religious marketplace, individuals use cultural issues to choose among religious traditions. In the political marketplace, people choose parties based in part on how they feel about abortion and gay rights. This is normatively satisfying.

But at another level, our book does not assuage those who fret that the public is not up to the task of policy-driven choice. For one thing, moral issue attitudes are not reasoned positions. They are the product of gut-level emotions, not careful deliberation. And while it may be true that moral issue attitudes are strong, this is but a single pair of issues. What is true for them is not true for most other policies.

Plan of the Book

Moral Issues unfolds as follows. Chapter 2 elaborates the theory of moral power. It begins by unpacking the stability assumption that undergirds identity-to-issue models of public opinion. The stability of identities is traced to formative socialization experiences during childhood and emerging adulthood. By the time people reach their mid- to late twenties, their central identities have crystallized. We then lay out the logic of identity-to-issue models of opinion formation, emphasizing the motives to conform and the importance of learning where groups stand on the issues of the day.

After this, we present the theory of moral power. We argue that people develop durable policy attitudes when they receive multiple policy messages from the information environment and automatic processing compels them to react the same way to these messages across repeat exposures. Both conditions hold for abortion and gay rights. Moreover, the information environment has long provided a steady dose of cues about where religious and political actors stand on these controversies, opening the possibility that people update group loyalties based on how they feel about moral issues. Lastly, we argue that core identities sometimes change in response to experiential and psychological pressures.

Chapters 3 through 7 constitute the empirical heart of the book. Chapter 3 presents a wealth of new content analysis data showing that abortion and gay rights messages have permeated the information environment, broadly defined, since the late 1980s. Our data cover every major party platform from 1972 to 2020; over 119,000 articles from national newspapers; over 56,000 congressional speeches; and over 6,100 congressional campaign websites. We also present data from analyses of over 6,600 TV episodes, 1,500 Christian sermons, and even roadside billboards. (Additional data and analysis are available in the online appendix at https:// press.uchicago.edu/dam/ucp/books/pdf/Goren_Chapp_Online_Appendix.pdf.) These data let us build the case that abortion and gay rights messages have infused popular discourse for a long time, implying that message reception has been high. We also show that anger and disgust language have permeated the ongoing discourse.

Chapter 4 begins by briefly describing our data. We then pivot to testing two empirical implications of our theory. Using data from a pair of national surveys, we show that disgust sensitivity predicts conservative positions on moral issues. We also review published work showing that progressive anger and disgust engender pro-choice, pro-gay sympathies. Next, we show that moral issue attitudes are as stable — often more stable — than religious and partisan IDs.

Chapter 5 addresses two paradoxes about the stability of moral issue attitudes. One objection to our claim about attitude stability at the individual level is that collective opinion on gay rights has changed a lot in recent decades. If individual attitudes endure, why has collective opinion swung so decisively in the progressive direction? And why has collective opinion on abortion changed so little? We show that generational replacement accounts for some, but far from all, of the macrochange on gay rights. The key to unpacking these paradoxes lies in seeing that while most individuals have remained stable in their personal views of gays, those whose views changed moved decisively in the progay direction. Small changes in one direction year over year can add up to big changes after a period of years. This explains how stable individual attitudes about gay rights have coexisted with significant change in collective opinion on the gay community as a whole. For abortion, most people have also stood pat in their personal views, but among the few whose opinions changed, pro-choice switchers mostly canceled out pro-life switchers. In other words, the net effect on collective opinion change is zero. This explains how stable attitudes about abortion at the individual level coexist with collective opinion that is stable on abortion and unstable on gay rights.

In chapters 6 and 7, we leverage data from multiple panel studies to model the dynamic relationship between moral issue attitudes and core identities. The datasets cover the years 1992 to 2020. Chapter 6 takes up the dynamic relationship between moral issues, categorical religious identities (i.e., affiliated or unaffiliated), and the strength of religious ties. We find that moral issues, rather than political identities, drive religious change. Issue-driven backlash therefore provides a better explanation for the rise of the nones than backlash rooted in political identities. Chapter 7 takes up party ID. There, we report that issue-driven sorting is more widespread than party-driven sorting. Said another way, moral issues are stronger than party ID. Along with chapter 4's stability results, the results from these two chapters affirm our key theoretical claims. Attitudes toward abortion and gay rights are unusually powerful. Indeed, these attitudes are powerful enough to alter American religion and the party coalitions.

Chapter 8 brings the book to a close. We review the theory of moral power, recap the evidence in its favor, and highlight the limits of what we can claim. The rest of the chapter takes up the larger theoretical, substantive, and normative implications our results have for understanding public opinion on abortion and gay rights, the state of American religion, party coalitions, and the future of American politics.

CHAPTER TWO

The Theory of Moral Power

The prevailing view in the social sciences is that core identities govern the positions people take on social and political issues. Most people neither know nor care enough to figure out where they stand on such controversies. For the most part, the positions they take depend on the positions advanced by the groups involved in the matter. When they learn where people like them stand, they adopt their group's stances as their own.

This assumption is true usually but not always. Consider the personal journey of "Autumn," a thirty-eight-year-old mother of six whom we interviewed in June 2018.[1] Looking back at life in her twenties, Autumn told us that she experimented with a number of different churches. At thirty-one, she and her husband settled on a Unitarian Church. Like many people around this age, she appeared to have found her religious and spiritual home. A big part of the church's appeal was politics: "they were liberals like we were." Autumn stressed that at the time, she was a Democrat and held liberal views on most issues. But within a few short years, Autumn and her husband switched to the Catholic Church, which they attend to this day.

What changed? The answer turns on the tension between her church and her feelings about abortion and gay rights. Autumn has "always hated abortion." The sexual revolution, she said, "has made feminism hedonistic. It is no longer about women's rights but about faux empowerment, . . . a symptom of women being disconnected from who we are as biological creatures." On top of that, Autumn has long condemned same-sex relations: "Biologically, we're not made for that. Anything outside of [heterosexual intercourse] reflects a deep psychological issue that has not been addressed." As America's culture war dragged on, the conflict in her mind between her stances on these issues and those of her Unitarian church

THE THEORY OF MORAL POWER

grew. After some thought, she resolved the conflict by selecting into a new faith tradition that catered to her moral tastes. Her political loyalties have also evolved. Given her negative feelings about abortion and gays, she left the Democratic Party for the GOP. In fact, she is now active in local GOP politics.

Around the same time, we interviewed a second woman. "Dawn" is a fifty-six-year-old mother of two. She has spent most of her adult life attending various Protestant churches. Until recently, church membership had more to do with finding community than anything else. Things began to change in 2009, following the mainline Evangelical Lutheran Church in America's (ELCA) decision to allow gay pastors. While Dawn's local parish had previously been apolitical, it broke with the ELCA over the decision. The move troubled Dawn, who thought that gays and lesbians should be able to serve. Dawn stuck with her church for a while but frequently emailed her pastor to express her concern with the church's position. In 2012, the state that Dawn lived in took up a gay marriage amendment. When Dawn's pastor delivered an "anti-gay" sermon, Dawn got up and left in the middle of the service. Following a "harsh" email exchange with her pastor, Dawn made the decision to leave the church permanently. She and her family joined a left-of-center United Church of Christ congregation. They have attended worship services there ever since.

Dawn's take on moral issues is the opposite of Autumn's. But, like Autumn, her views have not wavered over her life. Dawn doesn't view same-sex relationships as wrong or unnatural in any way. She has long believed that "God would have us support the marriage of loving committed people no matter what their gender." The only thing that has changed is the salience of these issues in her life. It was only after gay rights became salient, in the form of her church's ELCA departure and the gay marriage amendment in her state, that the tension between her moral views and her religious identity became apparent. Dawn's feelings about gay rights led her to break with her congregation once she learned that she was out of step with the group.

Autumn's and Dawn's stories contradict the standard social science claim that core identities govern the positions people take on issues. For Autumn, the country's culture war was never far from her mind, a reminder that the religious and political groups she identified with did not share her deeply held views on abortion and gay rights. In Dawn's case, her church's changing posture toward gay rights and her state's gay marriage amendment underscored the conflict between her church and her moral views. Their stories show that when group identities clash with feelings about moral issues, some people choose new identities that match their views on abortion and gay rights.

The key question this book tackles is whether untold Americans, like Autumn and Dawn, have chosen new identities to reflect their feelings about moral issues. We say yes. The theory of moral power advances four claims about the ability of these issues to engender identity change. First, for the past thirty or so years the information environment has given voters plenty of chances to evaluate abortion and gay rights and see where the key groups stand. Second, visceral moral anger and disgust guide responses to these messages. This process renders moral issue attitudes durable and impactful. Third, religious and party ID, though durable, are not fixed. Both identities may waver in response to pressure exerted by exceptionally strong attitudes and beliefs. Fourth, when identities conflict with how people feel about moral issues, some people resolve the cognitive dissonance by aligning their identities with their moral feelings.

This chapter unfolds in five parts. The first section defines the key concepts. The second section briefly summarizes the vast literature on the weakness of issue attitudes. The third section reviews the logic of identity-to-issue models of opinion formation. The fourth section elaborates our rival theory. It explains why attitudes toward abortion, gays, and same-sex rights are strong and then takes up how and why these attitudes affect core identities. The final section wraps things up and points to the path ahead.

Key Concepts

Attitudes toward Moral Issues

Before taking up the rival theories, we must first define the key concepts. To begin, moral issue attitudes are bottom-line judgments about abortion and gay rights. By bottom-line judgments, we mean positive or negative evaluations of each issue (Eagly and Chaiken 2007). Some people have very positive feelings toward both sets of rights. They favor the right to choose under any circumstance and equal rights for same-sex individuals (and couples) without exception. Others hold very negative feelings toward abortion, gays, and same-sex rights. They oppose it all without equivocation. And of course, many people take less extreme views, favoring abortion under some circumstances and the same for gay rights.

Our take blends multiple facets of each issue into one overarching dis-

THE THEORY OF MORAL POWER 19

position. We do not focus on a single abortion situation (e.g., when the woman's life is in danger) or a single civil right (e.g., same-sex marriage). Instead, we focus on multiple, interrelated elements. Someone who favors abortion under one scenario (e.g., the woman's life is in danger) is more likely to favor than oppose reproductive rights under a second scenario (e.g., the woman does not want another child). A person who favors abortion in these cases is also more likely than a staunch pro-lifer to favor same-sex marriage and adoption rights. By focusing on multiple aspects of both issues, we get a broad view of how people feel about core moral conflicts.

Some readers might object to our conceptual mélange. Although abortion and gay rights are distinct issues, we treat them as manifestations of the same evaluative disposition. To this objection we reply that prior statistical work suggests that opinions on abortion and gay rights derive from a single latent factor (see Jelen 2009 for a review). In the chapter 4 measurement appendix, we present new evidence that opinions on both issues derive from the same psychological impulse.

Readers may also be uneasy with our choice to limit "moral" issues to abortion and gay rights. What about school prayer, gun control, critical race theory, and immigration? Without denying the import of these and other issues, we focus on abortion and gay rights for several reasons. First, abortion and gay rights evoke universal concerns about human sexuality, gender roles, and family structure. By touching on the most intimate and personal of human concerns, abortion and gay rights attract closer scrutiny than less personally intrusive issues (Luker 1984; Hunter 1992).

Second, abortion and gay rights have been high on the US political agenda for the past thirty or so years and show no sign of losing their potency. We discuss this history and present content analysis data on moral issue messaging later in the book. For now, we note that school prayer, gun control, critical race theory, and other cultural issues cannot match the staying power of abortion and gay rights. Most issues surge onto the nation's agenda for a brief period only to fall away shortly thereafter. This often happens with gun control. Horrific massacres attract widespread attention that reignites the gun control controversy. Initial demands for action run rampant but little change actually occurs. Eventually, calls for gun control fade away as other issues move to the fore.

The third reason we equate moral issues with abortion and gay rights is that automatic, unconscious moral emotions shape how people respond to messages about both issues. Moral disgust and moral anger stabilize these attitudes and render them resistant to change (more on this in what follows). By contrast, the feelings people hold toward many other cultural issues do not seem to depend on moral emotions. This also holds true for many domestic and foreign policy issues (Terrizzi, Shook, and Ventis 2010; Gadarian and van der Vort 2018). This basis in moral emotions marks a key distinction between abortion/gay rights and other issues.

Lastly, we stress that in our usage "moral" denotes a characteristic of a specific, narrow class of issues. As just detailed, we label abortion and gay rights moral issues because they are grounded in discrete moral emotions (i.e., moral anger and moral disgust). This does not hold true for most other cultural and noncultural issues. It is important to note that other authors theorize moral issues differently. For example, Timothy Ryan (2014, 2017) argues that people vary systematically in how much moral conviction they attach to a given issue attitude. To illustrate, some people root attitudes toward abortion in their underlying core beliefs and values. Other people ground their attitudes toward Social Security in core moral convictions. For Ryan, *moral* describes a property of individual attitudes, akin to other attitude properties like certainty or accessibility. Again, in our usage *moral* describes a specific class of issues. We see value in both approaches but focus exclusively on our take.

Religious Identification

Most scholars see religion, broadly defined, as a multifaceted concept. They describe religion in terms of the three Bs — that is, belonging, belief, and behavior (Stark and Glock 1968; Layman 2001; Froese and Bader 2010). Scholars have devoted a lot of attention to beliefs, ranging from views that the Bible is infallible to the nature of God. Behavior denotes practices, such as worship attendance, saying grace, praying, and other religiously inspired acts. Elsewhere, we covered the relationships between moral issues, religious belief, and religious behavior (Goren and Chapp 2017). We do not repeat these exercises here.

Instead, we focus on one aspect of religious belonging. We examine whether people identify as a religious person. Those who identify with any religious tradition count as affiliated. Those who reject religion, whether actively or passively, are unaffiliated. These are the religious "nones." This label denotes the fact that when asked on a survey which religion they identify with (e.g., Protestant, Catholic, Muslim, Jewish, etc.), some people choose "none of the above."

THE THEORY OF MORAL POWER 21

We focus on the nones for two reasons. First, the rise of the nones speaks to a number of important questions such as the changing role of religion in American society and the evolving composition of party coalitions in the electoral arena. Second, it would take a companion volume to unpack the links between moral issues and denomination switching within and across the main traditions. This question merits investigation, but such a study also lies beyond what our book can accomplish.

As defined here, religious identity (religious ID) reflects a minimal level of attachment. To model the rise of the nones, this is what we need to examine. However, categorical attachment ignores variation in identity strength. To see what this means, imagine two Catholics. For the first, being Catholic is central to her self-concept. It defines how she sees herself, how she presents herself to others, and how she lives her life. She is raising her children in the faith and brings them to church every Sunday. She also prays daily and reads her dog-eared Bible several times a week. Our second person also identifies as a Catholic, but her attachment is weak. It is not central to how she sees herself and what she does on a day-to-day basis. While she had her children baptized, the family only attends services on Christmas Eve and Easter. She rarely prays and hasn't taken communion in years.

As these hypotheticals make plain, religious identity varies from strong to weak (and even nonexistent for some people). Since variation like this is socially and politically consequential, we take up the question of how feelings about abortion and same-sex rights affect religious identity strength. This two-track approach lets us study those who exit religion and those whose religious ID shifts by matters of degree. We take up the moral issues–religion connection in chapter 6.

Party Identification

Party ID reflects a psychological attachment to the Democratic or Republican Party (Campbell et al. 1960). For most people, it represents the primary group attachment in the political domain. Just as religious ID reflects how people see themselves in spiritual terms, party ID reflects their political self-concept. Party ties develop early in life and harden by the mid- to late twenties. During adulthood, political experience with the party label and stable social settings reinforce these ties. All of this renders party ID resistant to change (Green, Palmquist, and Schickler 2002).

The scholarly consensus holds that party ID is the strongest predisposition in the minds of American voters (Johnston 2006). Party ties color political perception, judgment, and behavior. These ties govern the ballots voters cast in all kinds of elections; the positions they take on all kinds of issues; and even their core political values (Bartels 2000, 2002; Goren, Federico, and Kittilson 2009). Party ID also shapes personal preferences, such as who we find attractive, who we want to date, and potential marriage partners for our children (Iyengar, Sood, and Lelkes 2012; Nicholson et al. 2016).

Chapter 7 comes at party ID from two angles. It starts with the link between moral issues and the standard seven-point scale, which sheds light on the direction and strength of party ties. We then pivot to categorical ID to see if moral issues affect the likelihood that someone identifies as a Democrat, an independent, or a Republican. This tells us whether feelings about moral issues push some to leave their party or even switch sides.[2]

Issue Attitudes Are Weak

Strong versus Weak Attitudes

A key argument we make throughout this book is that attitudes toward abortion and gay rights are more durable and impactful than attitudes toward other issues. In other words, the bottom-line judgments Americans make about moral issues last longer over time and shape key political choices to a much greater extent than virtually all other issues. This begs the question of how strong attitudes develop in the first place.

Strong attitudes develop with practice—that is, through the repeated expression of similar bottom-line evaluations about a given subject (Converse 1970; Eagly and Chaiken 2007). To acquire a strong political attitude, two things must happen. First, one must receive a series of communications about a political subject over some period of time. Message reception results when we encounter a topic and understand it. When this happens, we form snap impressions about the topic. The more messages we receive, the more snap judgments we make.

Second, given message reception one must render consistent evaluations about the goodness or badness of the topic. If we evaluate the subject the same way in response to a series of messages, the attitude crystallizes. An example: when someone receives a message about a new presidential candidate, such as Joe Biden in 2020, she makes a summary judgment about him (e.g., "I don't like Biden"). If she comes to the same conclu-

THE THEORY OF MORAL POWER

sion upon receipt of new messages (e.g., "Biden will be bad for America," "This guy . . . this is not my kind of guy," etc.), her attitude becomes entrenched. She will consistently express ill will toward Biden in the future. But if she reacts inconsistently to these messages (e.g., sometimes she is pro-Biden, sometimes she is anti-Biden, and sometimes she is unsure), her attitude does not crystallize. She does not really know how she feels about him.

In short, a crystallized attitude results when we evaluate a given topic the same way many times over. The snap judgments we make usually point to the same conclusion. We know where we stand. Given sufficient crystallization, an attitude like this persists, resists challenge, and guides judgment. It is a strong attitude.

Issue Attitudes Are Unstable and Lack Impact

When it comes to social and political issues, weak attitudes are the norm. Two lines of work sustain this conclusion. The first centers on an idea we introduced in chapter 1—response instability in issue opinions. Researchers use various statistical methods to quantify how stable attitudes are. Studies typically find that most people do not take consistent positions on issues year over year (Converse 1964; Converse and Markus 1979; Freeder, Lenz, and Turney 2019).

We use some of these methods later on in the book. For now, an anecdote from a study by John Zaller and Stanley Feldman (1992) reveals what response instability looks like in practice. They asked survey respondents to report their opinion on federal spending on education at two points in time. After giving their answers, respondents discussed the reasons for their choices. The following quote describes how one subject's position changed from one month to the next.

> When asked in the May interview about the proper level of government services, one respondent, identified as a teacher, emphatically favored higher levels of service and spending. The country was facing an educational crisis, the teacher said, and more expenditures for education were drastically needed. Any cuts in federal services or spending would inevitably reduce the already inadequate funds available for education. Just a month later, however, the same individual favored cuts in government spending. Government was too big and had to be cut back. There was no reference to the educational crisis that had preoccupied this individual just a few weeks earlier. (Ibid., 594)

This is a remarkable passage. In May, this person favored more spending on public services. In June, they reversed course completely. The responses seem to have come from two different people. In short, a perfect illustration of response instability.

Findings on response instability strongly imply that ill-formed policy attitudes are poor bets to guide the routine political choices that people make. Gabriel Lenz's 2012 book *Follow the Leader* confirms that issue attitudes lack behavioral impact. Lenz used panel data to test whether issue attitudes shape voter choice or the reverse. Issue-voting theories predict that when the media and campaigns lavish attention on a given issue, that issue should come to weigh more heavily on voters' choices. Contradicting this hypothesis, Lenz showed that after campaigns and the news media primed an issue, the issue did not come to weigh more heavily on voters' candidate preferences. Instead, many voters changed their issue positions to match the positions advocated by candidates they already favored.

The following is an example. During the 2000 presidential campaign, Al Gore and George W. Bush sparred over the future of Social Security. Bush proposed allowing workers to invest a share of their Social Security taxes in privately managed accounts. Gore rejected this idea out of hand in favor of using a "lock box" to safeguard Social Security funds. Each thinking their position more popular, the candidates stressed their differences during the first presidential debate in early October. Media coverage ramped up, thereby priming the issue in the public mind. Lenz showed that the heightened media coverage changed few votes. Instead, voters who already liked Bush came to appreciate the virtues of partial privatization. Voters who already preferred Gore moved closer to his take on the issue. Per Lenz (2012, 3), "voters first decide they like a politician for other reasons, and then adopt his or her policy views." The implication is clear. Ephemeral issue attitudes lack behavioral impact. This is why they do not affect voter choice.

The findings that issue opinions vacillate from one reading to the next and do not reliably predict voters' preferences suggests that large portions of the American public lack real preferences about salient political issues. These results are unsurprising in light of what we know about the American public's limited appetite for news about public affairs. Most people care little about politics. Few know anything about the origins, details, and likely effects of policy proposals (Converse 1964; Delli Carpini and Keeter 1996; Prior 2019). As such, it makes sense that most people do not hold strong feelings about most issues. Instead, issue attitudes are

THE THEORY OF MORAL POWER　　　　　　　　　　　　25

weak attitudes. They depend on stronger predispositions like core identities. The next section explains why.

Identity-to-Issue Theories

In politics, as in other areas of life, the groups we identify with shape what we believe. Identity-to-issue theories hold that group-ties structure the positions people take on issues that are relevant to the group (Campbell et al. 1960; Conover 1988; Kane, Mason, and Wronski 2021). Though they differ over the social and psychological mechanisms underlying group influence, these approaches share some assumptions that are relevant to our concerns. The first point of agreement is that core identities develop earlier in the life cycle and persist longer than issue attitudes. This helps set the stage for the identity-to-issue effects we describe later on.

Identities Develop Early and (Often) Hold Steady in Adulthood

The standard story begins with preadult socialization. A consistent finding in research is that social and partisan identities develop earlier in life and endure longer than issue attitudes. During the early and middle childhood years, parents teach their children which groups they belong to and why their groups are better than other groups (Hyman 1959; Jennings and Niemi 1974, 1981). Modes of parental influence include verbal instruction, informal signaling, and modeling attachments. At this stage of the life cycle, the transmission of identities from parents to offspring proceeds smoothly because children desire parental approval and lack the reasoning prowess to resist what their parents inculcate. In this way, children learn which groups they belong to, what members in good standing believe, and how they should behave (Bos et al. 2022).

Parents try hard to raise their children a particular way, but there is no guarantee of success. Growing children are not passive vessels who mindlessly absorb what grownups tell them. As any parent knows, children often vex them with their own ideas about who they are and what they believe (Wolak 2009). That said, many children do follow in their parents' religious and partisan footsteps as they age.[3]

As children meander through adolescence and early adulthood, forces outside the home begin to impinge on identity development (Sears 1983). Teens are open to novel influences in part because they have developed the cognitive capacity to think more critically about their attachments (Arnett 2000). On top of that, friends, peers, schools, and different types of media influence self-concepts. Young adults move into and out of different peer groups, subcultures, and romantic relationships. They explore new identities anchored less firmly in the past.

Once the tumult of adolescence and early adulthood has died down, group attachments crystallize. For many people religious and political identities have been in place since early childhood. Others have flirted with a range of different identities before returning to the fold. And some individuals have left one or more groups for other groups. Whatever the path, most have settled on core identities by their late twenties.

The more time people spend in a group, the less responsive their group ties become to new information (Converse 1969). There are several reasons for this. First, the imprint of early socialization is hard to shake. For many of us, group ties date back to childhood. Think about someone raised by devout Catholic parents. When the child reaches adulthood, her religious identity as a Catholic has been in place for as long as she can recall. Even if she no longer practices her faith, she probably still thinks of herself as Catholic. Second, the stability of social environments facilitates the stability of personal identities. When surrounded by others who share similar traits and beliefs for a long time, group ties grow stronger and more resistant to change. Given that group environments change slowly, if at all, it is not surprising that many identities persist over the long haul (Green, Palmquist, and Schickler 2002).

How Groups Shape Attitudes, Beliefs, and Preferences

Another common thread in these theories centers on the nature of group influence. The groups we belong to shape our beliefs and preferences. This influence is not unique to politics. It reflects a fundamental aspect of what it means to be human. For reasons detailed shortly, we all face emotional and instrumental incentives to adopt our groups' positions. The net result, as Christopher Achen and Larry Bartels (2016, 216) put it, is that "all the great issues of life—religion, nationality, gender roles, popular scientific ideas, partisan loyalties, the value of different occupations, the appeal of different foods—are taught to the vast majority of people by their family, their culture, and their subcultures. At a slower pace, socialization to group norms continues throughout adulthood."

Unpacking this logic begins with the recognition that human beings are social animals. We automatically categorize individuals we see as members of various groups, and we instinctively distinguish between "us" and "them" (Kinder and Kam 2011). We shower in-group members with preferential treatment. We dismiss out-group members and discriminate against them (Allport 1954). Groups form under the faintest pretexts and when the stakes are meaningless (Tajfel 1970; Tajfel et al. 1971). Group conflict increases when rival groups compete for coveted resources, such as wealth, power, prestige, and respect (Clark et al. 2019). To attain these spoils, group members need to stick together.

Groups confer benefits on their supporters. Membership improves individual well-being on numerous fronts. We enjoy the company of people like us, who like the same things we do, and who can lend a hand when we need one. Groups help us advance our interests and achieve our goals. Being part of a group also boosts our self-esteem when "we" prevail against "them" in social conflicts. It also buffers us from stress, provides us with social support, helps us avoid social isolation, promotes good health, and leads to longer, more fulfilling lives (House, Landis, and Umberson 1988; Putnam 2000; Holt-Lunstad, Smith, and Layton 2010; Jetten et al. 2015). Group life is central to the good life.

The emotional and instrumental benefits of group membership are substantial, but they come with a price. To signal that one is a member in good standing and thereby secure these advantages, members must generally accept the positions advanced by group leaders and endorsed by most followers. This increases group cohesion in the pursuit of common goals. The flip side is that sustained dissent imposes serious costs. Those who consistently buck the accepted view risk dissolving the bonds of sentiment that bind them to others. By internalizing the groups' positions as one's own, members reap the benefits. So long as people have a reliable means of learning what the group believes, most people in the group conform (e.g., Asch 1951; Cohen 2003).

Groups and Public Opinion

In politics, group members confront subtle pressures to go along with the policy positions advocated by opinion leaders in the group. The policy positions that people express in surveys reflect in part what they think people like them are supposed to say. This is most evident in the case of political parties. Republicans oppose economic redistribution because they learn from party elites and fellow Republicans that this is the party view, not because they have studied the matter on their own and arrived at this conclusion. Democrats favor redistribution because they discover that this is what fellow Democrats believe. They too have not studied the matter.

How do people ascertain where their groups stand on key issues? The information environment comes into play at this point. By information environment, we mean any network through which messages spread. We see these networks in the broadest terms. Political messages diffuse through news media, such as network and cable news; online, print, and radio news; political talk radio; campaign advertising; discussion groups; and so on. On occasion, some issues cross over into everyday discourse via popular media, such as TV sitcoms and dramas, morning and daytime talk programs, movies, pop music, and other apolitical diversions.

Opinion leaders and trusted sources take clear stands on issues, which they communicate to their followers through these networks. A steady stream of messages provides people with multiple opportunities to learn how rival groups line up on the matter. People take cues from both in-group and out-group sources (Nicholson 2012). When the information environment on some issue intensifies to an unusual degree, widespread learning occurs (Carmines and Stimson 1980; Zaller 1992).

Proponents of identity-to-issue models maintain that religious and partisan identities guide public opinion on abortion and gay rights. As chapter 3 shows, message volume on abortion and gay rights has been intense for a very long time. These messages have spread via political and apolitical media, providing Americans with numerous chances across multiple forums to see where key groups stand. These media communicate that religious people and Republicans are pro-life and protraditional family, and that nonreligious people and Democrats are pro-choice and pro-gay. When people learn this, they take the positions appropriate for their group. Chapters 6 and 7 describe religious and partisan information flows in detail. For now, we simply note that standard theories predict that the positions people take on abortion and same-sex rights, like the positions they take on other issues, depend in part on the groups they identify with.

The Theory of Moral Power

We now elaborate our theory of moral power. The theory explains, first, how strong issue attitudes develop and, second, how and why they come to shape core identities. The argument we make builds on four propositions. (1) The information environment has provided Americans with plenty of

THE THEORY OF MORAL POWER   29

chances to form crystallized attitudes. (2) The summary judgments people make about both issues are rooted in automatic, visceral emotional reactions that people experience in response to these messages. As a result, these attitudes endure and have impact. (3) Core identities can change when they conflict with other strong psychological dispositions. (4) When moral issue attitudes and core identities are at odds, some people resolve the conflict by updating their identities.

The Information Environment

The first proposition in our theory is that the information environment has furnished most voters with ample opportunities to form crystallized attitudes about abortion and gay rights. In American politics, multiple issues compete for space on the political agenda (Downs 1972). Most issues fail to make it. Among those that do, the lion's share remain visible briefly before vanishing. Issues with short shelf-lives limit the odds that people will form meaningful, long-lasting attitudes. By contrast, a few issues remain salient year over year. Clearly, chronically salient issues are much more likely to capture attention at some point than less visible issues. The more often people encounter a given issue, the more often they can evaluate it. Obvious examples here include racial and immigration issues (Carmines and Stimson 1989; Abrajano and Hajnal 2015).

Abortion and gay rights have also received a great deal of attention. Messages about both controversies have pervaded all forms of political discourse, such as broadcast, cable, print, and electronic news; talk radio; and, of course, political campaigns. The prevalence of these issues in political media is expected. Beyond customary political outlets, abortion and gay rights have, to an unusual degree, spilled over into popular media. These forums include prime-time shows, soap operas, movies, social media, pop music, and so forth. This has heightened Americans' exposure to moral issues to an unusual degree—and far more than what we witness for most other issues. Of course, most people miss most messages, but since messages about abortion and gay rights have saturated the information environment for so long, we surmise that message reception in the mass public is high.

A handful of studies have shown that different sectors of the information environment have conveyed abortion and gay rights messages to the general public for years (L. Bennett 1998; Rohlinger 2002; Carmines, Gerrity, and Wagner 2010; Moscowitz 2010; Sisson and Kimport 2017). In the next chapter, we present the most extensive analysis to date of the information environment surrounding moral issues. Our data, covering four decades of political and entertainment media, reveal that messages about moral issues have flooded the information environment. Put simply, the conditions for message reception across the public are favorable.

Moral Emotions and Attitude Strength

Given message reception, the next question to take up is how people respond to the inputs. Do they usually react the same way? If so, strong attitudes prevail (Krosnick and Petty 1995). Recall that political attitudes strengthen when two things happen. First, one receives a series of messages on some topic over a period of time. Second, one makes consistent bottom-line judgments about the topic across these repeated trials. The more issue messages one receives and the more frequently one evaluates the target the same way, the more crystallized the attitude becomes (Converse 1970; Eagly and Chaiken 2007). The amount of time it takes for a political attitude to crystallize surely varies, but it seems that a few months might be enough (Sears and Valentino 1997; Jacobson 2019). After that, subsequent exposure, even if sporadic, reinforces the attitude.

The key question we confront is what leads people to react to moral issue messages in a consistent way. To answer this question, we draw on research on emotions and moral psychology. We theorize that as people receive moral issue messages, automatic emotional reactions habitually push some of them to respond positively and others negatively to these primes (Haidt 2001).[4] The two key emotions are disgust and anger—two of the seven universal emotions (Ekman 1992).

Disgust is a feeling of aversion toward things we find offensive. Offensive things include physical objects we perceive with our senses, such as seeing maggot-infested roadkill; actions we become aware of, such as a seventy-year-old man having sex with an eighteen-year-old woman; and negative ideas, such as misogyny. We feel anger when something or someone frustrates our goals or treats us unfairly. We also get mad when people do these things to others, such as when we hear of someone who spouts racist propaganda (Rozin et al. 1999; Paul Ekman Group n.d.).

On cultural issues, some folks have been socialized to feel "conservative disgust" in response to specific actions seen as debasing society's moral order. Abortion and gay marriage violate what certain traditions deem morally acceptable, thereby arousing disgust among those who by disposition and enculturation accept these norms. For them, opposing abortion and gays just feels right.

Others have learned to feel "progressive anger and disgust" in response to things that infringe on the rights of others and strip them of their dignity. Attacks on the rights of women, gays, and lesbians arouse moral fury and revulsion because these acts violate the norms of autonomy and personal freedom and dehumanize the intended victims (Rozin et al. 1999; Rozin, Haidt, and McCauley 2008; Gadarian and van der Vort 2018). For those who have taken these lessons to heart, support for abortion and gays feels right.

It is beyond the scope of this project to unpack these socialization processes in detail. That said, we feel obligated to make a couple of points at this juncture. First, groups play a key role. People learn how to respond emotionally to things that violate moral codes from the central socializing agents in their lives, such as parents, close friends, peer groups, the local community, and so on. Primary groups and their associated subcultures take precedence over more distal groups such as political parties and organized religion. Second, while the effects of early socialization are critical, further socialization takes place once people leave home and move into new social groups. Social learning is a lifelong process (Haidt et al. 1997; Rozin, Haidt, and McCauley 2008; Chapman et al. 2009).

While cultural conservatives and progressives take different positions on moral issues, the psychological pathways that lead them to their distinctive positions are largely the same. Both groups experience automatic emotional reactions to issue messages in ways that strengthen the connection between their evaluations and the issues (Fazio 2007). Because these emotions arise automatically in response to violations of different moral systems, they constrain people to make the same bottom-line judgments (Graham et al. 2013).

In chapter 4, we extend this discussion and present evidence consistent with our claims. But for now, we use a pair of examples to illuminate how the information environment elicits moral emotions that bolster these attitudes. We begin with abortion in a seemingly apolitical context (chapter 6 provides multiple political examples).

On October 27, 1994, 28 million Americans tuned into the *Seinfeld* episode "The Couch." Abortion comes up several times during the show, the first time when Jerry and Elaine are dining at "Poppie's" restaurant. As they await the main course, their conversation turns to abortion (Dickson 2002).

32   CHAPTER TWO

ELAINE: Boy, I'm really looking forward to this duck. I've never had food ordered
    in advance before.
JERRY: Ah, I could've stayed home and ordered a pizza from Paccino's.
ELAINE: Paccino's? Oh no. You should never order pizza from Paccino's.
JERRY: Why not?
ELAINE: Because, the owner contributes a lot of money to those fanatical, anti-
    abortion groups.
JERRY: So, you won't eat the pizza?
ELAINE: No way.
JERRY: Really.
ELAINE: Yeah.
JERRY: Well, what if Poppie felt the same way?
ELAINE: Well, I guess I wouldn't eat here, then.
JERRY: Really!
ELAINE: Yeah. That's right.
JERRY: Well, perhaps we should inquire. Poppie! Oh, Poppie. Could I have a word?
    <Poppie comes over.>
POPPIE: Yes, Jerry. I just checked your duck . . . it is more succulent than even I had
    hoped.
JERRY: Poppie, I was just curious . . . where do you stand on the abortion issue?
POPPIE: When my mother was abducted by the Communists, she was with child . . .
JERRY: Oh, boy.
POPPIE: . . . but the Communists, they put an end to that! So, on this issue there is
    no debate! And no intelligent person can think differently.
ELAINE (offended): Well . . . Poppie. I think differently.
POPPIE: And what gives you the right to do that?
ELAINE (standing up): The Supreme Court gives me the right to do that! Let's go
    Jerry, c'mon.
WOMAN AT NEXT TABLE (to her date): I heard that. Let's go, Henry.
HENRY: But we just got here . . .
WOMAN AT ANOTHER TABLE: I'm with you, Poppie!
WOMAN AT YET ANOTHER TABLE (to her date): Let's go!
ELAINE (to Poppie): And I am not coming back!
POPPIE: You're not welcome!
JERRY: Well, I'm certainly glad I brought it up.

This scene illustrates how we think issue messages interact with moral
emotions to shape abortion attitudes. First, it provides a good example of
how abortion spills over into mainstream entertainment, thereby provid-

THE THEORY OF MORAL POWER

ing millions of Americans with incidental exposure to the issue. Millions more received exposure after the series went into syndication and then migrated to Netflix. Second, Poppie and Elaine's visceral reactions are telling. Poppie responds with a mix of revulsion and fury, shouting, "So, on this issue there is no debate!" Elaine snaps back, "Well . . . Poppie. I think differently" before storming off with a final "And I am not coming back!" For some viewers, Poppie's reaction mirrors their own. Like the restaurateur, a tinge of disgust at the mere mention of abortion reinforces their judgment that abortion is wrong, that it must be banned. This is conservative moral disgust in action. Other viewers react like Elaine. They feel a flash of anger. Poppie's attack on the right to choose and those who support it elicits different moral emotions that boost pro-choice views.[5]

Naturally, many other viewers fell somewhere in the middle of these extremes and thus had a more muted reaction. But the general point stands: messages like these prime moral issues and many people respond viscerally. The conservative disgust some people feel hardens their anti-abortion sentiments. The progressive anger and disgust felt by others when women's reproductive freedoms come under attack sustains pro-choice views. As these processes recur year over year in response to political and nonpolitical messages, extant attitudes strengthen.

We think the same process plays out with respect to gay rights. To illustrate via example, we turn again to an ostensibly nonpolitical setting—the thirty-year war between the Walt Disney Company and the religious and political right. Disney, of course, has no desire to be drawn into such conflict. As stated on their homepage, "The Mission of The Walt Disney Company is to entertain, inform, and inspire people around the globe through the power of unparalleled storytelling, reflecting the iconic brands, creative minds and innovative technologies that make ours the world's premier entertainment company." That mission has not insulated them from attacks. Religious groups and conservative politicians have clashed with Disney over its stance toward gay rights since the mid-1990s. One could author a book on this complicated history, but we stick to simple news stories drawn from various print and online news sources. Each snippet comes from the lede of the story.

> From the *New York Times*: Florida has become a battleground for the conservative Christian assault on the Walt Disney Company, whose recent decision to extend health benefits to the live-in partners of gay employees has fueled complaints that it can no longer be trusted to provide wholesome entertainment. (Navarro 1995)

From the *New York Times*: The Southern Baptist Convention called for a boycott of the Walt Disney Company today to protest that the creators of Mickey Mouse and an animated Snow White have gone astray, profiting from a liberated Ellen and offering health benefits to employees' homosexual partners. (Myerson 1997)

From *Forbes*: Disney promised Monday to support efforts to strike down Florida's Parental Rights in Education Act—known by critics as the "Don't Say Gay" bill—after Gov. Ron DeSantis (R) signed it into law, saying the law "should never" have been enacted after the company drew widespread criticism for not doing more to oppose it before the bill was passed. (Durkee 2022)

From *AP*: Around 200 to 300 Christian conservatives marched along Apopka-Vineland Road on Monday in protest of Disney. After that, they participated in a concert in a parking lot, with Christian music. The gathering was organized by TP USA Faith, Mom's for America, and a group called Hold the Line. They said Disney crossed the line by taking a stance in politics, so they too are holding their line. The group supports the Parental Rights in Education law, also known as the "Don't Say Gay" legislation. They believe Disney needs to focus on entertainment, rather than politics. (Boey 2022)

From *Fox News*: Gov. Ron DeSantis publicly attacked Disney, one of Florida's largest employers, on Thursday after its CEO voiced concerns with Florida's so-called "don't say gay" bill approved by the Florida Legislature this week. Florida Republican Gov. Ron DeSantis slammed the Walt Disney Company as "woke" on Thursday after the company came out against a Republican-led parental rights bill in the state that progressives have claimed is anti-LGBTQ. (Chasmar and Laco 2022)

In short, Christian conservatives have been complaining about Disney's pro-gay policies for some three decades. Conservative religious groups and their political partners have condemned the corporation for promoting a gay agenda and LGBT rights that somehow threaten children. Their objections, boycotts, and pickets outside park grounds have garnered a great deal of attention in the news, online, and by word of mouth.

When cultural conservatives find out about Disney's pro-gay policies or its opposition to Florida's "Don't Say Gay" law, the reminder of same-sex relations evokes unconscious distaste. Once activated, conservative disgust props up their anti-gay stances. When cultural progressives hear of this,

THE THEORY OF MORAL POWER   35

many of them feel anger and revulsion toward "Southern Baptists," "Christians," and Governor DeSantis who demean same-sex individuals and aim to curtail their rights. These emotions also buttress pro-gay beliefs.

We note that other causal mechanisms, beyond moral emotions, likely vest feelings toward abortion and gay rights with psychological power. For example, Lilliana Mason (2015) argues that abortion is an "issue-based identity" grounded in the types of foundations underlying partisan and religious ties. Unfortunately, we lack the data to disentangle "issues as identity groups" from "emotion evoking issues" as competing causal mechanisms. We suspect both factors are at play at some level. This tension notwithstanding, the broader point, as we see it, is that Mason's work supports our claim that moral attitudes are different from most other issue attitudes (also see Hobolt, Leeper, and Tilley 2021).

In chapter 4, we present and review evidence consistent with the claim that moral issue messages evoke different kinds of anger and disgust in the minds of cultural conservatives and progressives. For now, though, we simply recap this section's main points. Messages about moral issues have been ever present in political, popular, and other apolitical discourses going back to the end of the Reagan-Bush era. When people get these messages, they have gut-level emotional reactions. For those who by disposition and enculturation take on a conservative cast of mind, these messages evoke moral disgust that consistently leads to negative bottom-line evaluations of abortion and gay rights. For those with a progressively instilled outlook, attacks on abortion and LGBT persons bring forth different kinds of moral anger and disgust. Emotional backlash against these attacks nudges them to evaluate abortion and gay rights in an even more positive light. These affective increments to existing attitudes are surely small but as these processes recur, attitudes toward abortion and same-sex rights quickly stabilize. Subsequent exposure to messages reinforce the attitudes. As a result, we think these attitudes possess the power to induce identity change, the subject of the next section.

Core Identities Sometimes Change

The next proposition in our theory holds that religious and political identities are not fixed. While people do not update their identities on an ongoing basis, some conditions prompt recalibration. Theories of lifelong openness hold that people may rethink their identities when these conflict with other strong psychological factors (Sears 1983). When the conflict is self-evident, the decision to change becomes explicit. More often, the conflict remains subterranean. Here, latent processes operate to resolve the cognitive dissonance (Campbell, Layman, and Green 2021).

Here are examples. Sometimes, Catholics convert to Judaism when they marry Jews (Putnam and Campbell 2010). Some of the long-term unemployed are more likely to identify as Black relative to those who have been employed (Saperstein and Penner 2012). The same is true for people who have spent time in jail (Saperstein and Penner 2010). In politics, partisans sometimes drift away from their party when short-term conditions reflect poorly on the party (Fiorina 1981; Tucker, Montgomery, and Smith 2019). Many people have abandoned organized religion due to various conflicts over the past thirty years (Hout and Fischer 2002, 2014).

Since policy attitudes are fickle and weak, it is not surprising that relatively few works posit that issues might induce identity change. Stable, impactful identities have no problem repelling whatever pull unstable, ineffectual attitudes may have. But attitudes toward abortion and gay rights are not cut from the same psychological cloth as other issues. People really know how they feel about both issues. And identities—including central social and political identities—sometimes change. This leads to our final proposition.

Moral Issue Attitudes Can Induce Identity Change

Our theory proposes that moral issue attitudes shape core identities as long as people know where the groups stand and feel some tension between their policy and group preferences. Per the conventional wisdom, we still expect that religious and party ID shape views of abortion and gay rights. However, the standard approach holds that the influence runs largely or entirely from identities to issues. What is new here is that the theory of moral power insists that the influence runs the other way.

Chapter 6 takes up the relationship between religious ID and moral issues. To preview, we build on earlier work that identifies political backlash as the cause of the rise of the nones (Hout and Fischer 2002, 2014; Putnam and Campbell 2010). These efforts posit that political identities drive religious disaffiliation. We theorize that moral issue attitudes, not political identities, drive some people away from religion. To expand, issue-driven change centers on two flavors of backlash—one from the cultural right, the other from the left. In the religious marketplace, foes of abortion and gay rights find religion more alluring than those who are pro-choice and

THE THEORY OF MORAL POWER

37

pro-gay. Disgusted by abortion and "alternative" lifestyles, they gravitate toward appropriate religious communities. Like Autumn in our opening vignette, moral issue conservatives seek religious venues that cater to their issue tastes. This is backlash from the right.

Abortion and gay rights supporters behave quite differently. When religious groups attack these rights, some supporters of abortion and gays distance themselves from religion. Dismayed by the intrusion of religion into the private lives of fellow citizens, angered by religious attacks that demean gays and women and deny them dignity and rights, and disgusted by the injustice of it all, some people decide to leave organized religion. This is especially likely among those whose religious ties are weak. Others retain their religious identities but see the strength of these identities cool. This is backlash from the left. Recall the second vignette that opened this chapter: Dawn left her church when it took public positions against gay marriage that contradicted her views.

Chapter 7 takes up party ID. Prevailing theory holds that strong partisan predispositions guide weak issue attitudes. Because most Americans lack strong feelings about most issues, issue-based party updating is unlikely but not impossible. It happens among small slivers of the public that care about a given issue, know where the parties stand, and do not align with their party (Carsey and Layman 2006). Building on theories of party revision (Fiorina 1981; Franklin and Jackson 1983), we theorize that people in general bring their party ties into alignment with their feelings about key culture war issues. Since partisan messages about both issues routinely appear in the information environment, people receive overlapping cues about where the parties stand on each. Abortion and gay rights opponents draw closer to the GOP. At the same time, those who back abortion and gay rights pull closer to the Democratic Party. Because people feel strongly about abortion and gay rights, we anticipate meaningful party updating.

All told, the theory of moral power makes novel predictions about the nature of moral issue attitudes and their ability to affect identity change in the minds of American voters. If the data confirm these predictions, the field will need to rethink what idea elements lie at the heart of mass belief systems.

Chapter Summary

Most people hold weak attitudes on the issues that preoccupy political elites. This is what Phillip Converse concluded in his seminal 1964 essay

38 CHAPTER TWO

and what leading accounts of public opinion have concluded ever since (Kinder 1998; Achen and Bartels 2016). Here and there, analysts note that feelings about abortion and gay rights seem different somehow. They have said less about what makes these issues different and whether this difference matters. Opine Kinder and Kalmoe (2017, 166), the difference "has something to do with the intersection of politics and morality: when policy touches on the public's sense of right and wrong, real preferences are more likely to result." We have theorized what this something might be and why it matters for American religion and politics.

To recap, the theory of moral power rests on four propositions. (1) The information environment has primed Americans to form crystallized attitudes about abortion and gay rights. (2) These attitudes are grounded in gut-level moral anger and disgust that people automatically feel when they encounter moral issue messages. Moral emotions stabilize these attitudes and vest them with power. (3) Religious and political identities endure but sometimes change when they conflict with other strong psychological dispositions. (4) As these conflicts arise, some people adjust their identities to fit their moral issue tastes.

We think this theory provides a credible explanation for why moral issue attitudes endure and drive identity change. The first proposition asserts that the information environment changed in ways that helped strengthen these attitudes. The next chapter reveals how abortion/gay rights messages surged in public and popular discourses starting in the late 1980s and running up to the present, thereby setting the stage for the emergence of strong feelings about touchstone cultural controversies to have their powerful effects.

CHAPTER THREE

Moral Messaging

In December 2019, the Hallmark Channel found itself embroiled in a controversy it did not anticipate. The cable channel aired an advertisement for the wedding registry company Zola that included two brides kissing at the altar. The conservative advocacy group One Million Moms took notice and issued the following statement: "Parents need to know they could now come face-to-face with the LGBT agenda when they sit down to watch the Hallmark Channel. . . . One Million Moms is asking Hallmark to stay true to its family friendly roots that so many families have grown to love, and to keep sex and sexual content—including the promotion of homosexuality—out of its programming." In response to this campaign, Hallmark pulled the ad. LGBTQ advocacy organizations roundly criticized this decision, equating it to "capitulating to a hate group" (Rozsa 2019). Following the backlash, Hallmark reversed its decision. CEO Mike Perry said, "We are truly sorry for the hurt and disappointment this has caused."

The Hallmark controversy sets the stage for the argument we make in this chapter. In chapter 2, we asserted that messages about abortion and gay rights have diffused widely throughout political and entertainment discourses for many years. High message diffusion, combined with the activation of moral anger and disgust, have catalyzed the development of strong issue attitudes in the public mind. If our argument is correct, two patterns should emerge from our analysis of the information environment. First, moral issue messaging should be widespread in political and popular forums. Second, moral issue messaging should rely heavily on moral anger and disgust frames.

The Hallmark controversy is a fitting example because it did not involve an act of Congress or a Supreme Court decision. Instead, a cable channel generated a newsworthy storyline that captured the public's attention. Politicians battle over abortion and gay rights too, and party differences on these issues matter a great deal. However, parties differ on a lot of issues. A defining feature of moral issue messaging is that it penetrates ostensibly nonpolitical media ranging from television shows to outdoor advertising to Sunday sermons.

The Hallmark controversy also generated powerful emotional responses. A columnist at the American Family Association characterized LGBT advocacy as a "sexual corruption coalition" and accused that "the body count is piling up of those who've capitulated to sexual rebel demands" (Harvey 2019). The Human Rights Campaign scolded Hallmark's decision to pull the ad, stating, "By caving into the wants of a hateful group, you have worked to erase LGBTQ people from television screens across the country" (Voss 2019). The mere mention of same-sex intimacy rhetoric likely elicited conservative moral disgust in the minds of same-sex marriage opponents. At the same time, anti-LGBT language surely evoked progressive moral anger and disgust among many of those sympathetic to gays and lesbians.

We contend that moral issues have become more accessible as a basis of political evaluation since the late 1980s. They have remained on the political radar ever since. Other issues (e.g., taxes and healthcare) often command more attention from politicians, but Americans pay less attention to these debates. Moral issues appear regularly in places where Americans might not be expecting a dose of politics. Moreover, the emotive character of moral communication typically involves "anger" and "disgust," both of which sharpen the bottom-line judgments people make about abortion and same-sex rights. The diffusion of moral issue messages in political and apolitical media, coupled with emotive framing, sets abortion and same-sex rights apart from other issues.

This chapter begins by examining scholarship on moral issue communication. Existing research shows that moral issue coverage has grown (Terkildsen, Schnell, and Ling 1998; Chomsky and Barclay 2010; Rhodebeck 2015). Many works in this vein focus on a single mode of communication, such as newspapers or news magazines. By contrast, this chapter provides the most systematic and comprehensive analysis of messaging about abortion and gay rights to date. As far as we know, ours is also the first effort to explicitly connect the framing of abortion and gay rights to moral anger and disgust. Below, we lay out our strategy for studying the information environment. We examine a range of quantitative and qualitative evidence to understand moral messaging. The evidence is largely consistent with the argument set out in chapter 2. As moral communications became more prominent in the late 1980s and early 1990s, it took on a character that set it apart from other public policies. Abortion and gay rights fill the information environment more broadly and deeply than other prominent issues. Moreover, the frames describing these issues rely on distinct moral language.

The Information Environment

Rising Message Volume Affects Public Opinion

When the media focus on a particular issue, that issue becomes more accessible in the minds of message recipients and weighs more heavily on political judgments (Iyengar and Kinder 1987). For example, Amber Boydstun (2013) documented a large increase in the number of people seeking a living will following the wall-to-wall coverage of the "right-to-die" Terri Schiavo case (Caplan 2015).

Research suggests that neither abortion nor gay rights were viable candidates for sustained priming effects until at least the late 1980s because media coverage was sporadic before then. In a study of *Time* and *Newsweek* articles from 1947 to 1997, Lisa Bennett (1998) found very little focus on gays until the 1990s. In a similar vein, Daniel Chomsky and Scott Barclay (2010) found that gays and lesbians were invisible for much of the twentieth century. Strikingly, they note that "the Stonewall riots in 1969 did not make the front page of the *New York Times* despite the fact that they occurred over several nights within 35 blocks of the *Times's* own front door" (ibid., 389). Marc Hetherington and Jonathan Weiler (2009) examined *New York Times*'s coverage of gay rights in presidential election years from 1988 through 2004. The issue received little coverage in the 1980s. Coverage shot up in 1992 and remained fairly high through 2004.

Research on abortion coverage paints a similar picture. Nayda Terkildsen, Frauke Schnell, and Cristina Ling (1998) located only seventy-three abortion articles in *Time*, *Newsweek*, and *U.S. News & World Report* from 1960 to 1979. Coverage actually declined in the years following *Roe*. Elizabeth Perse and colleagues (1997) examined abortion coverage in the *Washington Post* and *New York Times* from 1970 to 1988. They too found limited coverage of the issue.

The lack of moral issue coverage before the late 1980s extended beyond political news. Gwendoline Alphonso (2015) showed that a rise in the use of the word *family* in party platforms roughly aligned with an increase in news media coverage in the late 1980s and early 1990s. Before then, platforms were largely silent on "the family." Gretchen Sisson and Katrina Kimport's (2014) review of abortion film and television plots from 1916 to 2013 showed a similar trajectory. In the sixty years before the *Roe* decision, only 68 total plotlines involved abortion. From 1993 to 2002, 58 plotlines did so. Between 2003 and 2012, the total jumped to 116.

In short, the relative dearth of moral issue messages until the 1980s presumably rendered these issues only intermittently visible to the American public. By the late 1980s, rising message volume presumably rendered feelings about both issues more accessible in the minds of message recipients. In addition to increasing message volume, issue framing affects the nature of moral issue attitudes.

Moral Emotions and the Framing of Abortion and Gay Rights

Message frequency is not enough to strengthen moral issue attitudes. Framing differences matter too. To elaborate, research on political communication has found that "frames in communication" (i.e., how the media presents an issue) can influence "frames in thought" (i.e., how someone understands the issue). When frames in communication alter frames in thought, we observe a "framing effect" (Druckman 2001). Scholars have documented framing effects in a variety of settings, including judgments about moral issues (Brewer 2003; Price, Nir, and Capella 2005).

Frames do not come about by accident. They reflect political intent. Interest groups play a central role in crafting frames. In the case of abortion, Deana Rohlinger (2002) found that the National Organization for Women worked to alter how the media framed the organization. Likewise, the arguments made by anti-abortion groups proved more successful when framed as "pro-family" and "connected to a perceived decline in moral values and the subversion of women's biological destiny to be mothers" (McCaffrey and Keys 2000, 47). Framing has also influenced the same-sex rights debate. Stephen Engle (2013) concluded that the media's introduction of the marriage equality frame in 2003 had a significant spillover effect, initially lowering public support for gay rights.

Frames—and their emotional resonances—influence public opinion (Gross 2008; Chapp 2012). Two moral emotions in particular—disgust and anger—are related to attitude strength. Recall the argument we introduced last chapter. Research on moral evaluation shows that messages about gays and abortion elicit different kinds of emotional responses. For some, messages about gays and abortion evoke conservative disgust. For others, attacks on gays and women elicit progressive anger and disgust. Hence, when the media frame moral issues in emotionally charged ways, it probably helps stabilize and crystallize moral issue attitudes.

Prior work contends that moral emotions shape political rhetoric on abortion and gay rights. Some work unpacks the "frames in communication" that appear in elite political rhetoric. Courtney Megan Cahill (2013) argued that the language of moral disgust has increasingly framed the abortion debate. She showed that since the *Stenberg v. Carhart* (2000) decision, the language of disgust entered the US Supreme Court's working vocabulary for abortion (citing phrases in judicial reasoning like *gruesome* and *shudder of revulsion*). Follow-up work concurs, arguing that pro-choice advocates generally fail to effectively counter the disgust frame (Kumar 2018). Scholars use similar reasoning to understand the debate over same-sex marriage. For example, norm violations, including direct and indirect references to disgust, were among the most common types of arguments made against same-sex marriage (Cole et al. 2012). Cahill (2005, 1548) made a similar case with respect to legal reasoning about same-sex marriage, arguing that we ought to "reappraise the extent to which disgust, rather than reasoned argument, sustains laws directed at sexual and familial choice."

Other works document framing effects that result when communication frames influence frames in thought. In one of the best examples of this work, Edward Schiappa, Peter Gregg, and Dean Hewes (2006) examined the consequences of tuning in to the popular TV show *Will and Grace*, which portrayed several gay characters in a positive light. Controlling for confounding factors, the authors discovered that watching *Will and Grace* decreased anti-gay prejudice (also see Rideout 2008; Jones et al. 2018).

All of the works we have discussed suggest that moral issue message intensity has varied and that it has a distinct emotional tenor. As such, we expect to see a sharp surge in moral issue messaging starting in the late 1980s. This pattern should be present in forums that are explicitly political, such as party platforms, as well as seemingly apolitical outlets, such as TV programs. We also expect that messages about abortion and gay rights will make heavier use of disgust and anger frames relative to other visible issues. The moral issues are distinguishable both by their prominence in nonpolitical media, and their distinctly emotional character. Since extant

44 CHAPTER THREE

work focuses on smaller pieces of the communication environment, a fuller picture of the moral issue information environment remains elusive. The next section outlines our strategy to paint that picture.

Data and Content Analysis Strategy

How We Built Seven New Datasets

To test these claims, we look at seven different data sources that run from 1972 to 2022. We include political content like speeches delivered on the House floor and seemingly apolitical content like TV shows. Each data source has strengths and limitations. For example, we examine roadside billboards. Unlike other forms of media that suffer from self-selection problems, billboards elicit the attention of anyone who drives a car (Iveson 2011). However, our study of billboards is, by necessity, small in scope and limited to a convenience sample of interstate highways. We also examine a large representative sample of congressional campaign websites, but it only goes back to the 2008 election. Thus, we are unable to use these data to test our expectation that moral issue content became increasingly abundant in the late 1980s. In this section we lay out our strategy for analyzing the information environment and explain the various trade-offs.

Our first step was to generate lists of "keywords" to identify moral issues in various communication networks. These lists differ depending on the data source. For instance, to locate abortion and same-sex issues in the news, we searched newspaper headlines for a limited set of terms like *homosexual* and *abortion*. The headline approach lets us identify articles focused on moral issues while avoiding incidental mentions (Althaus, Edy, and Phalen 2001). We also examine congressional candidate websites. Campaign websites have different conventions than news articles, and some website titles like "On the Issues" can be ambiguous (Chapp et al. 2019). For this reason, our campaign keyword search covered a broader set of terms (e.g., *Hyde Amendment* and *right to choose*) and scoured the complete website, not just titles or headings. The online appendix lists the data sources and keyword lists we used to identify abortion and same-sex rights messages for each data source along with a justification for our approach.

For most datasets, the keyword approach did a good job locating moral issues. However, for some data sources this approach fell short. Billboards, for example, are primarily images. Accordingly, we trained coders to evaluate billboards visually. When we had to rely on subjective judgments, we used multiple trained coders to ensure we scored material in a consistent manner. The appendix reports intercoder reliability details.

Now, to the data. We have posited that moral issue messages became more commonplace in the late 1980s and early 1990s. To assess this claim, we built three datasets that extend as far back as practical to capture a period before moral issues were of political import. First, to examine moral issue messaging in politics, we analyzed party platforms from 1972 to 2020. Reviewing party statements on abortion and sexual orientation rhetoric prior to 1972 is pointless because these issues never came up. We retrieved party platforms from the American Presidency Project (American Presidency Project n.d.).

Second, we examined a sample of newspaper articles from 1980 to 2022. Using newspaper search engines, we sampled every article in the Associated Press, the *Washington Post*, and the *New York Times* with a headline containing the words *homosexual, gay, lesbian, LGBT, pro-life, pro-choice*, or *abortion*.[1] Next, we cleaned the resulting sample by hand to remove obvious false positives (e.g., *Enola Gay*). We also created two comparison datasets—one containing any headline that included the word *taxes* and one containing headlines referencing "Medicare" or "Medicaid." The rationale here was to choose two domestic policy areas (one "owned" by Democrats, one "owned" by Republicans) to aid with the interpretation of textual data. These issues help put into context how a statistic like "fifty articles per month" compares to other prominent topics. In all, the sample included 45,489 moral issue articles, 63,521 articles on taxes, and 10,353 articles on Medicare and Medicaid.

Third, to capture popular media portrayals of moral issues, we examined the ten most popular TV shows for each year from 1980 to 2022 as determined by Nielsen ratings. While "top ten" is an arbitrary cutoff, our goal was to examine shows that were broadly popular and thus capable of influencing public feelings about these issues. We excluded nonscripted shows, such as sports programming and reality television. We also excluded infotainment "news" programming. To this sample we added the Emmy winner for best drama in every year, to include programming that might be less popular but still conversation-generating. To see if these shows referenced moral issues, taxes, or health policy, we scraped text from the Internet Movie Database (IMDb) episode descriptions and then examined coded descriptions for keywords that would indicate the presence of a moral plot element. Because these descriptions are often short, our keywords list for this exercise was intentionally broad. For example, we scored every plotline that used the word *pregnancy*, because this might include discussion of abortion. We then checked every episode flagged as such to determine if abortion or same-sex issues were plotlines, removing false positives.

This is a conservative approach. We missed several relevant episodes because the shows were not popular enough for our threshold. For example, we missed a significant episode of *Hill Street Blues* from 1985 that featured a prominent abortion storyline. We also missed the highly viewed 1997 *Ellen* coming-out episode because the series itself was not in the top-ten. We also missed passing references to moral issues that were not prominent enough to appear in an episode description. In total, we examined 6,665 unique episodes from 111 programs. Note that many programs appeared in multiple seasons (e.g., *Seinfeld*). Of these, 35.1 percent of the most popular programs, but a much smaller fraction of total episodes, dedicated at least one episode to abortion or LGB issues.

These novel datasets let us examine temporal changes in the volume and intensity of moral issue communications. On top of this, we constructed additional datasets that let us trace the prevalence and emotional tone of moral issues in other modes of communication. First, we examined text from every congressional campaign issue page from 2008 to 2022. For websites from 2008 to 2012, text was scraped from the Library of Congress's campaign website archive (Druckman, Kifer, and Parkin 2014).[2] For the remaining years, we scraped websites in real time in the month before the election. In all, we examined text from 54,686 unique campaign issue pages covering 6,154 congressional campaigns: 6.3 percent of all campaign issue pages contained abortion or same-sex relations/rights content; 35.9 percent of all campaigns dedicated space to at least one of these issues.

One might object that the political speech we look at involves campaign communication and not governance and thus misses a critical part of political messaging. To head this off, we examined congressional one-minute speeches from 1989 to 2014, using data provided by Kathryn Pearson (see Pearson and Dancey 2011 for details on data collection). In all, we scored 56,574 speeches using the same procedure we used to score webpages: 2.1 percent of congressional one-minute speeches focused on our moral issues.

To bolster the claim that moral issues are prominent in nonpolitical forums, we built two more datasets. First, we examined billboard advertising. Despite growth in the potential significance of outdoor advertising (Iveson 2011), little research has examined its content. Sampling billboards is inherently challenging. Luckily for us, the Florida Department of Trans-

MORAL MESSAGING

portation archives has photographs of all active billboards. We sampled three major interstates in Florida and coded each picture by hand for whether it involved a moral issue or any other political issue. In addition, we examined the billboards along 250 miles of I-70 in Missouri, thanks to a public art installation curated by artist Anne Thompson. We also scored a convenience sample of billboards along I-35 between St. Paul, Minnesota, and Duluth, Minnesota (152 miles). While these stretches of road are not random, they all involve frequently traveled interstates from politically diverse regions of the country.

Finally, we reviewed Christian sermons that mention abortion, gay rights, taxes, or healthcare. Sermon Central is an online repository of sermons that functions as a resource for Christians seeking sermon transcripts on a topic or a Bible verse. We used the website's search engine to download all sermons using keyword markers for abortion, gay rights, taxes, and healthcare. Because this list returned many false positives, we refined the sample by requiring additional political keywords. For example, sermons that commented on gays/lesbians also needed to reference "unions" or "marriage." We identified 1,567 sermons that contained substantive policy discussion on abortion, same-sex rights, taxes, or healthcare.

Our sermon sample has clear limitations. Sermon Central collects only those sermons that pastors choose to upload, and some denominational traditions post to the website more often. We applied weights based on the denominations that show up most often in the online repository, but this is an imperfect remedy.[3] Second, given prohibitions on tax-exempt churches engaging in political campaigning, we suspect that pastors are less likely to upload an overtly political sermon to an open internet repository. We also acknowledge that we adopt a very conservative sampling procedure that misses (for example) sermons on the "sanctity of life" that implicates abortion without directly mentioning it. To recount, while our approach allows us to test for moral issue messaging against other types of political preaching, we also think it undercounts the actual level of abortion and same-sex speech in American churches. Like our approach to TV programs, this sampling procedure leads us to suspect that, if anything, this chapter understates the prevalence of moral issue communication.

How Do You Know Moral Anger and Disgust When You See Them?

On the topic of how to define obscenity, Justice Potter Stewart famously opined that "I know it when I see it" (*Jacobellis v. Ohio*, 1964). This sentiment captures the fundamental problem faced by researchers when identifying

48   CHAPTER THREE

a particular frame or emotive content in political communication. What seems "angry" to one person might appear mild to someone else. Subjectivity can color how one responds to a particular statement.

We use the National Research Council (NRC) word-emotion lexicon produced by Saif Mohammed and colleagues to score texts for whether they contain emotion keywords (Mohammed and Turney 2013). The NRC lexicon uses a crowdsourcing approach to ask scorers whether particular words are associated with discrete emotions like anger and disgust. While everyone might not have the same reaction to a word, this lexicon captures a degree of consensus in how the public understands the emotive gist of language. Dictionary-based approaches like this can reliably capture distinctions in the emotional resonances of language (Soroka, Young, and Balmas 2015). Critically, the NRC lexicon includes both *anger* and *disgust*. Other lexicons do not. Disgust includes 1,060 words such as *abuse, disease,* and *evil*. Anger includes 1,250 words, including *fight* and *misleading*.

Abortion and Gay Rights in the Information Environment

Rising Message Intensity on Abortion and Gay Rights

There is no clear starting point for the story of moral issues in the public life of the nation. From the dress reform movement to the Nineteenth Amendment to the battle over the Equal Rights Amendment, many social movements have sought to mold our collective understanding of sexuality, gender roles, marriage, and procreation. While it is tempting to identify *Roe v. Wade* and the AIDS crisis as the beginning of rising press attention to moral issues, we have already seen that *Roe* did not spark an immediate public conversation. Likewise, the AIDS epidemic only garnered media attention in slow drips. While *Roe* and AIDS became central storylines in the culture wars, it took a lot more to move these issues to the forefront of the public conversation.

How did abortion and gay rights become mainstays in public discourse? Advocacy organizations are a key part of the story, though they alone were not enough. The Mattachine Society began advocating for gay rights in 1950. The Daughters of Bilitis pushed for lesbian civil rights as early as 1955. The National Conference of Catholic Bishops began actively advocating for abortion restrictions in 1969, the same year the National Abortion Rights Action League formed in Chicago (Rohlinger 2002; Smith 2015).

Despite their importance in the respective movements, these groups were initially unable to spark public conversation. This started to change slowly as the parties began to build coalitions with movement activists (Carmines, Gerrity, and Wagner 2010). Geoffrey Layman (2001) attributes much of the emergence of culture war politics to the Democratic Party's embrace of the "New Left" platform—a move George McGovern's campaign made to win the 1972 nomination. In response, Christian Right activists began forging alliances between culturally conservative voters and the GOP. Figures like Jerry Falwell and Paul Weyrich helped build and grow an electoral coalition during the Reagan administration and pressured him to deliver on conservative policy promises (Williams 2010). This coalition gained strength in the 1980s before really taking off in the 1990s. For example, parachurch organizations advocated on abortion and homosexuality using "voter guides" as well as using media savvy developed through video ministries (Chapp 2019). Once the parties began to ally themselves with moral constituencies, abortion and gay rights became larger parts of the national conversation.

Changes in party platforms reflect the rising salience of abortion and gay rights. Far from being obscure documents read only by party officials, platforms are a window into the changing nature of the parties and are broadly reflective of the party bases. Platforms foretell how members of Congress will vote on key issues (Payne 2013) and are the "single most representative document of group influences on the central parties" (Victor and Reinhardt 2018, 266). Platforms also "affect voters' perceptions of both parties' presidential candidates" (Simas and Evans 2011, 836). In short, party platforms signal party priorities.

Figure 3.1 plots the number of moral issue words that appeared in the Democratic and Republican Party platforms from 1972 to 2020. We begin by noting that the Democratic Party has always taken more progressive positions (albeit not fully progressive) on both issues than their Republican rivals. Democratic programs have consistently endorsed the right to choose, equal rights for gays and lesbians, and gay marriage starting in 2012. The GOP program has long attacked abortion, defended the right to life and traditional family values, and resisted same-sex rights (see Domke and Coe 2010).

In terms of message volume, both parties have devoted more attention to these issues as time passed. Neither side made any mention of abortion or gays in 1972. Following the 1973 *Roe* decision, the parties took up abortion but shunned strong, unequivocal stands. In 1976, Democrats backed

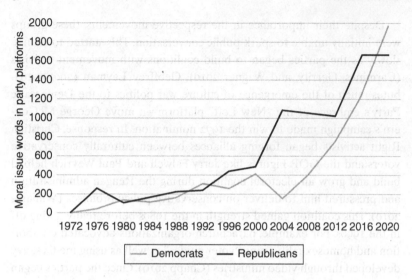

FIGURE 3.1. Moral issues in party platforms, 1972–2020
Notes: Y-axis is the word count of moral issue passages in Republican and Democratic Party platforms (n = 26). The 2020 Republican National Committee (RNC) data point replicates 2016, given a resolution at the 2020 RNC not to amend the 2016 platform.

Roe while acknowledging that "the religious and ethical nature of the concerns which many Americans have on the subject of abortion" would lead some in the party to disapprove. The 1976 Republican platform staked out a pro-life position, but with the caveat that abortion "is undoubtedly a moral and personal issue but it also involves complex questions."[4] In other words, while platform differences were evident, neither party was prepared to make abortion a litmus test.

In contrast to abortion, gay rights was not mentioned until 1992. That year, stark differences over gay rights emerged. Democrats professed support for "civil rights protection for gay men and lesbians and an end to Defense Department discrimination." Republicans declared that "we oppose efforts by the Democratic Party to include sexual preference as a protected minority" and "support the continued exclusion of homosexuals from the military as a matter of good order and discipline."

Figure 3.1 shows that the parties devoted increasing attention to both issues. GOP coverage rose steadily in the 1990s and then jumped sharply from 2000 to 2004. This jump coincided with debates over gay marriage (Tesler 2015). In early February, the Massachusetts Supreme Judicial Court ruled that same-sex couples could legally marry in the state start-

MORAL MESSAGING 51

ing on May 17 (Belluck 2004). One-week later San Francisco officials began performing marriages between same-sex individuals (Stout 2004). In response, President George W. Bush announced his support for a constitutional amendment to ban same-sex marriage. The GOP platform reflected that commitment: "We strongly support President Bush's call for a Constitutional amendment that fully protects marriage, and we believe that neither federal nor state judges nor bureaucrats should force states to recognize other living arrangements as equivalent to marriage." GOP moral issue language surged again from 2012 to 2016.

Figure 3.1 displays a similar trajectory in Democratic platforms. The number of mentions of abortion and gay rights ticked up from 1992 to 2000 before falling back in 2004. Because support for same-sex marriage was politically unpopular at the time, the party did not embrace it. The 2004 platform declared that states should decide the matter and repudiated "President Bush's divisive effort to politicize the Constitution by pursuing a 'Federal Marriage Amendment.' Our goal is to bring Americans together, not drive them apart." After the 2004 election, Democratic attention to both issues increased sharply every four years, peaking in 2020.

In the span of forty-four years, the GOP went from saying literally nothing about these issues in 1972 to over 1,600 words spread across multiple passages in 2016 and 2020. Democrats took a similar path. Between 1972 and 2020, their moral issue word count rose from 0 to nearly 2,000.

One interesting feature of these positions is how they moved from being stand-alone planks to positions woven throughout the entire platform. The 2020 Democratic platform now connects gay rights and abortion to healthcare, immigration, and the military (e.g., "We will . . . ensure that LGBTQ+ service members and families enjoy equal respect, benefits, and care"). The 2016 GOP platform connects moral issues to education, religious freedom, and the tax code (e.g., "American taxpayers should not be forced to fund abortion."). Figure 3.1 leaves no doubt that since 1992 both parties have worked assiduously to relay their positions on abortion and gay rights.

The rise of moral issue politics is also evident in the news media landscape. Figure 3.2 displays the monthly number of newspaper article headlines explicitly dealing with abortion and gay rights. For comparison, we also include headline counts for taxes and Medicare/Medicaid. While headlines that use the word *taxes* are clearly more prominent for most of the time series, several features of the moral issues trend line stand out. First, while not the most common news topic, moral issues are still quite

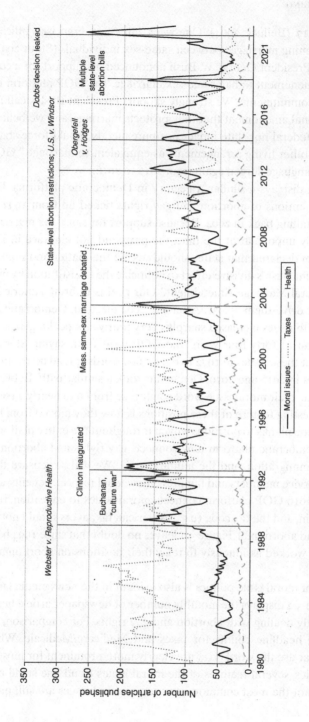

FIGURE 3.2. News content by story type, 1980–2022

Notes: Lines represent the number of articles of each story type published per month, smoothed with a six-month moving average (n = 119,363 news articles). The articles come from the *New York Times*, the *Washington Post*, and the Associated Press. Moral issues represent 38.1 percent of the sample.

common, surpassing stories about Medicare and Medicaid and occasionally eclipsing taxes—particularly in the last decade.

Second, the growth in moral issue news stories roughly parallels the changes we observed in party platforms. Moral issue articles became more conspicuous in the late 1980s and early 1990s. Apart from the occasional dip in coverage (e.g., during the onset of the Great Recession and the COVID crisis), moral issues have usually been present in the news. Before 1987, there were roughly forty-two stories per month dealing with moral issues. From 1987 to 2022, this total more than doubled to ninety-two stories per month. Indeed, since 2012, moral issue stories have kept pace with or surpassed headlines using the word *taxes* (with the exception of a few months of coverage of the Republican tax overhaul in late 2017). The 2022 *Dobbs* decision, coupled with state-level moral policymaking, has elevated culture wars to a new peak in the news cycle.

A complete accounting of this pattern lies beyond the scope of this chapter. However, the data invite some speculation. First, much of the increase in coverage originates from a political angle. Stories are more newsworthy if they involve some sort of conflict frame (W. L. Bennett 2005). Many spikes in news coverage coincided with major political events, including the 1992 GOP convention, Clinton's inauguration and subsequent unrolling of the "Don't Ask, Don't Tell" policy, and the debate over same-sex marriage in Massachusetts in 2004, to name only a few. In short, as politicians have elevated the status of moral issues, the media have followed suit.

Supreme Court decisions also contribute to increases in coverage. A decomposed time series of moral issue coverage reveals a seasonal spike in June that coincides with the high court's release of judicial opinions. Major decisions like *Obergefell* and *Dobbs* garner tremendous media attention. Recent coverage of *Dobbs* is particularly striking. We observed 294 articles in May 2022. This volume of coverage was sustained when the court officially reversed *Roe* in the summer of 2022 (324 articles in July) and continued through the midterm elections in November (158 articles), despite other salient issues competing for attention.[5]

While politics is one driver of media attention, it is not the only source. A share of the increase that began in the late 1980s is tied to the growing HIV/AIDS crisis, which became too widespread for the media to ignore (e.g., "Keeping Borders Closed to AIDS Sufferers Decried by Gay Groups," Associated Press, 1991). Likewise, acts of violence, from anti-gay hate crimes to abortion clinic attacks, have driven a substantial amount of coverage (e.g., "Abortion Bombings Suspect a Portrait of Piety and Rage," *Freedman*, 1987). The increase in coverage reflects changes in what the media considers culturally relevant. From celebrations of LGBT identity to coverage of films dealing with these issues to high-profile celebrities "coming out," the news media began to recognize abortion and gay rights in a way it did not in the early 1980s (Gibson 2004). Daniel Chomsky and Scott Barclay (2010) argue that Rock Hudson's AIDS diagnosis was a watershed moment in coverage of the issue. Headlines like "Gay Literature Comes Out of Closet as AIDS Memoirs Proliferate" (Kennedy, 1990) populate our dataset beginning in the early 1990s.

In addition to these watershed events, we also speculate that the news media was increasingly willing to cover moral issues. The *New York Times* provides an interesting case study. As Jack Mirkenson has argued, under the leadership of executive editor Abe Rosenthal from 1977 to 1986, the *New York Times* was unsympathetic to gay rights and the AIDS crisis, even going so far as to mandate the use of the word *homosexual* (as opposed to *gay*) unless the word appeared in a direct quotation (Mirkinson 2023). Given that the *Times* has an agenda-setting role for other media organizations (Golan 2006), it is not surprising that the spike in 1987 across all media sources coincides with Rosenthal's retirement.

Moral issues also show up in media sources viewed by the politically inattentive. TV is the most obvious example. The solid black line in figure 3.3 displays the percentage of popular programs with an abortion or LGBT plot element. The sharp jump in the early 1990s parallels the trends we observed with party platforms and news headlines. Moreover, unlike newspapers, where tax coverage outpaces moral issues, abortion and gay rights are essentially the only game in town when it comes to TV. While a few episodes of *The West Wing* and *Family Ties* dealt with taxation and medical dramas like *ER* occasionally broach health policy questions, these examples are few and far between.

In contrast, episodes that reference abortion and gays/lesbians are more commonplace. And oftentimes, single episodes have a reach that last long after the broadcast aired. To take perhaps the most famous historical example, in a 1972 episode of *Maude* the title character's choice to have an abortion at age forty-seven garnered an astounding 41 percent of the available audience. This episode generated much praise and backlash from viewers (Beale 1992). Decades later, abortion episodes continued to elicit similarly impassioned reactions. For a 2015 example, consider when the Olivia Pope character opted for an abortion on the TV drama *Scan-*

MORAL MESSAGING

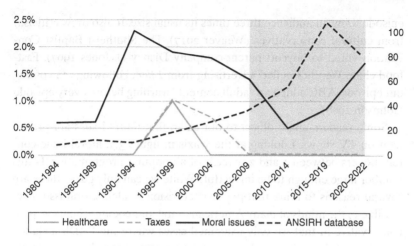

FIGURE 3.3. Moral issues on television, 1980–2022
Notes: The left axis reports the percentage of episodes among popular television programs containing moral issue plotlines (n = 6,665 unique episodes across 111 different programs). Moral issues are present in 1.3 percent of episodes and 35.1 percent of programs. The right axis corresponds to a count of all abortion programming in the Advancing New Standards in Reproductive Health (ANSIRH) database. The ANSIRH sample includes programming from streaming services and less popular shows. The shaded part of the figure represents the entry of streaming services into the market in (roughly) 2006.

dal: Planned Parenthood praised the episode for demonstrating that "our rights to reproductive healthcare are under attack." The conservative Media Research Center declared that "ABC's *Scandal* just crossed a sickening line" (Coombs 2015; Richardson 2015).

Popular shows do not treat abortion lightly. In 2010, *Friday Night Lights* portrayed abortion in a multi-episode story arc. A tenth-grade student—Becky—becomes pregnant and seeks advice from her high school principal, asking, "Do you think I'm going to hell if I have an abortion?" The principal, Tami, says no and offers support for whatever she decides. The school board pressures Tami to issue an apology for suggesting that abortion is a choice. Tami also received threatening phone calls from pro-life advocates. In the end, Tami loses her position as principal when she refuses to read a scripted apology, instead saying, "Listen, y'all, I've always put the welfare of the students over everything else. Every action I made was with that intent ... and that's all I have to say."

Similarly, shows that deal with gay rights issues do not seek to sidestep politics. When Ellen DeGeneres's character came out on *Ellen*, the episode drew an audience three times its usual size. It also drew criticism from cultural conservatives (Weaver 2017). The Southern Baptist Convention voted to boycott parent-company Disney (J. Jones 1997). Fastfood chain Wendy's pulled advertising from *Ellen*. Following the coming out episode, ABC added an "adult content" warning before every episode (Johnson 2008).

Some readers might object to our claim that moral issues are prominent on TV shows. Looking at the y-axis in figure 3.3, moral issue content hovers between 1 and 2 percent of all popular programming. Is this number large enough to be impactful? While we can only guess, there are several reasons to think that popular television renders moral issues accessible in the minds of many Americans. First, our coding scheme is quite conservative in that we only examined cases where the IMDb included abortion/gay issue keywords in a plot summary. These issues certainly came up more frequently. Our data only display episodes where the moral issues were significant plot elements.[6] Second, while we only sampled the most popular shows, this particular sample of episodes still attracted many viewers. This sampling strategy also means that we missed a number of culturally significant programs. Thus, only one season of *Will and Grace* made our sample, and *Ellen* never did. Third, viewership is not the only marker of impact. Many of these programs generated conversation, even among audiences who didn't watch them.

The trend line in figure 3.3 declines throughout the early 2000s, before increasing again from 2015 to the present. Does this signal, in any way, a diminished importance of moral issues in entertainment television? We don't think so. First, it is important to take stock of limitations in the data. Streaming services and cable have replaced a substantial portion of the networks' television audience. Because we cannot evaluate their popularity in a uniform way across the decades, we didn't examine these programs. We suspect that shows on streaming platforms (e.g., Hulu, Netflix, and Amazon) have elevated abortion and gay rights in the American consciousness. To take a few notable examples, *The Handmaid's Tale, Orange Is the New Black, The L Word, Heartstopper*, and *Veep* have all addressed moral issues in substantive ways and attracted sizeable audiences but are not included in our sample.

As a partial corrective for this omission, the dashed black line in figure 3.3 plots all television programs listed in the Abortion Onscreen Database. Gretchen Sisson developed this dataset (Advancing New Standards in Reproductive Health, or ANSIRH for short). These data do not use our "most popular" sampling frame and only chart abortions, not gay rights. Nevertheless, the trajectory of the line makes it clear that when cable and streaming programming are included, the prevalence of moral politics in popular television has risen over time. Sisson and Kimport (2014, 415) found that "since the 1973 *Roe v. Wade* decision, representations have increased each decade over the decade before by at least 31%."

We concede that the dashed line in figure 3.3 is partially a reflection of increased viewing options. This said, there is little doubt that abortion makes up a regular part of TV plotlines. Benjamin Toff and colleagues' (n.d.) study of political television corroborates this claim. While Toff's category of "family issues" is broader than our narrow focus on abortion and same-sex issues, the coding scheme includes abortion and LGBT storylines. Toff's analysis is consistent with our own. "Family issues" are the second most popular political theme on television, second only to "law and crime."

Finally, while our data runs through the end of 2022, it takes time to develop a show, making it unlikely that recent bombshell developments like *Dobbs* are reflected in these data. Evidence suggests that Hollywood producers are eager to incorporate more storylines dealing with the politics of abortion access (Galuppo et al. 2022). Likewise, the Gay & Lesbian Alliance against Defamation (GLAAD 2022) applauded record high LGBTQ representation on television in 2022. In short, it seems quite likely that moral issues will remain prominent on the small screen.

Party platforms, newspapers, and TV programs are useful because they allow us to track temporal change over the long haul. We can leverage other data we collected to paint a picture of where moral politics stands in more recent years relative to other political issues. To make this point, we add three more sources of data to bolster our case: congressional websites, outdoor advertising, and Christian sermons.

We start with campaign websites. These are ubiquitous in American political campaigns. James Druckman and colleagues (2018) have argued that campaign websites are the medium best suited to capture the campaign's general strategy. Our web data begins in 2008 and covers 6,154 Republican and Democratic campaigns for a seat in the US House. In total, these campaigns issued 54,686 unique issue pages on their websites. Moral issues are common, though far from the most popular issue: 36 percent of all campaigns issued statements on abortion or gay rights. At 6.3 percent of total issue pages in our sample, moral issues rank seventh. This lags behind the first-place topic of "jobs and the economy" (9.9 percent

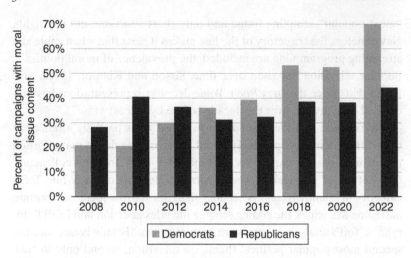

FIGURE 3.4. Moral issues on congressional campaign websites, 2008–2022
Notes: Bars represent the percentage of campaigns with moral issue content in a given year, separated by political party (n = 54,686 unique issue statements from 6,154 campaigns). Moral issues made up 6.3 percent of total issue statements and were present in 35.9 percent of all campaigns.

of all issue pages) but comes out ahead of web pages dedicated to "senior citizens" (3.9 percent of all issue pages) and "veterans" (4.2 percent of all issue pages).

While abortion and gay rights are not the most salient issues in congressional campaigns, their growing visibility in the space of the past eight elections is notable. Figure 3.4 displays the percentage of congressional candidates with an issue page at least partially dedicated to abortion or LGBT issues from 2008 to 2022. Republican candidates have been consistent over this period, with roughly one-third engaging in moral issue politics in any given year. From 2008 to 2012, GOP candidates made heavier use of moral issues on their websites. Democratic messaging has been more variable over time, but since 2014 Democrats have outpaced their GOP rivals in moral issue messaging. By 2020, 52.7 percent of Democrats had issued an abortion or gay rights statement, surpassing Republicans by ten points. In 2022, the impact of *Dobbs* loomed large, widening the partisan gap to a full twenty-five percentage points. Seven out of every ten Democrats featured moral issues on their campaign website, in stark contrast to 2008, when barely two in ten did so. This is evidence of a remarkable change in candidates' issue emphases in the space of fourteen years.

Qualitatively, these issue pages tend to be unambiguous, and partisan differences are sharp (Chapp et al. 2019). Republicans frame abortion in terms of *sanctity of life* and *protecting the unborn*. They also make frequent overtures to religion. The statement on Lisa McClain's (MI-10) 2020 campaign website is typical: "I am 100% pro-life. I believe in the sanctity of human life and that life begins at conception. I believe we must honor the first guarantee of the Declaration of Independence—which is a right to life." Pro-choice Democrats, in contrast, stress reproductive rights and women's bodily autonomy. As David Trone (MD-06, 2020) expressed it, "I'm 100% pro-choice. Medical decisions should be made by women and their doctors, not politicians like Donald Trump and Mike Pence."

Party stances on same-sex rights are equally clear and polarized. The GOP stresses traditional views about religion and family. Democrats emphasize equality. A typical Republican might issue a statement like "I believe that God defined marriage as between one man and one woman. I support traditional marriage and oppose alternative definitions of marriage" (Cynthia Lummis, WY-AL, 2010). Challenger Dana Cottrell issues a typical Democratic perspective: "I support the equal rights of all Americans, along with the privileges and freedoms afforded to all Americans without discrimination. I support gay marriage, along with transgender rights of free expression to live their lives in the manner befitting their personal identity" (FL-11, 2020).

We now move onto our last two datasets, both of which cover moral issues outside the context of partisan politics. As our discussion of television made clear, moral issues are prominent outside the political arena. To further buttress this claim, we examined billboards. In an age of digitization, social media, and smart phones, old-fashioned billboards might seem like an odd choice for analysis. However, the increasing complexity of the media environment is exactly what makes billboards attractive. As new media advertising opportunities have expanded and fragmented, businesses have more and more viewed outdoor advertising as a stable and cost-effective way to reach a broad cross-section of consumers (Iveson 2011). Nielsen reports that 81 percent of individuals aged sixteen and over have noticed a billboard in the last month; 85 percent of those engaged with the advertising (Nielsen 2019).

Figure 3.5 shows the percentage of billboards on a sample of interstate highways across three states that addressed moral issues and other issues. It covers select periods from 2014 to 2018. The figure underscores the potential for moral issues to reach politically inattentive Americans.

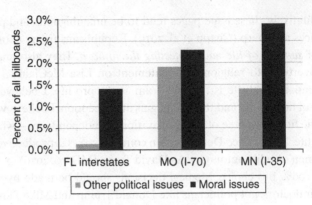

FIGURE 3.5. Moral issue billboards in three states, 2014–2018
Notes: Bars represent moral issue billboards as a percentage of total billboards observed for selected stretches of interstate. The Florida sample includes I-75 North, I-10 East, I-95 North; n = 2,086, collected in 2018. The Missouri sample includes I-70 East and West, St. Louis to Kansas City; n = 304, collected 2014–2016. The Minnesota sample includes I-35 North and South, St. Paul to Duluth; n = 470, collected in 2018.

While the percentage of abortion and LGBT billboards is low (between 1.4 percent and 3 percent), moral issues still make up the vast majority of all political messaging on the stretches of highway we sampled. Most of these billboards were "pro-life" in character, although we did observe pro-choice and gay rights messaging on occasion.

The low percentages on the y-axis might make some readers suspicious of billboards' significance. We offer two responses. First, at highway speeds, low percentages still equate to high visibility. If you spent the two-plus hours driving south from Duluth to St. Paul, you would see a moral issue billboard every twelve minutes. Second, billboard messaging is quite explicit, with statements like "I could feel pain before I was born," "God knew my soul before I was born," and "God's Definition of Marriage: One Man + One Woman For Life." Moreover, billboards use striking visuals to catch the eye. Two figures in the online appendix display a pair of anti-abortion billboards. Both imply that there is no distinction between a newborn baby like the adorable ones pictured and a developing fetus with language like "Smile 12 weeks from conception." Billboards like this are likely to capture the attention of many drivers and their passengers.

Just as moral issues dominate the political signals one sees on television and billboards, it is also the case that if a Christian worship service "gets political," it often revolves around moral issues. Figure 3.6 shows the number of Sermon Central sermons dedicated to abortion and gay issues. We also include taxes and healthcare for the purpose of comparison. Abortion and same-sex politics dominate the other issues in our sample. To be sure, moral issue sermons represent a small fraction of the topics about which pastors preach. However, abortion and gay rights are the primary issue-vehicles through which politics make its way into the pews.[7] Moreover, like other forms of media we have examined, moral issue sermonizing is unambiguous and nontrivial. Christian sermons tend to be pro-life in character, attributing bodily autonomy to a fetus from the point of conception, equating abortion with murder and denying women any choice in the matter.

To take an example, one evangelical pastor in the database argued "The unborn child is a visitor in a woman's body. Just because she decides the visitor is not welcome is no ground for taking its life." (Sermon Central 2004). And while we observed a few Christian defenses of gay rights, most sermons in the database reject same-sex marriage and relations. These sermons generally find a scriptural basis for "traditional" (i.e.,

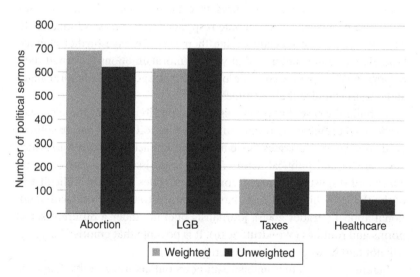

FIGURE 3.6. Political sermons by issue type, 2000–2020
Notes: Bars represent number of sermons in SermonCentral.com database with political content, sorted by issue (n = 1,567). Weights adjust for denominational differences in SermonCentral.com (which tends to underrepresent Catholics). Sermons retrieved in February 2020 (upload dates span October 2000 to February 2020).

heteronormative) relationships. One pastor, citing Romans I as justification, argues that homosexuality is "unnatural and a perversion." The sermon concludes that "marriage is based on the truth that men and woman are complementary, the fact that reproduction depends on a man and a woman, and the reality that children need a mother and a father" (Sermon Central 2015).

For the reasons we have given, the Sermon Central data are not gospel. We have concerns about the representativeness of the data. Reassuringly, survey research that asks churchgoers about sermon content is largely consistent with our claims. A 2016 Pew Research survey reports that next to the topic of religious liberty itself, abortion and homosexuality were the two most discussed political issues at worship services; 39 percent of churchgoing Americans reported hearing about homosexuality from clergy. Another 29 percent reported hearing about abortion. The results of the Sermon Central analysis are thus in line with evidence from polls.

Emotive Frames and Moral Issues

So far, our evidence suggests that the information environment provided Americans with plenty of chances to evaluate abortion and same-sex rights. We have argued that people responded in a consistent manner to whatever sample of messages came their way. We have further claimed (and elaborate in chapter 4) that visceral moral emotions governed their responses. When people come across these messages, a mix of moral anger and disgust stabilize their attitudes.

To build the case that public discourse contributed to attitude crystallization, we examine the frames in communication that disparate sources used to cover these issues. Specifically, we unpack the degree to which news media and political actors framed these issues in terms of moral anger and disgust. Newspaper coverage provides the most difficult test of the theory. While politicians have incentives to use rhetoric with emotional appeal (Brader 2006), journalists operate under a different set of norms and routines (Woodruff 2019). It is possible that emotive language will not find its way into news coverage.

Figure 3.7 shows that mainstream news outlets use emotive language to frame moral issues. We again compare abortion/same-sex stories to stories about healthcare and taxes. Moral issues contain more anger and disgust language. While some might object that taxes and healthcare are weak comparison categories, these issues do have the potential to elicit

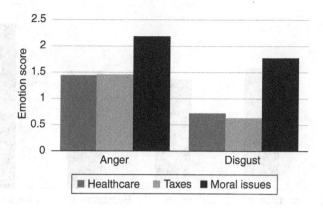

FIGURE 3.7. Moral emotions in the news, 1980–2022
Notes: Bars represent average emotion scores for each newspaper article type. Emotion scores are calculated as the total National Research Council (NRC) word count for a particular emotion dimension, divided by the total word count for the article and multiplied by 100.

strong moral reactions. Health issues revolve around discussions of disease and sickness. The denial of healthcare to others—especially those on the margins of society—evokes anger. Taxes often center on questions of government overreach, which angers some and disgusts others.

Using the NRC emotion keyword score described earlier in the chapter, figure 3.7 indicates that emotion-related language is more common in newspaper stories on moral issues than on healthcare and taxes. These differences are statistically significant ($p < .001$) and substantively large. Consider the moral issue anger score of 2.18 compared to a score of 1.44 for taxes. This means that in a typical seven-hundred-word article, we would expect to find about ten anger words if the topic is taxes and fifteen if the topic involves abortion/gays. Considering the intensity of moral language (*accuse, casualty, disgrace, furious*), this difference is meaningful.

These differences are even more evident for language that invokes disgust, which occurs at over twice the rate for moral issues versus healthcare and taxes. Qualitatively, these differences are evident even when we attempt to "control" for the article topic. For example, consider two 2016 AP articles previewing likely policy changes under the Trump administration. One article dealt with likely abortion policy changes; the other, likely tax policy changes. The abortion article detailed possible restrictions on abortion access using emotive language like *imperil, jeopardy, forced, tragic, hostile*, and *fight*. The tax article was similar in that it outlined some potential negative consequences of Trump's plan. The key difference is that the

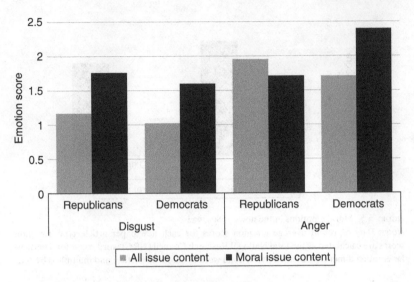

FIGURE 3.8. Moral emotions on campaign websites, 2008–2022
Notes: Bars represent average emotion scores for moral issue pages, compared with other policy discussions. Emotion scores are calculated as the total NRC word count for a particular emotion dimension, divided by the total word count for the issue page and multiplied by 100.

tax story used much softer language (*modestly cut income taxes, energize the economy*).

We have suggested that these moral frames will differ depending on which side produces the message. Cultural conservatives and Republicans are more likely to have a disgust reaction to same-sex relationships and abortion. Cultural progressives and Democrats are more likely to react with anger to anti-gay rhetoric (Gadarian and van der Vort 2018). It seems plausible that partisan messaging would follow suit.

Figure 3.8 tests this idea by comparing Republican and Democratic campaign websites that feature moral issues to all other campaign website issue pages. Results are consistent with expectations. The largely pro-choice and pro-gay rights Democratic pages used significantly more anger words than the other Democratic issue pages ($M_{MI\text{-}Others} = 0.7$, $p < .001$) and Republican moral issue pages ($M_{Dem\text{-}GOP} = 0.7$, $p < .001$). Democratic pages adopt a posture of moral outrage. Representative Ilhan Omar (MN-05, 2020) declared that she would "fight against any efforts to undermine LGBTQIA+ rights in the name of religious liberty." Sometimes the websites reference acts of violence/prejudice against those communities for whom Democrats advocate. Representative Omar's stance draws attention to "fatal violence against transgender people," "LGBTQIA+ youth...suicide," and "workplace discrimination."

The partisan pattern is quite different for disgust language. GOP candidates use disgust words more for abortion and gays than they do when talking about other issues ($M_{MI\text{-}Others}$ = 0.62, p < .001). They also use disgust words significantly more often than Democrats on moral issue pages ($M_{GOP\text{-}DEM}$ = 0.16, p = .003). On Republican pages, this disgust language often takes the shape of framing abortion as murder. Representative Clay Higgens (LA-03) said on his 2018 campaign page that "96 million children have been murdered in the womb in our country since the 1970s."

Figure 3.9 complements the campaign website study by looking at emotion words in party platforms. Here, we extracted the text surrounding moral issues and then compared it with the rest of the platform. The pattern in party platforms echoes what we saw on campaign websites. Democrats frame moral issues with more anger rhetoric than other issues ($M_{MI\text{-}Others}$ = 0.64, p < .06), while the GOP's anger score drops off ($M_{MI\text{-}Others}$ = −0.11, p ns). While both parties use significantly more disgust language when framing moral issues, the GOP stands out the most in this regard ($M_{MI\text{-}Others}$ = 1.77, p < .001). The party platform emotion

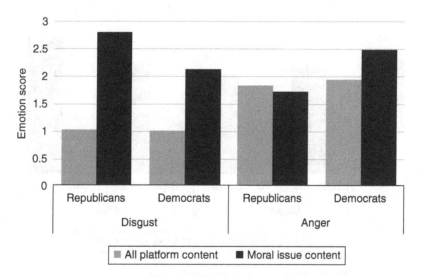

FIGURE 3.9. Moral emotions in party platforms, 1972–2020
Notes: Bars represent average emotion scores for moral issue passages, compared with total platform content. Emotion scores are calculated as the total NRC word count for a particular emotion dimension, divided by the total word count for the issue page and multiplied by 100.

word scores align closely with the emotion word scores we found on the campaign websites in figure 3.8. This shows a high degree of concordance (if not intention) in message construction. It surely reflects similar frames of thought operating in the minds of elites in the same party.

Figures 3.8 and 3.9 represent two different types of campaign rhetoric. It is possible that what politicians say in seeking office differs from what they say once they are in office. As such, we investigate the emotional language MCs use on the floor of the House. Figure 3.10 does this with data from congressional one-minute speeches. We examine links between emotive language, party, and moral issues. The pattern is largely consistent with figures 3.8 and 3.9. Democrats are angrier when talking about moral issues than when they talk about other issues ($M_{MI\text{-}Others} = 0.98, p < .001$). They are also angrier than Republicans about abortion and gay rights ($M_{Dem\text{-}GOP} = 0.46, p < .001$). Across the aisle, GOP members invoke disgust a lot more when talking about moral issues than when talking about other issues ($M_{MI\text{-}Others} = 1.06, p < .001$). They also invoke disgust more often than their Democratic counterparts ($M_{GOP\text{-}DEM} = 0.24, p < .001$).

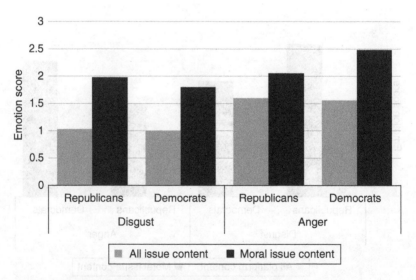

FIGURE 3.10. Moral emotions in congressional speeches, 1989–2014
Notes: Bars represent average emotion scores for moral one-minute speeches, compared with other one-minute speeches. Emotion scores are calculated as the total NRC word count for a particular emotion dimension, divided by the total word count for the issue page and multiplied by 100.

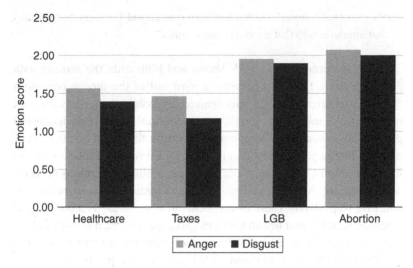

FIGURE 3.11. Moral emotions in Christian sermons, by issue type, 2000–2020
Notes: Bars represent emotion scores for Christian sermons, sorted by issue category. Emotion scores are calculated as the total NRC word count for a particular emotion dimension, divided by the total word count for the issue page and multiplied by 100.

Do the moral emotions at play in the political realm happen in other discourses? Answering this question presents unique challenges, though we think the answer is likely yes. The content analysis presented in this section is probably not replicable in the case of TV (character dialogue embedded in storylines is qualitatively different than political rhetoric) or billboards (which rely on images and contain limited text). This said, we suspect that the effect on audiences will be similar. Consider the TV show *ER*'s season twelve portrayal of an abortion. When a fifteen-year-old girl is raped and becomes pregnant, Dr. Neela Rosgotra has a heated exchange with the girl's religious father that hints at the father's moral disgust:

GIRL'S FATHER: "We don't believe in accidents ... it is God's will for her to have this child."
ROSGOTRA: "I only mean you might want to consider the other effects."
GIRL'S FATHER: "You might want to consider the spiritual effects of what you're suggesting."
ROSGOTRA: "It is my job to make sure the patient understands all the options available to her."

68   CHAPTER THREE

GIRL'S FATHER: "A human life has just been created and I'm sorry but anything
that interferes with that is morally indefensible."

While we cannot look at TV shows and billboards, the sermon data
permit analysis. Doing so presents a hard test of the theory, because a
"moral issue sermon" might have limited discussion of abortion. The rest
of the sermon might take the shape of scriptural exegesis or devotional
prayer. Do "moral issue" sermons stand out in the moral emotions they
convey? Figure 3.11 suggest that they do. Moral issue sermons tend to be
heavy on disgust and anger words relative to political sermons on taxes
and healthcare. Abortion and gay sermons register disgust scores of 2.01
and 1.89, respectively. These issues stand out as significantly more disgust-
oriented than tax and health sermons ($M_{MI\text{-}Others} = .72, p < .001$). Differences in anger between moral issues and comparison sermons are also
significant in the expected direction ($M_{MI\text{-}Others} = .52, p < .001$).

Taken together, the emotive construction of sermons parallels the patterns we observe in the political and other secular realms. When talking
about social and political issues, speakers invoke moral anger and disgust
more readily on abortion and gay rights than on taxes and healthcare. In
conclusion, moral issue messaging is seemingly everywhere in the information environment, framed in the language of anger and disgust.

Chapter Summary

The theory of moral power contends that messages about abortion and
gay rights have surged through the information environment, broadly defined, for decades. This chapter confirms that the volume of messages surrounding both issues has been high dating back to the end of Ronald Reagan's second term. The chapter also shows that moral anger and disgust
frames have structured moral issue messaging more deeply than messages
about other salient issues. Messengers from the right express conservative
disgust about same-sex marriage and abortion. Messengers from the left
express progressive anger and revulsion at attacks on women and same-
sex individuals that deny them their rights and basic human dignity.

Moral issues are now ever present across varied modes of public, entertainment, and private discourse. People see and hear about abortion and
gay rights while driving down the highway, watching a sitcom, going to the
movies, or sitting in the pews on a Sunday. The reach of moral issues goes

far beyond the sources examined in this chapter. In her pop song "TV," singer Billie Eilish sings, "The internet's gone wild watching movie stars on trial / While they're overturning Roe v. Wade." As of this writing, "TV" has over 25 million views on YouTube and 225 million listens on Spotify. It seems quite likely that Eilish has reached far more listeners than even the most loquacious politician or talking head.

In recent years social media has entered the fray, allowing moral issue messages to reach new audiences while using the familiar language of disgust and anger. After the Supreme Court overturned *Roe v. Wade*, celebrities took to social media platforms to weigh in. Invoking fear and anger, Taylor Swift wrote, "I'm absolutely terrified that this is where we are— that after so many decades of people fighting for women's rights to their own bodies, today's decision has stripped us of that" (@taylorswift13, August 18, 2018). Over 800,000 users liked this tweet. Again, messages about abortion and gay rights are seemingly everywhere. In the next chapter, we begin to explore how moral issue messages have affected public opinion.

CHAPTER FOUR

Moral Emotions and Attitude Stability

In the last chapter, we showed that messages about abortion and gay rights started ramping up in the information environment in the late 1980s. Both issues have featured heavily in political and popular discourses ever since. Americans have had plenty of chances to form impressions about both issues. We theorize that when they got these messages, automatic moral emotions shaped their reactions. Because these communications spontaneously evoked moral emotions that pushed them to evaluate moral issues in a consistent way, their feelings toward both issues stabilized in fairly short order.[1]

In this chapter, we investigate whether feelings about abortion and same-sex rights take root in moral emotions and endure for long stretches of time. We proceed as follows. First, we introduce our data and describe the survey questions we use to tap abortion and gay rights opinion. Second, we show that conservative moral disgust predicts opposition to abortion and same-sex rights. We then review research that shows that attacks on gays elicit progressive moral anger and disgust that reinforces pro-gay sympathies. We argue that similar processes play out for abortion. Third, we show that the positions people take on these issues endure as long as their religious and party ties. The last section sets the stage for what comes next.

Data and Variables

Data Sources

This chapter employs data from cross-sectional and panel surveys. Cross-sectional surveys capture public opinion at a single point in time. We use cross-sectional data to validate the moral issue scales. We then turn to the

2012 and 2016 Cooperative Congressional Election Studies (CCES) to test the hypothesis that disgust sensitivity predicts culture war issue attitudes.

With panel data, analysts measure how people respond to the same questions at two or more points in time. This facilitates the study of continuity and change in public opinion. By comparing the answers people give to identically worded questions in different years, any opinion change we observe results from changing attitudes, not changing questions.[2]

It takes a great deal of time and money to collect nationally representative samples from the same people at two or more points in time. Happily for us, we have access to a number of high-quality panel datasets that meet our needs. This book draws on seven different panels: (1) the 1992–1996 National Election Study (NES); (2) the 2000–2004 NES; (3) the 2006–2010 General Social Survey (GSS); (4) the 2008–2012 GSS; (5) the 2010–2014 GSS; (6) the 2006–2012 Portrait of American Life Study (PALS); and (7) the 2016–2020 NES. The panels furnish us with multiple opportunities to test the empirical implications of our theory. The appendix describes each dataset in more detail.

Measuring Attitudes toward Moral Issues

This section introduces the items we use to measure latent attitudes toward abortion and gay rights. Our measurement strategy is simple. Whenever possible, combine multiple abortion and gay rights items into simple additive scales. Multi-item scales are preferable to single items for two reasons. First, multi-item scales have greater measurement validity than single items (Bakker and Lelkes 2018). These scales do a much better job capturing the underlying attitude than single items do. Just as teachers use multiple questions to measure what students know, survey researchers use multiple items to measure how respondents feel about political issues.

Multi-item scales have a second virtue. They enhance the reliability of measurement scales. By this, we mean that the scales provide consistent, reproducible estimates of the underlying attitude. Multi-item scales help minimize random measurement error (RME) in survey responses. Moreover, they do so in ways that avoid some of the problems with "overcorrecting" for RME associated with more advanced statistical estimators (Ansolabehere, Rodden, and Snyder 2008).

Instead of describing every item in every scale, we provide an overview to convey their content. To begin, the GSS surveys pose seven yes/no questions on the circumstances under which a woman should be able to obtain an abortion. These items include both "elective" and "traumatic" abortion circumstances, an important distinction in abortion opinion (Cook, Jelen, and Wilcox 1992). One item reads "Please tell me whether or not you think it should be possible for a pregnant woman to obtain a legal abortion if she is married and does not want any more children." This gets at the "elective" dimension in abortion attitudes. The GSS also asks about abortion if "the woman's own health is seriously endangered by the pregnancy"—an example of a "traumatic" circumstance.

The elective-traumatic distinction aligns with reporting in the wake of the *Dobbs* decision, revealing considerable nuance in public attitudes. For example, a recent report from Pew (2022a) shows that among those who say that abortion should be illegal, a sizeable majority believes that exceptions should be made for traumatic circumstances. In contrast to the GSS surveys, the NES panels contain a single abortion item and the PALS survey contains three items.

Turning to gay rights, the panel studies contain a mix of items. The GSS surveys ask about the morality of "sexual relations between two adults of the same sex" and whether "homosexual couples should have the right to marry one another." The NES surveys ask at different times about feelings toward homosexuals/gays and lesbians, gays in the military, support for civil rights, and same-sex marriage. The PALS survey contains a lone item on support for traditional heterosexual marriage.

As this brief review reveals, we have a cornucopia of items. Question content, wording, and response options vary across the instruments and over three decades of political history. Some surveys contain more abortion items. Others tilt more toward gay rights. In our judgment, this variation constitutes a design strength. The theory of moral power asserts that people hold crystallized attitudes on both issues. If this is so, we should find that diverse sets of items combine to form valid and reliable scales, regardless of the items contained therein. Moral issues, however measured, should endure and predict change in core identities.

The number of items in a given scale varies from three to nine. We invite readers who want to peruse the questions to consult the measurement appendix at the end of the book. The appendix also contains a statistical analysis and discussion of measurement reliability and validity. There, we provide evidence that the items combine to form valid and reliable scales of latent attitudes (see online appendix tables A4.1 and A4.2). In a nutshell, we have very good measures of how people feel about abortion and gay rights.

Public Opinion on Moral Issues, 1992–2016

Before moving on to the initial tests of our theory, we believe it would help readers to see the distribution of opinion on moral issues in all of our datasets. In each survey, we combined all available items into a simple additive scale. Here and elsewhere in the book we fix the moral issues scale to range from zero to one. Higher values reflect stronger opposition to abortion and gay rights. Figure 4.1 presents the opinion distributions for the three NES datasets. Figure 4.2 does the same for the three GSSs and the PALS data. In each plot, the data comes from the first wave in each panel.

To start with the NES data in figure 4.1, two points jump out. First, collective opinion on abortion and gay rights leaned slightly to the left in 1992 and 2000. The respective means are 0.45 and 0.42 on the 0–1 scale. In 2016, Americans' opinions tilted more decidedly to the left (mean = 0.34), pulled there by the large number of respondents who took the most progressive position. Figure 4.1 suggests that from 1992 to 2016 the US public became more progressive on moral issues. This shift is consistent with data reported elsewhere in the book and in other forums. However, since we use different questions to construct the scales we cannot rule out question wording as a possible explanation for some of this observed change.

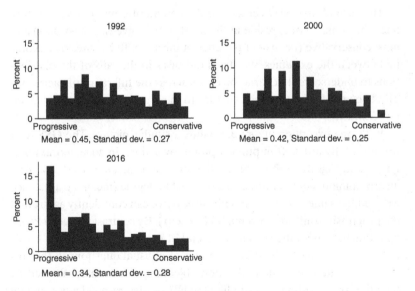

FIGURE 4.1. Public opinion on moral issues, NES data
Note: The data come from the first wave in each NES panel.

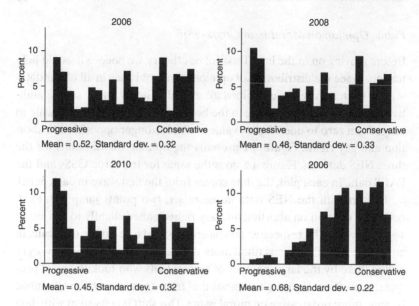

FIGURE 4.2. Public opinion on moral issues, GSS and PALS data
Note: The data come from the first wave in each GSS panel and the PALS panel (lower right histogram).

The second takeaway centers on the spread of opinion. Every survey finds that some people reside in the most progressive (i.e., 0.00–0.05) and most conservative (i.e., 0.95–1.00) ends of the scale. To be sure, most scores lie between the extremes. We stress the cases in the tails of the distributions to underscore that variation exists across the full range of each scale. This becomes important when we turn to the regression estimates in chapters 6 and 7.

With one exception, figure 4.2 paints a similar picture. The GSS data reveals a leftward shift in public opinion over time. In 2006, moral opinion leaned slightly in the conservative direction (mean = 0.52). By 2010, macro-opinion had liberalized to a noticeable degree (mean = 0.45). Since we used the same questions in both surveys, we can confidently assert that the progressive shift was meaningful ($p < .001$). By contrast, the 2006 PALS data tilts heavily to the conservative end of the scale (mean = 0.68). This right skew is in part a function of a pair of unusual questions in the survey that elicited strong anti-abortion objections not counterbalanced by the other two questions.[3] Lastly, like the NES scales, respondents populate the extreme points in the GSS and PALS samples.

Moral Emotions Shape Public Opinion on Abortion and Gay Rights

In chapter 2, we argued that moral anger and disgust are the emotional substrates that underlie moral issue attitudes. We theorized that when people encounter messages about moral issues, automatic emotional reactions habitually push some of them to favor, and others to oppose, abortion and gay rights. Visceral conservative disgust nudges some to take pro-life, anti-gay stances. Instinctual progressive anger and disgust prod those turned off by anti-woman, anti-gay attacks in the pro-choice, pro-gay direction. Here, we test whether conservative disgust predicts disapproval of abortion and same-sex rights. We then review published work that shows that progressive anger and disgust feed back into pro-choice, pro-gay sentiments.

Conservative Disgust

We begin with conservative moral disgust. Recall that people feel disgust—that is a sense of aversion—toward different classes of objects. These include physical things (e.g., spoiled meat), acts (e.g., incest), and people (e.g., sexual deviants). Disgust originated as a rejection response to protect the body from ingesting potentially harmful foods and other contaminants. Disgust continues to serve this survival function, but it has expanded to protect us from interpersonal and moral threats posed by others (Rozin, Haidt, and McCauley 2008; Graham et al. 2013). Valarie Curtis (2011, 3478) put it well when she wrote, "Sometime in our evolution toward human ultra-sociality, disgust took on an extended role—providing a motive to punish antisocial behavior and to shun the breakers of social rules." Interpersonal and moral threats do not dampen our survival odds. Instead, some see them as threats to the soul, the moral order, and society at large.

Psychologists refer to these kinds of reactions as "moral disgust" (Haidt et al. 1997; Chapman and Anderson 2013). Disgust motivates withdrawal in the face of threats, whether real or not, and the adoption of hygienic behaviors to ward off contamination, whether physical or spiritual. Said another way, physical *and* moral hazards that threaten to infect the self and society motivate flight and containment efforts.

How does moral disgust arise in a given situation? The answer depends on innate sensitivity to core disgust elicitors *and* what people have picked up from their groups, their cultures, and their subcultures (Haidt et al.

1997; Chapman et al. 2009; Graham et al. 2013; Casey 2016). In many conservative and traditional cultures, group members have learned that abortion and gays represent existential threats to the moral order. Abortion is murder. Homosexuality is a sin. Both acts violate long-standing norms about gender, procreation, and family, thereby debasing society (Cahill 2013). We see evidence for this line of thought in the gay bashing that accompanied the AIDS crisis and the rationales proffered by pro-life activists in their crusade against abortion (Luker 1984; Herek and Capitanio 1993). As a result of socialization processes like these, many cultural conservatives find abortion and same-sex relations distasteful if not morally repugnant. The solution lies in eradicating these practices. Doing so safeguards public morality and preserves social stability.

People vary widely in their susceptibility to feeling disgust in the presence of its established elicitors. Some of us are quite sensitive to revolting stimuli; others have stronger stomachs, so to speak (Schaller 2006; Curtis 2011). To measure this predisposition, researchers have devised a standard battery of survey questions. The seminal works in moral psychology validated disgust sensitivity scales containing some two to three dozen or so items (Haidt, McCauley, and Rozin 1994; Olatunji et al. 2007). Political scientists have deployed five to eight item scales in their work (Kam and Estes 2016; Aarøe, Petersen, and Arceneaux 2017).

The standard hypothesis is that high scores on disgust sensitivity scales will predict conservative positions on the core moral issues. This is just what prior work finds (Inbar et al. 2009; Terrizzi, Shook, and Ventis 2010; Smith et al. 2011; Koleva et al. 2012; Kam and Estes 2016). At the same time, self-reported disgust sensitivity does not predict views on issues such as government spending, taxes, affirmative action, the death penalty, and other issues. This implies, but does not prove, that pro-life and anti-gay attitudes are uniquely rooted in moral disgust. We now seek to replicate this work.

We expect that those who score high on disgust sensitivity will react more negatively to abortion/gay rights than those who score low on it. To test this proposition, we use the 2012 and 2016 CCES data. The common content and the Vanderbilt University modules contain the necessary items.[4] For moral issues, the 2012 survey contains one abortion item and two gay rights items. The 2016 instrument has four abortion items and one gay rights item. We use the Kam and Estes (2016) eight-item measure of disgust sensitivity. Respondents reported how disgusted they feel about various scenarios (e.g., "I never let any part of my body touch the toilet seat in public restrooms."). They also indicated how disgusting they find various experiences (e.g., "You are about to drink a glass of milk when you smell

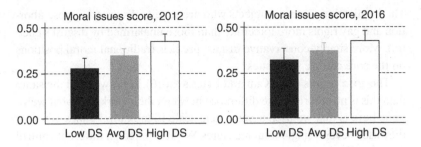

FIGURE 4.3. Disgust sensitivity predicts moral issue conservatism, 2012 and 2016 CCES data
Notes: Bars represent the mean moral issue score on the moral issues scale. This scale ranges from 0.00 (pro-choice/pro-gay) to 1.00 (anti-choice/anti-gay). The effect of disgust sensitivity is significant both years (p < .01). Estimates derived from 2012 and 2016 CCES models in table A4.3.

that it is spoiled."). The scale runs from zero (least sensitive) to one (most sensitive). Again, the responses people give to questions like these predict their views of abortion/gay rights, with the more easily offended taking more conservative positions. The chapter appendix provides the question wording for these variables.

We use the disgust sensitivity scale to predict policy opinions in an ordinary least squares (OLS) regression model, controlling for various background variables and traits.[5] Appendix table A4.3 reports the OLS estimates for interested readers. Here, we use a graphic to illustrate the main quantities of interest. Figure 4.3 displays two bar charts, one for the 2012 data and the other for 2016. Each bar graph shows how variation in disgust sensitivity on the x-axis correlates with moral issue opinion on the y-axis, all else constant. Higher scores on moral issues denote stronger pro-life/anti-gay sentiments. Higher levels of disgust sensitivity should predict stronger opposition to abortion/gay rights.

As called for by our theory, figure 4.3 shows that disgust sensitivity does indeed predict moral conservatism. In both datasets, those repelled by revolting things in daily life take more conservative positions on abortion/gay rights than those who are not so squeamish. We can see this by looking at the predicted moral issue scores for respondents at low, average, and high levels of disgust sensitivity.[6] Movement from low to high values on disgust sensitivity on the x-axis predicts more right-wing positions on moral issues on the y-axis. The effect is significant in both datasets (p < .01) and sizable in magnitude. To take the 2012 data as an example, the moral conservatism score is 0.28 for the disgust insensitive, 0.35 for those with average levels of disgust sensitivity, and 0.43 for those who are highly sensitive to disgust.

The implication is clear. Subjects who are readily disgusted oppose abortion and gay rights more forcefully than those unalarmed by disgust's elicitors. More simply, conservative disgust predicts traditional moral positions on the core culture war issues.

The 2012 results echo Kam and Estes's (2016). Since we used the same data this is no surprise. One difference between their work and what we've done here is that we used a multi-item scale to tap moral issues, whereas they used several single-item measures. We also relied on different control variables. Given the fragility of many social science inferences, our replication adds value. The 2016 estimates provide further confirmation that disgust sensitivity and moral conservatism covary. Of course, the data we use cannot prove these links are causal.

Acknowledging this uncertainty, we conclude that conservative disgust seems to play a key role backstopping opposition to abortion and gay rights. The spread of moral issue messages through sundry communication channels evokes flashes of disgust in the minds of disgust-sensitive individuals. These flashes generate consistent evaluative responses to abortion and gay primes. We think this process renders opposition to abortion and gays durable. But before taking up stability, we must consider the role moral emotions play in crystallizing progressive attitudes on gay rights and, more speculatively, abortion.

Progressive Anger and Disgust

Conservative disgust cannot explain why some Americans favor abortion and same-sex rights or why these impressions grow stronger with repeat exposure to communiques about the issues. Something else must be going on. But what, precisely? Recall that the violation of social norms and individual rights evokes moral emotions. We feel some combination of anger and disgust when people violate our rights, when they treat us unfairly, when they disrespect us, and when they do so to others—especially those we sympathize with (Rozin et al. 1999). Our concern lies with harm done to others.

How do people who are sympathetic toward women, gays, and lesbians respond when these groups come under attack? Work by Shana Kushner Gadarian and Eric van der Vort (2018) speaks directly to this question. In innovative research, they discovered that attacks on gays provoke different kinds of emotional reflexes among pro-gay and anti-gay subjects. Said another way, progressive anger and disgust is different from conservative disgust. Because this research bears directly on our argument about moral emotions, we take some time to unpack their results.

In one experiment, Gadarian and van der Vort randomly assigned subjects to one of three conditions (positive, neutral, disgust) to read a news story about a constitutional amendment to ban same-sex marriage in Indiana. In the disgust condition, subjects read, "Two men will never be able to reproduce. Anal penetration can never result in the creation of new life." A picture of an anti-gay protester holding up a sign that read "The Anus Is a Grave" accompanied the text. For some subjects, this treatment heightened opposition to gay rights relative to subjects in the neutral condition, via moral distaste. This is conservative disgust playing out.

For other subjects, the disgust treatment evoked moral anger, relative to those in the neutral condition. Morally angered subjects subsequently reported *more* support for gay rights. Gadarian and van der Vort (2018, 537) speculated that "this indignation is fueled by a reaction to the anti-rights rhetoric present in our disgust treatment. . . . disgust rhetoric may be a powerful tool but it does not come without a price. This price may be found in a form of emotional backlash among segments of the population who are supportive of rights and who react with indignation and in ways that anti-gay elites would not want them to." It appears that anti-gay messages trigger conservative moral disgust that stokes opposition to gay rights among some people and progressive moral anger that reinforces support for gay rights among those with different predilections. The finding on progressive anger echoes research that has found that the violation of individual rights, such as stealing from a blind person, activates moral anger among those who bear witness to such acts (Rozin et al. 1999).

In another experiment Gadarian and van der Vort asked subjects to write down their feelings about gays and lesbians given different primes. In the neutral condition, subjects wrote down what came to mind when they thought about gays and lesbians. In the treatment condition, subjects described something about gays and lesbians that disgusted them. The treatment prompted some to deliver vivid expressions of anti-gay disgust relative to neutral condition subjects. Example: "I think it is disgusting because life should be about a man and a woman and they should be able to reproduce offspring." Once again, we observe primal conservative disgust.

The prompt also elicited anger and revulsion among subjects who decried the way gays suffer at the hands of the legal system and bigots, and the toll such patently unfair treatment inflicts on them. One sympathetic subject noted, "I felt disgusted by the lack of compassion some people choose to show for gays and lesbians because of their hatred for those who are different from them." (Gadarian and van der Vort 2018, 533). Responses like these imply that anti-gay rhetoric in politics and everyday life repulses and outrages many people, leaving them more sympathetic toward gays and lesbians. Across both experiments, the emergence of pro-gay backlash rooted in moral anger and disgust supports our argument that progressive moral emotions underlie pro-gay attitudes.

All told, the Gadarian and van der Vort experiments show that messages disparaging gays and lesbians evoke distinct emotional reactions in different slices of the public. For some people, moral disgust foments anti-gay attitudes. For others, anti-gay messaging engenders sympathy and support for gays and same-sex rights. As people from different backgrounds encounter these messages and experience automatic emotional responses, their attitudes crystallize in the direction of the emotional inputs. Conservative disgust motivates anti-abortion, anti-gay sentiments. Progressive anger and disgust motivates pro-choice, pro-gay feelings.

So much for same-sex rights, but what about abortion? Do some people find attacks on a woman's right to choose infuriating? Revolting? Worthy of censure? Given the close correspondence between people's attitudes on both issues, it seems plausible that what generates emotional backlash against anti-gay attacks might do the same work for anti-abortion messages. The resulting emotional backlash would then bolster pro-choice attitudes. With that said, we are unaware of studies that confirm links between backlash anger/disgust and pro-choice views. Kristin Luker (1984) provides qualitative evidence that such processes play out among pro-choice activists. But we cannot be sure that this plays out in the mass public. We freely acknowledge we are making a strong assumption here. This is an area ripe for future work.

To bring this section to a close: messages about abortion and gays have appeared regularly in political, popular, and other discourses going back several decades. These messages automatically evoke distinct affective reactions among different parts of the electorate. For some, moral disgust bolsters conservative issue attitudes. For others, conservative messages elicit progressive moral anger and disgust. These reactions rebound into pro-gay and, we speculate, pro-choice sensibilities. In this way, attitudes toward abortion and gay rights, whether left- or right-leaning, harden. The next section explores just how durable these attitudes really are.

Moral Issues Are as Stable as Core Identities

The theory of moral power predicts that attitudes toward moral issues will persist as long as core identities. To convey the intuition here, we circle back to the stories of Autumn and Dawn that opened chapter 2. As noted there, Autumn's religious journey led her to try out a few different faiths and churches in her twenties and thirties. Her party ID also changed as she switched from Democrat to Republican. The one thing that remained the same is her implacable opposition to abortion and same-sex relations. In a similar way, Dawn's history couples stable views on gay rights with flux in her religious identity. Dawn told us that she always favored gay rights. When her local parish opposed a gay marriage amendment in her state, she left for another church. Like Autumn, Dawn's views on moral issues outlasted her group ties.

These stories are suggestive, nothing more. They shed no light on whether views on abortion and gay rights endure in the minds of most people. We need better evidence to build the case for attitude stability as the rule for most people. We can gauge stability by looking at the statistical relationship between the answers people give to the same survey question at two points in time. Social scientists often do this by calculating continuity correlations. The correlation for a perfectly stable identity or opinion variable is 1.00. For a completely unstable variable, the correlation is 0.00.[7] Thus, the higher the correlation, the more stable the attitude.

How do we know what counts as stable? The correlations for religion and party ID provide a useful baseline. Researchers report that core identities are more stable than the positions people take on most issues (Converse and Markus 1979; Kinder and Kalmoe 2017). Identity correlations often fall in the 0.70–0.80 range. We expect the stability of moral issues to match that of the religion and party variables. This would confirm that attitudes toward abortion and gay rights are indeed durable.

We use our panel data to calculate Pearson r correlations for our moral issue scales, religious identity strength,[8] and the seven-point party ID item.[9] Figure 4.4 plots the correlation for each variable in each dataset. Note that the religious strength variable appears only in the GSS datasets. Each dot represents a correlation between responses given in the first and last wave of a survey. The bands around the dots are 95 percent confidence intervals (CIs). They represent uncertainty around each estimate.[10] Dots further to the right indicate larger continuity correlations (that is, more stability). The higher the correlations, the more that people like Autumn and Dawn, who have unchanging views of moral issues, populate the samples.

Recall that we are looking for values in the 0.70–0.80 range (or higher), which denote substantial stability. Figure 4.4 reveals that sixteen of the seventeen correlations are greater than 0.70. The lone exception is the moral issue scale in the six-year PALS dataset ($r = 0.66$). For fourteen of

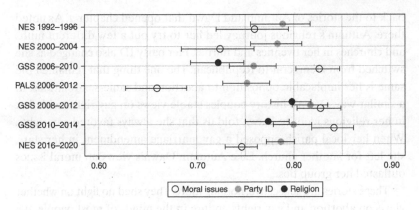

FIGURE 4.4. Continuity correlations in seven panel studies
Note: Pearson *r* correlations bounded by 95 percent confidence intervals.

the seventeen correlations, the lower confidence limit falls above the 0.70 threshold—more evidence of high stability. The three exceptions are the PALS issues scale (95 percent CI = [0.63, 0.69]); the 2000–2004 NES issues scale (95 percent CI = [0.69. 0.72]); and the 2006–2010 GSS religion variable (95 percent CI = [0.69, 0.75]). The latter two are near misses.

Note that when we break down the full scale into separate abortion and gay rights mini-scales, these mini-scales prove highly stable and equally stable. The mean continuity correlation comes in at 0.71 for abortion and 0.69 for gay rights. These results imply that people persist in their views on abortion and gay rights to the same impressive degree.

These results validate the stability hypothesis in two ways. First, they affirm that feelings about abortion and same-sex rights persist for periods lasting four-to-six years. Across the seven panels, the average issue correlation equals 0.77. With the exception of the PALS data, which spans six years versus four in the other panels, the high continuity correlations from the early 1990s until 2020 are striking.

Several data points in figure 4.3 merit added comment. The first period in which we are able to examine the stability of moral issues occurs between 1992 and 1996. As the 0.76 correlation makes clear, moral issues in the early 1990s were already durable. This dovetails with the argument we advanced in the previous chapter. In the late 1980s, the information environment began to fill up with policy messages in a way that prompted the emergence of strong policy views. By the early 1990s, moral issue attitudes were very stable. In an ideal world we would have panel studies that included measures of abortion and gay rights from the 1970s/1980s. Given the dearth of media coverage of abortion and gay rights at the time, we would expect *lower* correlations in this era (though not necessarily low, see Converse and Markus 1979). Absent panel data from that era, we cannot be sure.

Another finding merits a bit of discussion. We direct readers to the trio of GSS issue estimates, which all eclipse 0.80 and average 0.83. Remember from our earlier discussion that the GSS scales include seven abortion items, one item on same-sex morality, and one on gay marriage. These scales do a better job covering the essential elements of both issues than the other scales at our disposal. The abortion items ask about a much wider range of elective and traumatic circumstances than the single NES item and the idiosyncratic PALS items (see the appendix). And while some of the NES panels have more questions about gays and lesbians, we believe that the two GSS items do a better job getting at the heart of these views. If we could only ask two questions about gays on a survey, we would ask about the morality of same-sex relations and gay marriage—the very questions that appear on the GSS.

The point is this. The GSS opinion scales are the best we have. They are more valid and reliable than the NES and PALS scales. The GSS scales show that feelings about abortion and gay rights proved remarkably stable during a period of high issue salience and political volatility. There was a lot going on at the time. Consider this sample of events: (1) Obama's 2009 commencement speech at Notre Dame that aroused some opposition to his pro-choice stance; (2) the appointments of Sonia Sotomayor and Elena Kagan to the US Supreme Court in 2009 and 2010; (3) Obama's 2012 declaration of support of gay marriage; (4) multiple state ballot initiatives on gay marriage. Against this backdrop, few people altered their views of abortion and same-sex rights.

The results confirm our theoretical intuitions about the stability of moral issue attitudes in a second critical way. Standard theories hold that core identities last longer and evolve less than issue attitudes. Figure 4.4 affirms that religious ID and party ID endure for long periods of time. The Pearson correlations vary from 0.72 to 0.80 for religion and from 0.75 to 0.82 for party. However, the data fail to affirm the claim that identities outlast issues. Over all seven panel studies, the mean correlation for moral issues (0.77) is indistinguishable from that of religious ID (0.76) and party ID (0.78). These findings deviate from the conventional view that identities are strong and issue attitudes are weak. The findings fit with the theory of moral power.

84

To be sure, there is important variation within and across the panels. Take party ID as an example. Party is more stable than issues in some of the datasets. This is true in 2000–2004 (0.78 > 0.72). It also holds true in 2006–2012 (0.75 > 0.66) and 2016–2020 (0.79 > 0.75). But the pattern reverses elsewhere. Moral issues seem more durable than party ID in 2006–2010 (0.83 > 0.76) and 2010–2014 (0.84 > 0.80). No one should make a big deal about any of these differences. They reflect modest differences in degree rather than meaningful differences in kind. Again, the mean correlation is 0.77 for issues and 0.78 for party ID—no real difference.

To wrap up, the way people feel about moral issues holds as steady as their ties to organized religion and political parties. Studies show that the latter two identities are among the firmest orientations in the minds of Americans. As a baseline for assessing stability, they pose a tough test for issues. Moral issues pass this test with flying colors. We conclude that most Americans are like Autumn and Dawn. Their feelings toward abortion and same-sex rights persist to an impressive degree.

Chapter Summary

This chapter has covered disparate ground. To review, we described our data and the items we use to capture how people feel about abortion and gay rights. The online appendix shows that our scales are valid and reliable measures of latent feelings about abortion and gay rights. Next, we found that disgust sensitivity predicts the positions people take on these issues. This provides some support for the claim that conservative disgust affects and presumably stabilizes attitudes about these issues. Other evidence suggests similar processes play out for progressive moral anger and disgust in the case of same-sex rights (Gadarian and van der Vort 2018). We also showed that moral attitudes are as stable as religious ID and party ID, the benchmarks for what counts as standing predispositions in mass belief systems. This sets the stage for examining the relationship between issue change and identity reconstruction in chapters 6 (on religion) and 7 (on party ID).

But before we take that up, we must address a pair of questions that many readers have likely asked themselves in the preceding pages. If most individuals hold stable views about moral issues, then how did collective opinion on gay rights change so much in recent years. And how can stable attitudes coexist with instability on macro gay rights opinion and stability on macro abortion opinion? Chapter 5 resolves these paradoxes.

CHAPTER FIVE

Stand Patters, Switchers, and Collective Opinion

In the last chapter, we provided some evidence that the attitudes people hold on moral issues persist as long as their partisan and religious identities. We also saw that their views of abortion and same-sex rights are equally stable. Recall that the mean continuity correlation equals 0.71 for the abortion scales and 0.69 for the gay rights scales. These estimates imply that most people, like Dawn and Autumn, hold stable views on abortion and gay rights. Yet this conclusion sits in tension with what we know about collective opinion on both issues.

Polling results make this tension plain. According to a 2004 survey from the Pew Research Center, 31 percent of the American public favored same-sex marriage. Thirteen years later, 62 percent of the public did (Pew 2019). This is an enormous change in a relatively short period of time. Shifts this large are extremely rare in the annals of public opinion (Page and Shapiro 1992). Nothing comparable has happened on abortion. In 1995, Pew reported that 60 percent of the public favored legal abortion in all or most cases. Twenty-seven years later, 62 percent took that position one month after the US Supreme Court's 2022 *Dobbs* decision overturned the 1973 *Roe* decision that guaranteed a constitutional right to abortion (Pew 2022b). While collective opinion on gay rights changed dramatically in just over a decade, collective abortion opinion has barely moved at any point during the thirty-year history of the culture war.

The Pew numbers challenge the theory of moral power on two fronts. First, our theory contends that individual Americans hold stable views on gay rights. This seems hard to square with the rapid change in collective opinion on gay rights. On the face of it, big change at the collective level implies lots of change at the individual level—more than the theory of moral power allows. Put simply, how can the American public have changed so much if most individuals changed so little?

To answer, we focus on cohort replacement and one-sided opinion change. Drawing on data from GSS cross-sectional surveys, we show that the changing composition of the US public explains a portion of this collective shift. As younger, more tolerant adults replaced older, less tolerant elders in the electorate, macro opinion liberalized. But cohort replacement takes us only so far, so attitude change at the micro level must account for much of the collective shift in favor of gay rights. The question remains: How can stable individual opinions coexist with massive collective change?

To resolve this seeming paradox, we need to know how many people stand pat—that is, don't change their position—how many people change, and how these switchers change (Key 1966). Consistent with our claim of attitude stability, we show that gay rights "stand patters" outnumber gay rights "switchers" by a 5.67:1 ratio. However, the switchers who move in the pro-gay direction outnumber the anti-gay switchers by a large enough margin to help push collective opinion to the left. In short, the inference that macro instability on gay rights implies micro instability is an ecological fallacy. For this issue, widespread stability at the individual level coexists with lots of churn at the collective level.

The Pew data pose a second challenge to the theory of moral power. If the attitudes that individuals hold toward abortion and same-sex rights are equally stable, why doesn't the same hold for collective opinion? In other words, how can the American public change so much more on gay rights than on abortion when individuals change so little on either issue? Our panel data analysis shows that abortion stand patters outnumber switchers by a 4.25:1 ratio—much like gay rights. The key difference between the issues lies in what the switchers do. On gay rights more switchers moved in the pro-gay direction, leading to a progressive shift in collective opinion. On abortion, pro-choice switchers canceled out pro-life switchers, leading to no meaningful change in macro opinion. The net result is that collective opinion on abortion is far more stable than for gay rights even though micro opinion on both issues is highly and equivalently stable.

Chapter 5 is organized like this: First, we estimate how much of the change in macro opinion on moral issues is explained by cohort replacement. Next, we leverage the GSS panels to show that change in collective gay rights opinion and stability in collective abortion opinion rests on stable individual-level views of both issues. The last section looks at how

STAND PATTERS, SWITCHERS, AND COLLECTIVE OPINION   87

the behavior of the switchers have transformed the size of America's rival moral factions between 2006 and 2014. We find that moral progressives became ascendant in surprisingly short order.

Changing People versus Changing Minds

We start with cohort replacement as a possible explanation for increased public support for gay rights. Cohort replacement means that successively younger pro-gay generations replace older anti-gay generations. Since cohort replacement involves the composition of the electorate, it could produce macro opinion change with no individuals changing their minds. This is a simple way to reconcile our claim of stable individual attitudes with the large swing we saw in the Pew data. The evidence in this section will show that while we cannot ignore cohort replacement, large-scale attitude change remains on the table as a serious challenge to our theory.

The Pew data discussed is not unique in showing that the public has become more progressive on gay rights while holding steady on abortion. We can confirm this using GSS data. Figure 5.1 tracks collective opinion on same-sex intimacy, gay marriage, and abortion. Because the GSS did not regularly ask questions related to same-sex marriage until 2004, we employ a dichotomized version of the "same-sex relations" item here and later on in the chapter. This question dates to 1973 and tracks closely with views on gay marriage.[1]

Figure 5.1 highlights the twin challenges faced by our theory. Public opinion on same-sex relations began to liberalize in the early 1990s. Opinion on gay marriage followed a similar trajectory from the early 2000s on. By contrast, there is much less movement on abortion opinion.[2] From 1973 to 2016, it ebbed and flowed by limited amounts before trending in a pro-choice direction during the Trump years.

It is not self-evident from figure 5.1 why US public opinion on same-sex relations evolved. It may be that contrary to our claims, many people simply changed their minds. However, it is important to remember that many of the respondents in the later cross-sections were not part of the electorate in the early 1990s when the progressive shift began. Also, some respondents from the 1970s–1990s had passed away by the 2010s. If the generations entering the electorate were more tolerant than those departing it, the changing composition of the public might explain a significant portion of collective change on gay rights. If that portion is high enough,

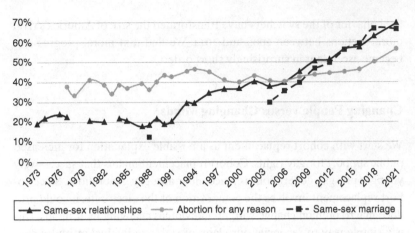

FIGURE 5.1. Public opinion on abortion, same-sex relationships, and gay marriage over time
Notes: All data comes from the GSS Cumulative Data File. Lines represent the percentage of respondents in favor of "same-sex relations" (dichotomized), "same-sex marriage" (dichotomized), and "abortion for any reason." The same-sex marriage item was introduced in 1988 but then not asked again until 2004. Note that the 1988, 2004, and 2021 items use slightly different question wording, asking if same-sex couples *should* have the right to marry.

it would suggest that cohort replacement, not individual attitude change, drove this progressive shift. But if cohort replacement is not primarily responsible for this trend, the micro-macro paradox lingers.

It would be nice if there was an easy way to disambiguate cohort replacement from attitude evolution. Unfortunately, understanding temporal change via time-series cross-sectional data is a thorny statistical problem.[3] This is known as the "age-period-cohort" problem. "Age" refers to some sort of underlying life-cycle process. For example, the incidence of arthritis increases with age, and this might be due to biological processes that go along with getting older. "Period" refers to change that affects all individuals in a population evenly, regardless of age. If a population transitions rapidly from heavy manual labor to office work, the incidence of arthritis in the population might decrease over time. "Cohort" refers to effects on one or more generations. Perhaps because of changes in childhood diet and nutrition, all cohorts born after a certain date will have higher rates of arthritis. As a result, we might observe changes in arthritis rates due to cohort replacement, as generations with nutrient-deficient diets replace generations with high-quality diets. Age, period, and cohort influences are not prime movers of attitudes and behaviors but, rather, proxy for broader social forces (Fosse and Winship 2019). In the arthritis example, period is a stand-in for changes in the labor economy that have downstream effects on individual health.

Previous chapters hint that distinct age, period, and cohort mechanisms might shape attitudes on moral issues. For example, the work we did in chapter 3 suggests that political messages might produce period and cohort effects. Once politicians began deploying emotively charged rhetoric, it is possible that voters in all cohorts began thinking about abortion and gay rights in fundamentally different ways. Then again, given that different cohorts consume different media, it is possible that political communications impact generations in different ways (Lee and Hicks 2011; Nielsen Insights 2016).

A growing body of work has sought to disentangle these forces in order to explain the liberal shift on gay rights. Using GSS data, Dawn Baunach (2011, 2012) found that cohort replacement explains roughly one-third of the change between 1988 and 2006. The remaining change was attributable to intracohort factors—that is, evolving attitudes. Philip Schwadel and Christopher Garneau (2014) found that period effects explain rising tolerance toward gays much better than cohort effects (see Sherkat et al. 2011; Twenge and Blake 2021). This line of research suggests that the patterns in figure 5.1 depends more on attitude change than cohort replacement.

To take a first cut at isolating these influences, we regressed same-sex opinions on both cohort and period. We looked at separate models for "same-sex marriage" 1988–2021 and "same-sex relations" 1988–2018 and 1973–2021. We model "same-sex relations" for the entire range of time for which we have data as well as the shorter time frame 1988–2021 so we can compare it to same-sex marriage on even footing. These models are simplified versions of the linear decomposition procedures used by Glenn Firebaugh (1989) and Dawn Baunach (2011).[4] These models help us partition the variance explained by birth cohort and period.

This strategy has limits. Because of linear dependencies, we cannot account for life-cycle effects. Moreover, this approach does not allow us to compare abortion and gay rights on an even footing. Looking at the trend line for abortion in figure 5.1, it is clear that opinion mostly ebbs and flows rather than moving in a clear direction. Thus, the method we deploy provides a useful baseline for assessing opinion change but yields no definitive answers.

Figure 5.2 uses a pie chart to display the results of the analysis. The dark gray portion represents change due to cohort succession—good news for our claim that moral attitudes are stable. The light gray slices represent

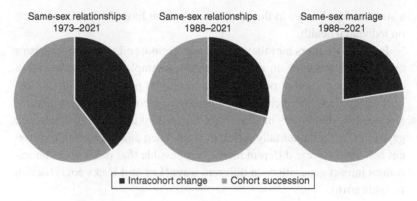

FIGURE 5.2. Decomposing change in collective opinion on gay rights
Notes: All data comes from the GSS Cumulative Data File. Pie slices represent estimates of age and birth cohort regressed on each of three dependent variables, adjusted to equal 100 percent. Estimation calculations can be found in table A5.1.

intracohort change—that is, evidence of people changing their minds within a cohort.

As expected, both period and cohort predict views of same-sex relationships.[5] Looking at "same-sex relations" opinion from 1973 to 2021, we estimate that cohort replacement accounts for roughly 39 percent of the change. Intracohort factors account for the remaining change. On balance, this is good news for our theory because cohort replacement, not attitude change, explains almost 40 percent of the collective change we see in public opinion.

However, much of the recent research has focused on a different GSS survey question—same-sex marriage. The GSS introduced this item in 1988 and returned to it from 2004 to 2021. Restricting the analysis to the more recent timeline weakens the case for cohort replacement. For same-sex relations from 1988–2021, cohort replacement explains 27 percent of collective opinion change. For gay marriage, cohort replacement accounts for less than a quarter of the observed change. These estimates support the conclusion that generational churn does not explain much of the recent dramatic change in LGBT opinion.

What can we conclude about cohort replacement versus attitude change as explanations for the liberalization of gay rights opinion that we see in figure 5.1? While both dynamics are at play, since the early 1990s changing minds have outweighed changing people as an explanation for rising pro-gay sentiment. We think the best explanation involves different mechanisms driving opinion change in different eras. When we examine the entire time series (1977–2021), roughly 40 percent of the change comes from cohort replacement. This is consistent with the idea that during the 1970s and 1980s, the rise of more progressive generations played a major role in driving macro opinion change on same-sex relations. However, something changed in the early 1990s. When we focus on this part of the time series, the cohort replacement estimate drops, which means that a noticeably larger portion of the public was updating its position. This coincides with the rising message intensity surrounding moral issues documented in chapter 3.

Figure 5.3, which divides GSS respondents into birth cohorts, reinforces this point. The figure displays the percentage of respondents in a cohort who answered "sometimes" or "not at all" to the same-sex relations is wrong question.[6] Before 1990, the "slopes" of the lines are largely flat, with all the differences in progressive same-sex attitudes occurring between generations. However, since the early 1990s, every birth cohort except the GI generation has become more accepting of same-sex relationships. For example, in 1987, just 24 percent of Baby Boomers (most of whom were in their thirties at the time) approved. By 2021, over 60 percent of them now approved.

This said, each successive cohort still entered the electorate holding more liberal views than their predecessors. For example, in 2006, the first

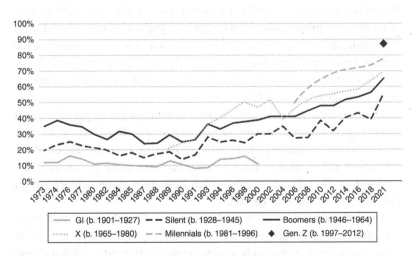

FIGURE 5.3. Support for gay rights, by birth cohort and year
Notes: All data comes from the GSS Cumulative Data File. Lines represent the percentage of respondents in favor of "same-sex relations" (dichotomized), by birth cohort.

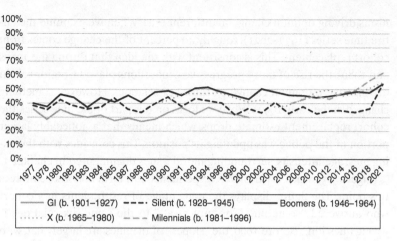

FIGURE 5.4. Support for abortion rights, by birth cohort and year
Notes: All data comes from the GSS Cumulative Data File. Lines represent the percentage of respondents in favor of "abortion for any reason," by birth cohort. The GSS does not ask every question of every respondent. For this reason, Gen Z sample sizes are too low to include in this figure.

year Millennials enter our sample, twenty-three points separates them from the Silent Generation. The gap is still present in the 2021 wave of the GSS, even though both cohorts have become more liberal by roughly twenty-five points. Lastly, note that Gen Z enters our analysis in 2021; 87 percent of them prove progressive on gay rights, the highest number recorded for any cohort in the history of the GSS. This visual inspection makes it clear that the time-series variation observed in figure 5.1 is at least partially due to cohort replacement, even after the 1990s. Before then, cohort replacement played a more prominent role.

Abortion provides an important point of contrast. Figure 5.4 displays the percentage of respondents who agree that a woman has a right to an abortion under any circumstance. Cohorts in figure 5.4 are less distinct from each other, and at times younger generations prove more conservative than their parents. To take one example, Gen Xers are sometimes more pro-life than their Baby Boomer parents.

Overall, collective opinion on abortion is stable within cohorts. This implies that neither attitude evolution nor cohort replacement occurred at the same pace relative to the public's views on gay rights/relations. What change is occurring is nonmonotonic, and patterns differ across the generations. Millennials have become over twenty points more liberal on abortion between their first appearance in the time series in 2006 and 2021. In contrast, the Gen X cohort fluctuates a great deal between 1988 and 2021, a pattern that reflects a group coming of "age at a time when most of the United States was divided into factions for and against specific moral claims" (Barringer, Sumerau, and Gay 2020, 283).

Let us tally up where the theory of moral power stands at this point. Consistent with the work done by others, our analyses suggest cohort replacement played a role in pushing gay rights opinion in the progressive direction—especially in the 1970s and 1980s. While we are confident that cohort-replacement explains some of this change, we still need to contend with attitude evolution. Contrary to Dawn and Autumn, some people are changing their minds.

Resolving the Paradoxes

We have argued that individual opinions on abortion and gay rights change quite modestly year over year. We have also seen that the public's collective view on abortion has changed little while its view on gay rights has changed a great deal. This seems paradoxical. The purpose of this section is to answer two questions about these cross-level differences. First, how can the American public have changed so much on gay rights when most individuals change so little? Second, how can the public have changed so much more on gay rights than on abortion when individuals rarely change their position on either issue?

To sort all this out, we return to the GSS panels introduced in chapter 4. Our analysis is simple. For every respondent in the 2006–2010, 2008–2012, and 2010–2014 surveys, we tracked their views of abortion and same sex relationships.[7] We then tallied up how many "stood pat," how many moved in a conservative direction, and how many moved in a progressive direction. The latter two categories are our "switchers."

We rely on the same abortion (any circumstances) and same-sex relation items used earlier in this chapter. Figure 5.5 displays the resulting distributions. The black bars represent the stand patters. These are voting-age adults who gave the same responses to a question in both panel waves. For example, someone who says "no" to the abortion question at $time_1$ and $time_2$ is a stand patter. For abortion, 81 percent of respondents on average took the same position at both points in time—high stability. We find the same thing for gay rights. In fact, these views prove a tad more stable than abortion attitudes, averaging 85 percent across the datasets.[8] Looking at the data this way shows that attitudes toward abortion and gay rights are

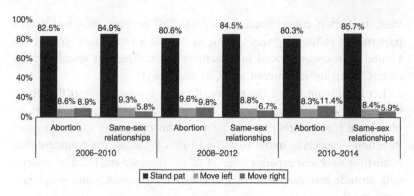

FIGURE 5.5. Stand patters and switchers on moral issues
Notes: Data come from the three GSS panels. Bars represent the percentage of respondents who "stood pat" on "abortion for any reason" or "same-sex relationships," those who moved to the left on these issues, and those who moved to the right.

very stable at the individual level, just like we saw with the continuity correlations in chapter 4. Grounded in moral emotions, such stability comes as no surprise.

At first glance, the high percentage of stand patters on abortion and same-sex relations seems to sit in tension with figure 5.1. That figure shows that macro abortion opinion changed much less than macro opinion on gay rights. The key to resolving this puzzle is looking at how figure 5.5's switchers behaved on each issue. For abortion, the percentage who moved left and moved right are nearly identical in all three panels. We can see this in the first set of bars at the figure's left. From 2006 to 2010, 8.6 percent of the panelists moved from a pro-life to a pro-choice stance. They were canceled out by the 8.9 percent who moved from a pro-choice to pro-life position. Averaging across the three panels, we find that switchers moved 1.1 points in the conservative direction. Since pro-life and pro-choice switchers essentially nullify one another, collective opinion holds steady. On abortion, most people do not change. Among those who switch sides, the moves cancel out. The bottom line here is that attitude stability and modest change at the individual level coexist with stability at the collective level.

On gay rights, stand patters also greatly outnumber switchers. But among the few who updated their positions, more shifted to the left than the right. From 2006 to 2010, 9.3 percent switched from anti-gay to pro-gay while only 5.8 percent switched from pro-gay to anti-gay. In contrast to abortion, the switchers here do not cancel out. Across the three panels, pro-gay opinion averaged a 2.7-point shift to the left.[9] This shift may seem small, but keep in mind that only four years separated the waves in each panel. As time passes, small but steady micro-level shifts add up to bigger shifts at the collective level. Here, the data suggest that collective opinion moved over 5 percent in a pro-gay direction between 2006 and 2014. While this change does not fully mirror the increase in collective opinion we saw in figure 5.1, it is important to note that this survey includes only people who were present for both waves of a survey. It does not factor in cohort replacement, thereby understating the changes we observe in that figure.

We relied on the same-sex relations item because its four scale points make it comparable to the abortion item when dichotomized. However, when we turn to the gay marriage item, the results lend stronger support for our claim. We dichotomized the marriage item so that "agree" and "strongly agree" responses count as progressive. On the flip side, the "neither" and the two "disagree" options count as traditional. Across all three GSS panels, 79 percent of respondents stood pat, 6.4 percent moved in an anti-gay direction, and 14.6 percent moved in the pro-gay direction.

All told, our evidence suggests that the micro-macro paradoxes are more apparent than real. No conflict exists between our claims about the stability of moral issues in the minds of individuals and the divergent trends in collective opinion. In the twenty-first century, the American public has changed more on gay rights than on abortion because there has been one-sided movement in the liberal direction among the relatively few gay rights switchers, while abortion switchers have usually canceled out. And of course, cohort replacement explains some of the macro change.

To recap the data: figure 5.5 indicates that (a) 81 to 86 percent of individuals stood pat on abortion and gay issues in a given panel, reaffirming our claim that these attitudes are stable; (b) those who moved left on abortion offset those who moved right, leading to macro stability; and (c) those who moved left on same-sex relations—and gay marriage too—outnumbered those who moved right, leading to greater public support for gay rights with the passage of time. Hence, micro-level stability on both issues is compatible with macro-level stability on abortion and macro-level change on gay rights.

The Changing Size of America's Moral Camps

The last task we take up in this chapter is to explore how individual opinion shifts on moral issues have transformed America's moral factions.

Changes in the size of these factions affects religious and party change—topics we take up in the next two chapters.

As figure 5.1 reveals, the pro-gay rights share of the electorate has increased over the last fifteen or so years. From 2004 to 2021, support for gay marriage rose from 30 percent to 66 percent. At the same time, acceptance of same-sex relations grew from 38 percent to 69 percent. The GSS data also show that support for abortion under any circumstances increased, albeit unevenly and less dramatically, from 41 percent to 56 percent. Recall that much of this change happened during the Trump years.[10]

Cohort replacement accounts for some of this change, but figure 5.5 revealed individual opinion churn going on beneath the aggregate statistics. For example, between 2010 and 2014 19.7 percent of panelists changed their mind (one way or another) on abortion, while 14.3 percent did so on same-sex relationships. This mix of some collective-level liberalization and individual-level churn implies one of two things: either the moral camps are becoming fractured on these issues or moral progressives are growing at the expense of moral traditionalists. Which is it?

To answer this question, we return to the 2006–2014 GSS panels. Figure 5.6 reports the percentage of respondents who fall into one of three categories in each panel wave, one panel at a time. The black bars reflect "mismatched respondents," such as those who disapproved of "same-sex relations" while supporting "abortion for any reason" (or the reverse pattern). The dark gray bars capture respondents who reported pro-life and anti-gay positions—what we call "consistent moral conservatives." The light gray bars capture respondents who reported pro-choice and pro-gay views—"consistent moral progressives." By tracking the same respondents from, say 2006 to 2010, we can see how the opinion shifters altered the size of the moral constituencies.

Here are the key takeaways from figure 5.6. First, in two of the three panels, the percentage of mismatched respondents ticked down between waves. In 2006, 29.1 percent of respondents held inconsistent attitudes. This dropped to 26.7 percent four years later. Likewise, between 2010 and 2014, mismatched respondents declined by over a percentage point. In the 2008–2012 panel, inconsistency rose by about a point and a half. Overall, there is no significant change in the size of the mismatched group across the panels.[11] These data tell us that individual views of abortion and gay rights are not moving in opposite directions.

The second takeaway is that moral progressives are growing at the expense of moral conservatives. Conservatives saw their fortunes wane from

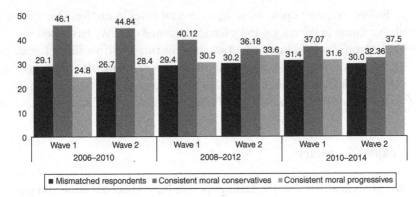

FIGURE 5.6. Mismatched and consistent moral issue opinions across panel waves
Notes: Data come from the three GSS panels. Bars represent the percentage of respondents with mismatched or consistent attitudes. We use the abortion under "any circumstances" question and dichotomize the same-sex relations question. Consistent respondents gave traditional (progressive) answers to both questions. Mismatched respondents gave a traditional answer to one question and a progressive answer to the other.

wave to wave in each panel, and from earlier panels to later panels. In the 2006 wave of the first panel, consistent conservatives were the largest moral group at 46.1 percent of the public. Moral progressives were the smallest at 24.8 percent. By the 2014 wave of the third panel, the pattern switched. Moral traditionalists had fallen to 32.4 percent of the public.[12] The progressive camp had grown to 37.5 percent. To put this another way, conservatives outnumbered progressives by 21 percent in 2006 and trailed them by 5 percent in 2014. These are substantial changes in a relatively short period.

Speaking broadly, most Americans—some seven in ten—remain committed to their moral camp. A small number have changed their views. A few have moved to the right. More have moved to the left. These person-level changes have altered the size of the rival moral factions. In eight short years, traditionalists declined from being America's largest moral faction to its smallest (based on the GSS measures we used). Simultaneously, their progressive antagonists grew from being America's smallest moral camp to the largest (by a small margin). Progressives are drawing in more recruits via conversion while the ranks of the traditionalists are dwindling. As the Gen Z cohort supplants the Silent Generation, we expect that the progressive camp will continue to grow at the expense of traditionalists. As we will see in the chapters to come, these changes have reverberated throughout American religion and politics.

Before wrapping up, we must inject several notes of caution. Our speculative forays in figures 5.5 and 5.6 rest on limited data. We have used single measure items in three panel studies covering a narrow slice of time. The need for replication using other measures and datasets over longer time spans is clear. We look forward to future research that builds on what we have done here, hoping for confirmation while awaiting the verdict.

Chapter Summary

We have theorized that the feelings people have about abortion and gay rights endure and change under limited circumstances. Most voters are dug in on abortion and gay rights, but some do evolve. The evolutionary path matters for our theory and our understanding of politics. This chapter has confronted two challenges to our theory. First, to the extent that collective views on gay rights liberalized quickly, our attitude stability claim seems suspect. Second, the much faster pace of aggregate change on gay rights vis-à-vis abortion also seems at odds with our claim that attitudes toward both issues are stable at the individual level. The results of our analyses in this chapter suggest neither criticism holds up.

So, what have we learned? First, cohort replacement explains a fair share of collective change in gay rights opinion in recent decades. New generations are joining the electorate with far more progressive views on gay rights than the generations that depart. This said, changing minds is the bigger driver of the public's embrace of gay rights. That change comes from the small share of the public that has reliably moved in a pro-gay direction. For gay rights, micro-stability goes hand-in-hand with collective change. For abortion, the handful who shift in the pro-choice direction cancel out those who shift to the pro-life position, thus rendering macro opinion stable. To conclude, attitude stability at the individual level can lead to either continuity or change at the collective level. It all depends on how the small number of switchers break. Finally, we showed that the behavior of the switchers is altering the size of America's moral camps. Progressives are ascendant.

In this and the prior chapter, we made the case that most people hold stable views on the core issues that constitute America's long-running culture war. In the next two chapters, we take up the question of whether these views affect Americans' ties to organized religion (chapter 6) and political parties (chapter 7).

CHAPTER SIX

Moral Issues and Religious Disaffiliation

In the summer of 2018, Evangelical leader Franklin Graham tweeted, "To everyone who has had an abortion, it is murder in God's eyes. But I'm happy to tell you that God will forgive you, take away the shame & guilt you've carried all these years, and save you for eternity if you turn to Him and put your faith and trust in His Son Jesus Christ" (@Franklin_Graham, August 18, 2018). Eight months later came this: "As a Christian I believe the Bible which defines homosexuality as a sin, something to be repentant of, not something to be flaunted, praised or politicized. The Bible says marriage is between a man & a woman—not two men, not two women." (@Franklin_Graham, April 24, 2019).

Franklin Graham betrays no reluctance expressing his opposition to abortion and gay marriage. His political pronouncements stand in marked contrast to the reluctance evinced by his father—Billy Graham—to enter the political fray. Billy Graham simply preached the Gospels and avoided the kinds of rhetoric that leaders on the Religious Right routinely employ. This difference between father and son illustrates how moral issues and organized religion have become inextricably linked in public life.

By demonizing abortion and homosexuals, the Religious Right quickly became a major political force. Ironically, after the movement rose to power in the 1980s millions of Americans left organized religion—slowly at first and with greater speed later on (Baker and Smith 2015; Burge 2021). Today, the country is much less religious than it was when the Religious Right launched its crusade to save America's soul.

It is difficult to overstate the importance of this trend. As Ruth Braunstein (2022, 293) recently put it, "Among the most significant changes in the

FIGURE 6.1. The rise of the nones, 1972–2021
Notes: The figure plots the percentage of respondents who did not identify with any religious tradition in a given survey. The data come from the GSS Cumulative Data File.

American religious field over the past few decades has been the rise of the 'nones.'" Researchers have documented this trend by asking survey participants to identify their religious preferences. For example, the GSS asks, "What is your religious preference? Is it Protestant, Catholic, Jewish, some other religion, or no religion?"

In figure 6.1, we use GSS data dating back to 1972 to chart the rise of the nones. Back then, nearly everyone was part of some faith. Only 5.1 percent of the public chose "no religion." This number barely budged for twenty years, but things began to change in the early 1990s when the share of nones jumped from 6.2 percent in 1991 to 8.9 percent in 1993. This upward drift continued for another quarter century, reaching 23.2 percent in 2018. By the time Joe Biden took office three years later, the share of the public with no religious affiliation had surged to 29.3 percent. The nones have morphed from a tiny sliver of the electorate to the largest religious bloc in the nation.

Why have so many Americans abandoned organized religion? Generational replacement explains part of this trend (Schwadel 2010). As churched cohorts passed away, unchurched cohorts took their place. More surprisingly, politics helps explain the rise of the nones. In pathbreaking work, Michael Hout and Claude Fischer (2002, 2014) showed that backlash against the Religious Right drove many political liberals and moderates away from religion. A more recent study by David E. Campbell, Geoffrey C. Layman, and John C. Green (2021) affirms that politics has driven a secular surge that has weakened organized religion. Their backlash thesis maintains that "many Americans turn away from a religious affiliation precisely because of cognitive dissonance between their religion and their politics" (Campbell, Layman, and Green 2021, 109). These works attribute the rise of the nones to a broad-based backlash against religion as a whole (also see Putnam and Campbell 2010; Burge 2021).[1]

In these accounts, political identities drive antireligion backlash. This class of variables provides a credible explanation for the rise of the nones. As Hout and Fischer (2002, 188) explain, "Organized religion linked itself to a conservative social agenda in the 1990s, and that led some political moderates and liberals who had previously identified with the religion of their youth or their spouse's religion to declare they have no religion." For political moderates and liberals who maintain ties to some faith, the symbolic association between a conservative social agenda and religion is disconcerting. The easiest way to resolve this tension is to renounce religion. Though plausible, we think there is more to the backlash story than political identities. We theorize that feelings about abortion and gay rights, not political identities, fueled the rise of the nones. We argue that once religion became linked to the Religious Right's social agenda, feelings about the core issues on that agenda—abortion and gay rights—led rising numbers of Americans to leave the religious fold.[2]

In the pages to come, we argue that the Religious Right played the critical role in symbolically aligning religion with opposition to abortion and gay rights. Although the Religious Right took the lead in forging these connections, these links emerged from varied sources. Christian televangelists like Jerry Falwell and Pat Robertson did a great deal to cement religion to pro-life/anti-gay positions. But one need not have any awareness of these figures to see these links. From religious figures outside of the Religious Right to popular TV shows to roadside billboards, plenty of cultural markers signal where religious and nonreligious people stand on moral issues.

This chapter takes up the dynamic relationship between religious ID and moral issue opinions. The data we examine shows that religious ID predicts moral opinion change. This evidence is consistent with group-based explanations of public opinion. We then demonstrate that moral progressives prove more likely to exit religion than moral conservatives. This evidence supports our theory of moral power. Critically, political identities do not appear to affect religion once we take issues into account. We also show that moral progressivism predicts waning religious identity strength.

Here, too, political identities fail to predict religious change. Together, these findings suggest that moral issues, not political identities, have fueled anti-religion backlash. These results suggest that moral issue attitudes are stronger than political identities.

The Religious ID to Issues Model

Religious ID and Identity Strength Defined

We define religious ID as affiliation with a religious tradition. Some of us identify with broad traditions (e.g., Protestant, Catholic, Jewish, and so on). Others identify with specific denominations (e.g., Southern Baptist, Lutheran, Shia Muslim, etc.). And others shun these labels, instead describing themselves as "Christian" or "spiritual" or something else (e.g., "Pagan"). All of these folks count as religious identifiers. On the flip side lie people who do not see themselves as part of any religion—organized or self-defined. They choose the "none of the above" or "no preference" option on surveys. These are the nones.

While there is a lot of value in conceptualizing religious ID this way, it has some limits. By lumping people together into one of two categories, we ignore the variation within each category. The affiliated category includes mainline Protestants, evangelical Protestants, Catholics, Jews, Muslims, Hindus, "spirituals," "Christians," and other faiths. These groups differ in their beliefs, practices, and political commitments. Likewise, the unaffiliated/none category lumps secular humanists, atheists, agnostics, and unaffiliated believers together. These groups differ in their reasons for rejecting religion. What unites the nones is their refusal to self-identify with a religious tradition.

Categorical attachments tell us little about how much these attachments matter psychologically or behaviorally. Some individuals identify very strongly with their tradition. Their faith is central to their self-concepts. It affects how they see themselves, how they present themselves to others, what they believe, and what they do. For others, the bonds are weaker. Being part of some faith is not central to how they see themselves and how they view the world. It does not affect their life at all. Differences like these shape behaviors ranging from volunteering at the local level to participating in national politics (Verba, Scholzman, and Brady 1995). In light of its importance, we examine religious identity strength in the pages to come. We will explore how this variation affects—and is affected by—differences in opinion on moral issues.

How Religious Identities Shape Public Opinion

To set the stage for our issue-based theory of antireligious backlash, we must first unpack the logic of the standard religious ID to issues model. Doing so helps illuminate how and why moral issue attitudes depart from the standard model. When we are part of a group, emotional and instrumental incentives motivate us to absorb the beliefs espoused by the group. Doing so feels good ("I'm not alone," "My group is good") and yields benefits ("I need a favor," "I need advice"). The price of these benefits is conformity to group beliefs. Conformity signals that one is a member in good standing, that she can be relied upon for solidarity and support. As long as group members can find out where the group stands, they typically conform.

In the religious domain, those who identify with a given faith or church often absorb core religious tenets of the group (Steensland et al. 2000). Beyond religious matters, these identities sometimes shape political perception and judgment. Opinion leaders bundle the ideas that comprise the group's political ideology and spread the word to their followers. They invoke religious tenets to justify political positions. Within congregations, small groups reinforce these stances (Wald, Silverman, and Fridy 2005; Bean 2014). Once religious group members discover where the group stands on political matters, they often adopt these positions as their own.

This two-step flow of influence from opinion leaders to followers works through multiple channels (Katz and Lazarsfeld 1955). Regional (e.g., megachurch pastors) and national religious leaders (e.g., televangelists) shape public opinion through the pulpit, TV, radio, direct mail, and social media (Chapp 2019). While such leaders wield influence, it is important to recognize that friends and peers do the same in small groups. This happens in local churches, Bible study groups, coffee klatches, and other informal get-togethers (Djupe and Gilbert 2009; Bean 2014). The conformity pressures at this level are intense. Whatever the source, members of religious groups receive cues from opinion leaders about the positions people like "us" should take on the issues "we" care about.

When organized religious groups press their demands on policymakers, they become more visible in the political arena. The conflict draws politicians and media to the fray. When religious movements succeed in politicizing grievances, backlash inevitably ensues (Layman 2001; Putnam and Campbell 2010). Pushback may come from rival religious groups, social movements, allied interest groups, and others who feel threatened by religious issue advocates. As message volume amps up, the public takes stock.

104   CHAPTER SIX

Individuals discern where their groups stand and absorb their group's positions. In this way, religious group identities come to shape the views people take on both sides of contested issues.

The Politicization of Abortion and Gay Rights

We now apply this logic to the case of moral issues. By the early 1990s, the Religious Right had pushed its moral grievances onto the national agenda. Messages that linked religion to pro-life and anti-gay beliefs took hold in the information environment. The public began to associate organized religion in general—not just the Religious Right—with conservative social views. Americans heard a steady drumbeat of messages telling them that religious people opposed abortion and gay rights.

Scholars trace the origin of the Religious Right to revolutionary cultural and social changes that began in the early 1960s.[3] Back then, the public's growing embrace of new self-expressive values that defied older norms about sex, gender, family, and religion transformed American culture and society. Alarmed by these changes, grassroots activists fought back in isolated locales ranging from Kanawha County, West Virginia, to Dade County, Florida, to Orange County, California.

Sensing that millions of conservative Christians and other socially conservative Americans were morally outraged by cultural change, a cadre of political activists and religious leaders banded together to create the New Christian Right (NCR) or, alternatively, the Religious Right. Their goal was to mobilize discontented religious (mostly evangelical) and culturally conservative (mostly white) Americans to push the GOP to the right on a range of social issues. These issues included the tax status of private Christian Schools, teaching evolution in public schools, feminism, the defense of traditional family values, and pornography. Without denying the import of these issues, abortion and gay rights have long been central to the Religious Right's agenda. As David Domke and Kevin Coe (2010, 113) have written, "Not all symbolic issues are created equal, of course. In particular, the political mobilization of Christian conservatives has been powered by two engines: opposition to abortion and to same-sex relationships."

During the late 1970s, Baptist televangelist Jerry Falwell and his allies built political organizations to get their message out, make policy demands on politicians, and mobilize voters on behalf of these causes. By the early 1980s, the Falwell-led Moral Majority had become the leading NCR organization in the country. Falwell lamented the country's moral decline in sermons at his Lynchburg, Virginia, megachurch; on his *Old Time Gospel Hour* television show; in direct mailings; and in conversations with elected officials. Falwell repeated the same jeremiad over and over, that America had become "one of the most blatantly sinful nations of all time" (Domke and Coe 2010, 52). Across these outlets, he preached that abortion was murder and homosexuality a sin. Here is a typical example from a 1981 direct mail appeal: "homosexuals do not reproduce! They recruit. And, many of them are out after my children and your children. . . . This is why the Old-Time Gospel Hour speaks out against the sin of homosexuality" (UNT Digital Library n.d.). While the Moral Majority and allied groups struggled to expand beyond the base, there is no doubt that their initial efforts paved the way for bigger things to come.

In the 1990s and beyond, NCR groups such as the Christian Coalition and Focus on the Family pushed the GOP to the right on moral issues by organizing at the state and local levels, endorsing candidates, capturing GOP organizations, lobbying, and mobilizing Christian voters. Echoing Falwell, allies in the cause delivered a relentless stream of socially conservative messages to large radio and television audiences and also in newsletters mailed to supporters. All of this was part of the information environment, with much of it occurring in ostensibly nonpolitical arenas.

In one memorable incident from 1999, Reverend Falwell claimed in a newsletter that Tinky Winky, a character in the *Teletubbies* children's show that aired on PBS, was homosexual (Applebome 2007). The basis of the claim? Tinky Winky had a young boy's voice, carried a red purse, was purple ("the gay pride color"), and had a triangle antenna atop his head ("the gay-pride symbol"). Falwell's ludicrous attack attracted a lot of attention—and much ridicule—in both political and nonpolitical media outlets (Mifflin 1999).

To take another example, James Dobson, the Evangelical Christian founder and former leader of Focus on the Family, wrote this in a 2003 newsletter: "the Holy Scriptures set forth the Creator's plan for marriage and family. To deviate from that model is to invite disaster. As early as the second chapter of Genesis, we learn that God created Eve as a "suitable companion" for Adam who would complement him physically, spiritually, and emotionally. This 'marriage' was the very first institution that God created, and it continues to be the primary institution of society to this day" (cited in Domke and Coe 2010, 117).

In this passage, Dobson explicitly connects belief in God to opposition to gay rights. This rhetorical construction is common. Take religious broadcaster and former presidential contender Pat Robertson's comparison of abortion and homosexuality to murder on his *700 Club* television show: "God knows your sin. Some of you have been involved in homosexuality, some of you have had an abortion, some of you have actually committed murder, you have lied, you have been disobedient to your parents, you have stolen money from your business, and God says if your repent and come to me I'll wash the slate clean, you can get rid of it all" (GLAAD n.d.).

Electronic and social media also connect religion to cultural conservativism. In a 2004 newsletter emailed to over 130,000 ministers, megachurch pastor Rick Warren declared that opposition to abortion and homosexual marriage is "non-negotiable" and "not even debatable because God's Word is clear." Warren indicated that opposition to abortion rights was the best reason to support political candidates that election season (Domke and Coe 2010, 113). Warren's pro-life stance has not changed. In 2013, he tweeted, "Planned Parenthood is the McDonald's of abortion. It's the #1 baby killing franchise" (@JohnPiper, March7, 2013).

It is essential to recognize that many religious figures not affiliated with the Religious Right stake out conservative positions on moral issues. Consider Jim Wallis, a well-known theologian, activist, and founder of the progressive *Sojourners* magazine. Wallis is a frequent critic of the Religious Right, arguing that religious communities should focus more on social justice issues like poverty and healthcare. However, while Wallis doesn't agree with the criminalization of abortion, he is also clear that the "number of unborn lives that are lost every year is alarming. It's a moral tragedy" (Olsen 2008).

Pope Francis, current head of the Catholic Church, provides a second example of how conservative issue messages emerge from sources outside of the Religious Right. Pope Francis has staked out liberal positions on a range of issues. And while he has advocated for the dignity of those in the LGBT community, he also characterizes homosexuality as a sin: "It's not a crime. Yes, but it's a sin" (Winfield 2023). On abortion, the Pope pulls no punches, characterizing it as "hiring a hitman" to take care of an unwanted pregnancy" (Winfield 2019). While it is a gross caricature to call Pope Francis and Jim Wallis the "religious left," they are certainly not the Religious Right either.

In this way, prominent voices outside the Religious Right routinely signal where religious people ought to stand on these issues, yoking together "organized religion" in the most general sense with culturally conservative politics. Hence, backlash against disparate religious traditions and figures discredits all organized religion in the eyes of many Americans.

Top-down opinion leadership like this happens routinely. At the same time, opinion leadership flows through channels closer to home. In local churches, clergy mobilize religious resources on behalf of various political causes (Chapp 2019). They do so despite legal prohibitions against certain political activities (Guth et al. 1997; Wilcox and Robinson 2011). Sometimes their views are unequivocal. Consider these quotes from the Sunday sermons database that we described in chapter 3. One pastor argued, "God destroyed Sodom because of its utter sinfulness. Clearly, theirs was homosexual sin" (Sermon Central 2017). Another preached, "To kill someone created in God's image is to indirectly attack the God who created life. Abortion must be defined as the destruction of a human life in violation of the 6th Commandment: 'You shall not commit murder'" (Sermon Central 2008). Statements like these justify opposition to abortion and gay rights on religious grounds. While clergy often refrain from being so direct, the fact that it happens at all is telling.

Opinion leadership happens on an even smaller scale. Lydia Bean's (2014) case study of evangelical churches makes this clear. Her fieldwork in two churches showed that volunteer lay leaders exert significant pull over their peers in small group settings—more so than those in formal leadership positions. She discovered that political conformity goes hand in hand with group membership. "To be a good member of the group one had to acknowledge 'our' shared stances on the 'moral issues.' These moral stances were impossible to challenge without violating these customs of group interaction—and branding oneself as a cultural outsider" (Bean 2014, 87). Moreover, these "captains in the culture war . . . reinforced a particular prototype of the 'good' group member: an ideal Christian is politically conservative. They also drew boundaries against out-groups, by identifying liberals, pro-choice activists, LGBT people, and Democrats as the adversaries to Christian influence in society" (ibid., 163). At the smallest scale, guidance flows from a church pastor or lay leader to one congregant at a time (Harding 2002).

Outside of in-group communications like these, messages that linked moral issues and religion reached the broader public through various media. Peter Kerr and Patricia Moy's (2002) review of 2,243 newspaper articles showed that coverage of the Christian Right increased fifteen-fold from 1980 to 2000. Coverage was limited at first before it picked up steam in 1983–1984. It then spiked between 1991 and 1994. Kerr and Moy also reported that hundreds of articles linked fundamentalist Christians to politics (also see Hetherington and Weiler 2009). Peter Kerr's (2003) content analysis showed that television network news stories (ABC, CBS, NBC, Fox, and CNN) about Fundamentalists and Christians often centered on political conflict. In short, the increasing volume of moral issue messages coincided with increasing coverage of the Religious Right's objections. These messages drew connections between religion and moral issues for both religious and nonreligious news consumers.

Our data speak to this as well. The content analyses in chapter 3 showed that message intensity on abortion and same-sex rights has remained high for decades. For example, our tally of media stories on moral issues is 39 in June 1980, 175 in June 1992, 109 in June 2004, 185 in June 2016, and 284 in June 2022. These figures indicate a 448 percent increase from 1980 to 1992 and a 728 percent increase from 1980 to 2022. These results imply that Americans had many chances to ascertain where the parties and religious groups stood on both issues. As message volume increased, moral issue attitudes presumably hardened.

Our data further indicate that news and political messages linked abortion and gay rights to religion on a routine basis. To explore this, we used a program called Linguistic Inquiry and Word Count that includes a predefined set of common religious words like *church*, *pope*, and *prayer*. We figured out how frequently these words appeared in conjunction with moral issues, relative to other issues. We found that moral issues invoked a religious frame far more often than other issues. In our newspaper data, 54 percent of articles on gay rights and abortion included some sort of religious word or phrase. The comparable percentages for taxes and healthcare were 25 percent and 16 percent. In our data on one-minute House speeches, 28 percent of culture war speeches use a religious term, relative to 14 percent of speeches about taxes and 11 percent of healthcare speeches. Religious language is more common on the GOP side, occurring in 35 percent of all such speeches.

The story is similar in our campaign website data: 38 percent of moral issue statements on websites use a religious term, compared to 21 percent of all other congressional issue statements. Again, religious language is more common among Republicans: 45 percent of all Republicans taking a stance on a moral issue include some sort of religious term in their policy justification. In short, our data affirm the claim that religion tends to be strongly associated with moral issues, particularly in the GOP.

Finally, recall that moral issues often come up in seemingly apolitical outlets like TV shows and movies. Consider an episode from *House*, a medical drama show that landed in our Nielsen top-ten database three times (2005–2007). In a 2007 episode, a young rape victim discovers that she is pregnant but refuses to consider an abortion for religious reasons. Dialogue between Dr. House and the young woman plays as a confrontation between faith and reason. Dr. House argues that there is no God, and the woman should only consider the immediate worldly realm in her abortion decision. When asked why a loving God would put her in this position, the woman muses, "Maybe he was challenging me." House responds by saying, "He hurts you to help you?" The traumatized woman responds, "You're trying to convince me there is no God. Why would you even say something like that?" House retorts, "Because you're throwing your life away."

To sum up, the politicization of abortion and same-sex rights followed a clear path. The rise of the NCR and its subsequent forays into politics ignited intense social conflict. Messages that symbolically fused religion, abortion, homosexuals, and gay rights flooded the information environment. This informational milieu taught many Americans where religious and nonreligious people stood on moral issues. Even largely inattentive citizens got cues about how well their moral issue positions aligned with their faith. If asked where they stood on these issues, they knew what to say. In this way, membership in religious groups has come to shape the positions Americans take on abortion and equal rights for gays.

Expectations

We now lay out the hypotheses that follow from the identity-to-issue framework. Throughout the culture war, the vast majority of Americans have identified with a faith tradition, most of which have opposed abortion and gay marriage (at least until recently). Members of these traditions confront expressive and instrumental motivations to toe the line on these issues. Doing so requires knowing where the groups stand. People learn this from various sources. They may receive a steady diet of cues from worship services, lay leaders in small group settings, friends and peers, religious broadcasters, media coverage, and even popular TV shows.

Religious identifiers ascertain that people in their faith—or religious people in general—are cool toward abortion and gay rights. In some traditions, opposition is absolute. In other traditions, opposition is less extreme but ever present. But across most traditions, the general stance toward moral issues is conservative. Religious ties shape the positions people take on moral issues.

What about people who do not identify with any faith? Many if not most of the unaffiliated passively reject religion rather than actively embrace identities like atheist or secularist (Baker and Smith 2015; Campbell, Layman, and Green 2021). How do they learn what positions are appropriate for people like them in the absence of strong group pressures to go along?

For starters, nonreligious people take cues from close family members, good friends, or other peers. If someone they trust is areligious, pro-choice, and pro-gay, they can simply follow suit. In addition, a small sliver of the public follows the lead of organized interests like the National Organization for Women and the American Humanist Association. When these groups signal their commitment to abortion and same-sex rights, their nonreligious followers toe the same line.

That said, it seems likely that large numbers of nonreligious folks formulate their views by rejecting the positions associated with religious groups. How does this process shake out? Social categorization is an elemental part of the human condition, and we know that people feel tremendous pressure to go along with the views of prototypical members of any group. Pressures to conform can happen even when formal group ties are weak or absent (Hogg 2002).

This process is especially likely to occur when group categories are socially salient—much like religious groups in the information environment since the 1980s. As messages about what the prototypically religious believe about abortion and gays flow through public and private channels, the nonreligious reject these stances and align their views with what they take to be the nonreligious group prototype. More simply, nonreligious people reject the positions advocated by religious sources even in the absence of external pressure to do so. In this way, passive identification as a none can color issue attitudes.

To take an example, when a religious leader like Pope Francis calls abortion an "absolute evil" and equates it with "the murder of children," nonreligious people might think to themselves, "The pope should stick to religion and stay out of politics. If he wants to outlaw abortion, I can't go along with that, so I guess that means I'm pro-choice" (Mares 2021). Here's another example: a nonreligious person might think "the religious guy on *Friday Night Lights* is pro-life. I ain't religious like him; I don't believe what he believes." Again, even the most banal group identities can influence the uptake of policy attitudes (Chapp 2012). In ways like this, the unchurched take progressive positions on abortion and gay rights.

The Moral Issues to Religious ID Model

Scholars have known for some time that the positions people take on moral issues change much less over time than their positions on other issues, suggesting that these attitudes are stronger than most other policy attitudes. The question of whether public opinion on these issues can induce identity change has received less attention over the years. The theory of moral power represents a first cut at the answer.

Here is a brief recap of the theory. The three-decade spread of messages about abortion and gay rights in political and popular discourse has provided most people with opportunities to evaluate both issues many times over. These messages, often framed in terms of moral anger and disgust, spontaneously evoke distinct emotional responses from different subgroups of the electorate. Those who are sensitive to conservative moral disgust—by virtue of personality and socialization—recoil when exposed to messages about abortion, same-sex relations, gay marriage, and the like. The moral disgust they feel stokes negative evaluations about both issues. Strong pro-life, anti-gay attitudes crystallize in response. Those who have been socialized to feel anger and revulsion in response to the denial of equal rights for and attacks on women, gays, and lesbians react quite differently. When exposed to attacks on these groups, the moral anger and aversion they feel elicits emotional backlash that engenders pro-choice, pro-gay attitudes. As these reactions recur, their attitudes crystallize. People know where they stand because it just feels right. The net result is stable moral issue attitudes.

But why, specifically, should these attitudes affect ties to religious and party groups? The final pillar in our theory is that core identities generally endure but sometimes change. Theories of lifelong openness posit that people may rethink long-standing ties to groups when these ties conflict with other strong psychological forces (Sears 1983). Whether explicit or implicit, the discomfort that arises from these tensions leads people to reduce or eliminate the source of cognitive dissonance. On most issues, people resolve any tension they feel by adjusting their policy attitudes to fit that of their group. But for abortion and gay rights, we think, people often respond the other way round.

We see anecdotal evidence of this in the news all the time. To take an example, politicized church defections have become routine. Recall from Dawn's story in chapter 2 that the mainline Evangelical Lutheran Church in America decided in 2009 to ordain gay and lesbian clergy. In the two years following this decision, over seven hundred congregations bolted from the denomination. During this period, the socially conservative Lutheran Congregations in Mission for Christ grew by nearly five hundred congregations, including many of the former ELCA churches—Dawn's among them (Lutheran Congregations in Mission for Christ 2020). This is why Dawn left her congregation.

Here's a second example that illustrates how LGBT politics compel religious change. In 2015 when the Mormon Church banned baptisms of the children of same-sex couples, over 1,500 Mormons lined up outside the Salt Lake Temple in Salt Lake City to resign en mass. In the words of one participant, "We're supposed to love our children like God loves us. . . . To ask someone to turn their back on their own child or for a child to turn their back on a parent, that's unnecessary" (Santoscoy 2015).

For some people, the positions their church takes on moral issues can be at odds with their personal views. This leads to cognitive dissonance, which, as a general rule, most people seek to avoid (Festinger 1957). Some of those who hold centrist or left-leaning views reevaluate their ties to their faith. Some go further, questioning their attachments to organized religion. If being part of a religion symbolizes being pro-life and anti-gay, they'll have nothing to do with it. This is why some people exit religion to become a none. Others do not go so far. Even if they do not abandon religion, it becomes less central to who they are and how they present themselves to others. While not renouncing their religion, the strength of their ties to religion recede.

Although we have devoted this section to the political causes of religious exit, conservative issue stances lead to some religious entry. As Michael Hout and Claude Fischer (2002, 179) have noted, "this religiously tinged political atmosphere . . . brought some religious people out of apathy into politics." We think those people were moral issue conservatives rather than political conservatives or Republicans. As abortion and gay rights moved onto the political agenda, issue conservatives embraced religious faiths that catered to their moral tastes. In this way, conservative issue views motivate religious attachment.

To sum up, the standard theories hold that religious identities guide the positions people take on abortion and gay rights. Contrary to this view, revisionist theories hold that political identities affect the decision to engage with religion (Hout and Fischer 2002, 2014; Patrikios 2008; Putnam and Campbell 2010; Margolis 2018; Budge 2021). We agree that politics shapes religion but think that moral issues are the main factor in this calculus. Moral issues, not political identities, drive disaffiliation.

Since moral issues endure and religious identities change in response to some pressures, the theory of moral power posits that the former shapes the latter. We predict that those who take progressive positions on moral

MORAL ISSUES AND RELIGIOUS DISAFFILIATION

issues will be more likely to exit religion than those who take conservative positions, even when we take political identities into account.

Analysis

Modeling and Measurement Details

We are now ready to test the rival hypotheses. But first, this section briefly reviews the variables and methods we use to test them. Readers uninterested in the details can skip to the next section without any loss of continuity.

We measure religious ID in two ways. First, we rely on questions that ask whether or not someone identifies with a religion, coding identifiers as 1 and nones as 0.[4] This covers categorical ID. Second, to tap religious identity strength we use a pair of items that appear on the GSS panels. One item follows the religious tradition question: "Would you call yourself a strong (tradition) or not very strong (tradition)." The response options are "strong," "somewhat strong" (volunteered), "not very strong," and "no religion." The other item asks, "To what extent do you consider yourself a religious person?" The response options are "very religious," "moderately religious," "slightly religious," or "not religious." The two-item strength scale is reliable (ordinal α averages 0.85 across the GSS surveys). The scale ranges from 0.00 to 1.00. Higher scores indicate greater identity strength.

Chapter 4 described the abortion and gay rights questions we used to build multi-item issue scales. That chapter's appendix presents the question wording for all items that make up these scales. The scales range from 0.00 (most progressive) to 1.00 (most conservative). We remind readers that every scale includes abortion and gay rights items, is reliable, and contains enough cases in the endpoints to make informative comparisons across the full 0.00–1.00 range (see figures 4.1–4.2).

We control for several demographic variables that covary with religion and moral issues.[5] At this point, we do not include political identities in the model because our goal is to isolate the effect of moral issue attitudes on religion. If, as we have theorized, moral issues also shape political affinities, then including, say, party ID in the statistical models may bias the estimated issue effects. Further tests reveal that the effect of issues on religious ID holds when we take political identities into account (more on this below).

To estimate the dynamic relationship between religion and issues, we use cross-lagged regression (CLR) models (Finkel 1995). We model moral issues$_t$ as a linear function of moral issues$_{t-1}$, religious ID$_{t-1}$, and the control variables. We then use logistic regression to model religious ID$_t$ as a function of religious ID$_{t-1}$, issues$_{t-1}$, and the controls. The t-1 subscript stands for a variable measured in the first wave of the panel (e.g., 2010). The t subscript stands for a variable measured in the second wave (e.g., 2014).

Two things must happen to validate the religion-to-issues hypothesis. First, religious ID$_{t-1}$ will manifest statistically and substantively significant effects on moral issues$_t$ across the datasets. Second, moral issues$_{t-1}$ will not affect religious ID$_t$. Results like this will suggest that religious ties shape moral issue positions without being affected by these positions. For our moral issues to religion hypothesis to hold, moral issues$_{t-1}$ will have significant effects on religious ID$_t$ across the datasets. This will suggest that public opinion on abortion and gay rights conditions the choice to enter or leave organized religion.

Religious Exit Results

In this section, we present the results of our tests. To keep things simple, we do two things. First, we confine the full set of model estimates from the twelve CLR models to the appendices at the end of this chapter (see Tables A6.1–A6.2). Second, we use forest plots and meta-analyses to summarize the key quantities of interest. We then use a pair of graphics to illustrate these effects.

The top forest plot in figure 6.2 shows the effect that religious ID$_{t-1}$ has on moral issue opinion$_t$ in each dataset, holding the other variables constant. Each circle represents the CLR point estimate for a model (see table A6.1). The lines extending out from each point are the lower and upper 90 percent confidence limits.[6] These confidence intervals tell us if religious ties reliably predict change in moral issues. We can infer religion shapes issues when the confidence intervals do not cross the vertical 0.00 reference line.

The top pane of figure 6.2 indicates that, compared to the nones, religiously affiliated Americans moved right on culture war issues over time. This evidence supports the religion-to-issues hypothesis. Each point estimate falls to the right of the 0.00 reference line and none of the 90 percent confidence intervals cross that line. All else equal, adults who identify with religion in the earlier period oppose abortion and gay rights to a greater degree later on than do the wave$_1$ nones. The largest effect appears in 2008–2012. There, anti-abortion/gay sentiments rose by 10 percent among

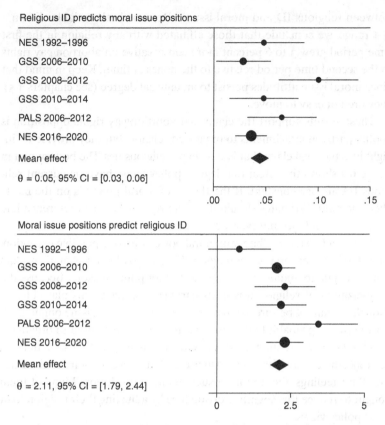

FIGURE 6.2. Forest plot summarizing the effects of religious ID and moral issues on each other

Notes: Each point estimate comes from the cross-lagged model results reported in table A6.1 (the top plot presents OLS regression estimates) and table A6.2 (the bottom plot presents logistic regression estimates). The point estimate for each study is bounded by 90 percent confidence intervals (CIs). The mean effect θ represents the precision-weighted point estimate across all six datasets. We also report the 95 percent CI for θ. The weight of each study is proportional to the size of the point estimate circle.

the religiously affiliated relative to the nones—a solid effect. The other effects are a bit smaller. For example, the difference is 5 percent in 1992–1996 and 7 percent in 2006–2012.

What is the average effect across the panels? Meta-analysis takes each study's point estimate and standard error to calculate a precision-weighted mean. Figure 6.2 shows that this effect is 0.05. The 95 percent confidence interval equals [0.03, 0.06], suggesting a meaningful if modest relationship between religious ID and moral issues.[7] Because both variables lie on a 0–1 range, we conclude that those affiliated with any religion in the first time period grew 3 to 6 percent more conservative on abortion/gay rights in the second time period relative to the nones at $time_1$. Keep in mind that since moral issue attitudes persist to an unusual degree (see chapters 4-5), they are not easy to move.

These results support the claim that abortion/gay rights opposition is rooted partly in attachments to organized religion, but they provide no insight into the rival claim that issues shape religious ties. The bottom plot in figure 6.2 shows the effect that lagged policy views have on current religious ID, all else constant. If the theory of moral power is on the mark, then the point estimates should lie to the right of the 0.00 reference line while the confidence intervals do not cross it.

The data bolster the theory of moral power with one possible exception. Moral $issues_{92}$ fails to predict religious ID_{96}. It may be that Americans had not yet begun to update their religious ties for policy reasons. Because the politicization of religion was in its early stages, this seems plausible, although we cannot be sure. Across the five other datasets, issue opinions alter the future probability that Americans remain connected to organized religion (all $p < .01$, one-tailed test). Our results suggest that sometime after 1996, the tension that some Americans felt between their religious ties and their feelings about moral issues required resolution. Many of them sought to reduce this cognitive dissonance by adjusting their religion to fit their policy views.

On to the average effect: the meta-analysis returns a mean value of 2.11 ($p < .01$). Recall that these are logistic regression coefficients. They do not have an intuitive interpretation. Fortunately, it is easy to transform this estimate into a mean probability of identifying with any religion. Doing so reveals that, on average, the most morally progressive respondents in the first wave of the panel are 12 percent less likely to identify with religion in the second wave, compared to the most morally conservative in wave one. The 95 percent CI shows that movement from the most progressive to the most conservative point on abortion/same-sex issues predicts a 0.07 to 0.17 increase in the future probability of identifying with religion. Put in an alternative way, as the positions people take on moral issues move in the pro-choice/pro-gay direction, the odds of identifying as a "none" go up. Pro-choice/pro-gay sentiments push some people away from religion.

To convey this relationship another way, we turn to a simple bar graph. We use the 2010–2014 GSS estimates to plot the probability that moral progressives, moderates, and conservatives who identified with a religion in wave one left it in wave two.[8] Doing so indicates that moral progressivism helps explain the rise of the nones.

We begin with progressives in the left-most bar. These folks backed abortion and same-sex rights to the hilt in 2010. Their probability of abandoning the religious field four years later is 0.12. Those who took moderate positions on these issues were less likely to exit. Their probability of leaving sits at 0.05. Moral conservatives were the least likely to withdraw from religion. For them, the predicted probability of identifying as a none down the line is 0.02. Note that relatively few people took the drastic step of leaving their religion. Given that religion is a "sticky" identity, this is not surprising. The key thing to keep in mind is that gut-level support for abortion and gay rights predict who is most likely to leave the fold.

Excepting 1992–1996, what we see in figure 6.3 is typical of what we see in other panels. All told, our evidence shows that politics shapes religion. But in contrast to some prior work, which credits liberal and Democratic identities for religious exit, our results suggest that it was progressive views on moral issues that dislodged people from their religious moorings. Given that the public has moved in a progressive direction on moral issues—principally same-sex rights—it seems that issues have played a critical role in the thirty-year rise of the nones.

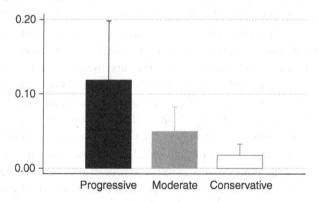

FIGURE 6.3. Public opinion on moral issues predicts religious exit, 2010–2014
Notes: Data come from the 2010–2014 logistic regression estimates reported in table A6.2. The figure shows the predicted probability that religious identifiers in 2010 who held progressive, moderate, or conservative moral issue positions identified as a "none" in 2014. Progressives, moderates, and conservatives score at the tenth, fiftieth, and ninetieth percentiles on our moral issues scale.

What about Political Identities?

So far we have seen that opinions on moral issues predict religious identity reconstruction over time. This result is consistent with the kinds of political backlash explanations offered elsewhere for the rise of the nones (e.g., Hout and Fischer 2002, 2014; Putnam and Campbell 2010). These accounts identify ideological and party ID as the main drivers of religious change. Since we did not account for political identities in the statistical models, readers may wonder about the power of moral issues to affect disaffiliation. To build the case for moral issues, we take political identities into account in this section.

We do so by adding the standard seven-point measures of liberal-conservative (LC) ID and party ID to the issue-to-religion equations. In each dataset we estimate three logistic regression models: ($Model_1$) background controls + party ID; ($Model_2$) background controls + LC ID; and ($Model_3$) controls + party ID + LC ID + moral issues. M_1 and M_2 tell us whether political IDs predict religious exit when we ignore moral issues. M_3 tells us what happens when we add in moral issues. If moral issues drive the decision to leave religion, then whatever effects identities have in M_1 and M_2 should wash out in M_3.

This is precisely what the data reveals. First, party ID predicted religious ID in five of the six M_1 models. Second, LC ID predicted religious change in four of the six M_2 models. Thus, in the absence of moral issues identities seem to matter. Third, and most importantly, *the political ID effects no longer hold once we add moral issues to the model.* Controlling for all three political variables, neither party nor ideology come close to reaching significance at conventional levels (see appendix table A6.3). By contrast, the moral issue effect holds in every single panel save 1992-1996 (as we saw above). In fact, the impact does not diminish at all. This becomes evident when we compare the logit coefficients for moral issues in table A6.2 to their table A6.3 analogues. They are, in a word, indistinguishable.

To sum up, the inclusion of political identities does not alter our conclusion about the power of moral issues to predict religious change. What does change is the conclusion about political identities and religious disaffiliation. When we account for the influence of moral issues, the influence of political identities wanes and perhaps even disappears. In big picture terms, these estimates suggest that moral issues, not political identities, motivate religious exit.[9]

This concludes our primary tests of the rival theories. Consistent with the classic view, religious ID predicts issue-attitude change. That is, reli-

MORAL ISSUES AND RELIGIOUS DISAFFILIATION   119

gious ID shapes policy views. Consistent with the theory of moral power, moral issue attitudes predict religious change. That is, issue attitudes seem to shape religious ID. In conjunction, this pattern of results implies reciprocal causation. When the Religious Right pushed its concerns onto the national agenda, everyday Americans noticed. Some people updated their views of abortion and gay rights to better reflect the preference of their religious groups. Others renounced religious identities to better reflect their issue tastes. Lastly, progressive takes on moral issues, more so than left-leaning political identities, drove antireligion backlash.

The Religious Identity Strength Tests

To this point we have treated religious ID as a dichotomous variable. We now move on to the links between issues and identity strength. We swap religious ID strength (our roughly interval-level measure) for religious ID (our dichotomous measure), repeat the analyses, and report what we find.

Three preliminaries to note. First, given a seven-point measure of identity strength, we model it using cross-lagged regression. Second, the ID strength variable appears only on the three GSS panels, which limits our analyses to these surveys. Third, note that roughly 11 percent of respondents have the lowest score on identity strength (0.00), while nearly 15 percent have the highest score (1.00) on the surveys. This lets us talk about movement across the full range of the ID strength scale in substantively informative ways.

On to the forest plots: the upper plot in figure 6.4 lists the CLR coefficients for the effect of religious ID strength$_{t-1}$ on moral issue opinion$_t$, ceteris paribus.[10] The bottom plot displays the CLR coefficients for the issue opinion$_{t-1}$ effect on religious ID strength$_t$, all else constant. Mean effect sizes appear at the bottom of each plot (the full set of estimates appear in Tables A6.6 and A6.7).

As called for by identity-based models, the top plot shows that lagged religious ID strength predicts current issue positions in all three datasets. When people pick up cues in public discourse about where "religious people" stand on abortion and gay rights, they adjust their policy views to conform to their religious priors. The point estimates from the individual studies range from 0.09 to 0.14 (all p < .01, one-tailed test) and average 0.11.

What does this mean in practical terms? It means relative to people with the weakest religious ID (i.e., mostly the nones), the strongest religious identifiers score 11 percent more conservative on moral issues four years later. Put differently, once we account for initial positions on moral issues,

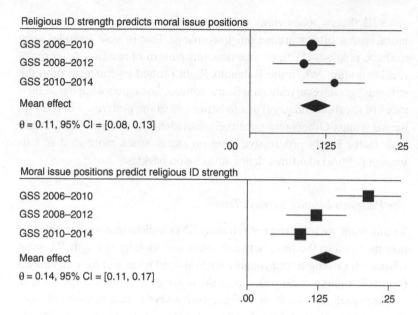

FIGURE 6.4. Forest plot summarizing the effects of religious ID strength and moral issues on each other

Notes: Each point estimate comes from the cross-lagged OLS results reported in table A6.6 (top plot) and table A6.7 (bottom plot). The point estimate for each study is bounded by 90 percent CIs. The mean effect θ represents the precision-weighted point estimate across all six datasets. We also report the 95 percent CI for θ. The weight of each study is proportional to the size of the point estimate circle.

the subsequent gap on issues between the most and least religious respondents grew by 11 percent (95 percent CI = [0.08, 0.13]). This is a sizeable effect. It attests to the continuing power of religion to induce attitude change.

The bottom plot takes up the moral issues hypothesis. There, wave₁ beliefs about abortion/same-sex rights predict how strongly people identified with religion in wave₂ (all $p < .01$, one-tailed test). As expected, the more strongly they favored abortion and gay rights, the more their religious attachments weakened down the line. The CLR coefficients vary quite a bit, ranging from 0.09 to 0.22. The mean effect equals 0.14. In plain language, the difference in religious ID strength between the most progressive and most conservative subjects grew by 14 percent on average. The corresponding 95 percent CI puts the effect in the 11 to 17 percent range—a somewhat larger effect than the reverse.

To help readers understand how these variables affect one another, figure 6.5 displays two bar graphs based on the 2008–2012 data. The graph to the left shows the predicted score on moral issues in 2012 for subjects who had weak, average, and strong religious identities in 2008.[11] Stronger religious identities$_{08}$ correlate with more opposition to abortion/same sex rights$_{12}$. Those with the weakest attachments to religion scored 0.40 on moral issues in 2012—a slightly progressive take on abortion and gay rights. The most religiously committed scored 0.49 on issues—a more moderate stance. Religious ID, in short, predicts issue opinion change, affirming the standard religion-to-politics model. The graph on the right shows that moral issues predict religious change four years later on. Pro-life/anti-gay respondents identify more strongly with religion than pro-choice/pro-gay respondents (0.62 vs. 0.51).[12]

To sum up the results of the identity strength tests, we find support for the standard theory and our rival theory. Per the usual view, religious ties engender issue attitude change. Consistent with the theory of moral power, issue attitudes predict a bit more change in religious ID strength. As was the case for categorical religious ID, this pattern of results suggests (but doesn't prove) reciprocal causation.

We have argued that the gut-level feelings people have toward abortion/gay rights shape religious ID and fuel anti-religious backlash. As the Religious Right politicized these issues, they precipitated moderate and progressive flight from organized religion. Appalled by the way some religious leaders and some of their followers maligned women and gays, some Americans have kissed religion goodbye. At the same time, a smaller

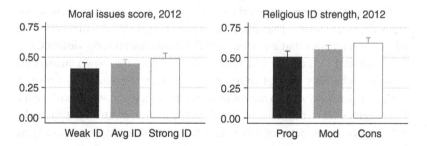

FIGURE 6.5. The relationship between religious ID strength and moral issues, 2008–2012
Notes: Data come from the 2008–2012 regression estimates reported in tables A6.6–A6.7. The bar graph on the left shows the predicted moral issue score in 2012 for weak, moderate, and strong religious identifiers in 2008. The bar graph on the right shows the predicted religious ID strength score in 2012 for issue progressives, moderates, and conservatives in 2008. On each x-axis, the values are for respondents at the tenth, fiftieth, and ninetieth percentiles on each variable.

A Final Test

Before wrapping things up, we undertake one final test. This section presents some additional statistical work that less technical readers may wish to avoid. They can do so with no loss of continuity because the results reaffirm what we have already reported.

The above results point to a two-way relationship between religious ID and moral issues. However, the results only account for between-person differences in religious ID over time. They do not adequately cover within-person change. It is important to get at within-person change because doing so brings more persuasive evidence to bear on the claim that moral issues shape religion. To get at this, we turn to the two-period fixed effects (FE) estimator (Allison 2009). In FE models, each person serves as their own control for all observed and unobserved covariates that do not vary over time. By definition, things that do not change cannot produce change in outcome variables. This means we can rule out a wide range of dispositional factors as rival explanations for religious change.

We look at religious ID strength instead of categorical ID for two reasons. First, there is not enough within-person change on categorical ID to model with FE tools. For example, in the 2006–2012 PALS 92 percent of the panelists did not change their affiliation. Second, there is enough variation on religious ID strength to model effectively.

We measure change on moral issues by subtracting the $time_{t-1}$ issue score from the $time_t$ score. The difference score ranges from −1.00 to +1.00, where −1.00 means that a person with the most conservative views in, say, 2006 switched to the most progressive views in 2010 and +1.00 means that someone who fully backed abortion and gay rights in 2006 fully opposed both in 2010. A score of 0 means that one held identical views both years. For religious ID strength, −1.00 signals movement from strongest to weakest identity; +1.00 denotes movement from the weakest to the strongest identity.

To estimate the model, we need to posit a causal order. Since the religion-to-issues and issues-to-religion models are both plausible on theoretical grounds and our empirical results do not yield evidence of a one-way relationship, it is not clear what to assume. As such, we pursue a more modest goal. We aim to show that issue opinion change predicts religious

MORAL ISSUES AND RELIGIOUS DISAFFILIATION

change, holding all time-invariant factors constant. If a relationship exists, we have a stronger basis for concluding that the variables are related.[13]

To cut to the chase, the results are encouraging (see table A6.8 for the details). Moral issue change predicts religious change in the first two panels but not the third. Because a one-point shift on a −1.00 to 1.00 scale is large and stability is the rule for moral issues, standardized coefficients do a better job conveying the effect sizes. The standardized coefficients are 0.08 for 2006–2010, 0.13 for 2008–2012, and −0.01 for 2010–2014. In plain language, when issue positions change, religious commitments also change.[14] Morally progressive folks become a little less religious over time. Morally conservative folks grow a bit stronger in their religious ties.

To finish up, we reiterate that none of our results prove that issues drive religious change. What the CLR and FE estimates do suggest is that the issues-to-religious ID model merits serious consideration moving forward. Feelings about abortion and gay rights seem to be strong enough to drive some toward organized religion and push many more away.

Chapter Summary

Many people believe that religion drives political change. Max Weber (1930) made this case in *The Protestant Ethic and the Spirit of Capitalism*. He theorized that a nation's religious character charts the course of its economic and political development. In his words, "in a time when the beyond meant everything . . . the religious forces which express themselves through such channels are the decisive influences on the formation of national character" (ibid., 102). Less well remembered is that Weber remained open to the prospect that the secular might influence the spiritual, writing that it is "necessary to investigate how Protestant Asceticism was in turn influenced in its development and its character by the totality of social conditions" (ibid., 125).

Our work affirms Weber's insights. Religion and social conditions respond to one another in dynamic fashion. We have shown that religious ties induce opinion change on moral issues. At the same time, we have shown that feelings about abortion/gay rights lead some people to embrace—and many more to walk away from—organized religion.

Our findings contribute to a growing body of work that demonstrates that politics shapes religion (Hout and Fischer 2002, 2014; Putnam and Campbell 2010; Margolis 2018; Egan 2020). But in contrast to most of this work, we have shown that the key psychological force driving religious identity change is not political identities but, rather, visceral feelings about abortion and same-sex individuals (also see Campbell, Layman, and Green 2021). Now, one might counter that the effects of party ID work through moral issues. If so, the inferences we have drawn from our data understate the power of party ID and overstate that of issues. To sort this out, the next chapter investigates the relationship between moral issues and party loyalties.

CHAPTER SEVEN

Moral Issues and Party Change

Today, nearly all Democratic politicians are pro-choice and pro-gay rights. At the same time, virtually every Republican official is pro-life. Many also favor some limits on same-sex rights or carving out religious exemption laws for those who oppose gay marriage. These stances define the current party brands. It was not always this way. Consider where the parties stood on abortion in the 1970s. The Democratic Party's congressional wing included many pro-life members. The GOP wing had its share of pro-choice legislators. As we detail later in the chapter, abortion split the parties the first time the anti-abortion Hyde Amendment came up for a vote in 1976.

The muted difference between the parties was also apparent on the presidential campaign trail that year. In a July 1976 television broadcast of *Meet the Press*, Democratic nominee Jimmy Carter called abortion "wrong" (NBC News 1976). It is hard to imagine a Democratic candidate for president saying the same thing today. In 1980, George H. W. Bush sought the GOP nomination as an abortion moderate—meaning that he opposed public funding without favoring an outright ban (McCammon 2018). Any candidate who adopted Bush's stance would have no chance to make it in the contemporary GOP.

What changed? The rise of the Religious Right and its success in politicizing moral issues during the Reagan-Bush years altered the course of American history. In a bid to mobilize previously apolitical Christians and siphon off support from culturally conservative Democrats, the GOP embraced the Religious Right's pro-life, anti-gay agenda. The Bush campaign injected the phrase "culture war" into the American political lexicon and clarified where the parties stood on its defining moral issues. Since then, pitched battles have raged at the local, state, and national levels over abortion and

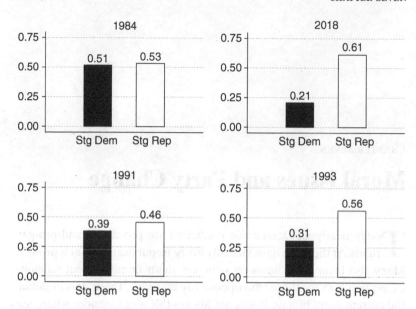

FIGURE 7.1. Strong Democrats and strong Republicans became polarized on moral issues, 1984–2018

Notes: Data come from the GSS Cumulative Data File. Bars represent the mean moral issue score on the seven abortion and one same-sex relations items. This scale ranges from 0.00 (pro-choice/pro-gay) to 1.00 (pro-life/anti-gay). Strong Republicans are significantly more conservative than strong Democrats in 1993 and 2018 (p < .01). Strong Republicans are marginally more conservative than strong Democrats in 1991 (p < .07). Strong Republicans and strong Democrats do not differ on moral issues in 1984 (p < .38). These are one-tailed tests.

gay rights. Supreme Court decisions that legalized same-sex marriage in 2015 and revoked a federal right to abortion in 2022 have not settled matters. Instead, the *Obergefell* and *Dobbs* decisions have poured more fuel onto the cultural fires. New controversies have erupted over state abortion referenda, religious exemption laws, "don't say gay" laws, and transgender rights—even on who can use bathrooms.

Americans have responded to these elite signals. They have brought their partisan identities in line with their feelings about moral issues. To make this point clear, we compare the positions that strong partisans have taken on these issues at different points in time during the culture war. Figure 7.1 deploys GSS data to plot the average moral issue score for strong Democrats and strong Republicans in 1977, 1991, 1993, and 2018. The moral issue variable ranges from zero to one. Respondents who score zero favor abortion without any exceptions and strongly approve of same-sex intimacy.

MORAL ISSUES AND PARTY CHANGE

Those who score one oppose abortion without exception and strongly disapprove of same-sex relations. Scores below the midpoint denote progressive leanings. Scores above the midpoint reflect conservative sentiments.

Let us begin with the two bar graphs in the top row. The top left graph reveals that there was no daylight between strong Democrats and strong Republicans on moral issues in 1984. Four years after Ronald Reagan embraced the Religious Right during the 1980 campaign, the most partisan Democrats and Republicans shared virtually identical, moderate outlooks on abortion and same-sex relations (0.51 ≈ 0.53, p < .38). Over the next three decades, these partisans polarized sharply on both issues. By 2018, strong Democrats had shifted dramatically in the progressive direction, from 0.51 to 0.21, while strong GOP partisans shifted to the right, from 0.53 to 0.61 (p < .01 in both cases). The country has moved from an era in which partisans completely agreed on abortion and gays to an era in which strong Republicans are three times more conservative than strong Democrats. Put simply, in the space of one generation strong partisans moved from moderate consensus on abortion and same-sex relations to extreme moral polarization.

The bar graphs in the bottom row reveal how the party–moral issue alignment began to shift after the 1992 presidential campaign. The left graph hints that the partisan divergence was underway by 1991: strong Republicans stood slightly to the right of strong Democrats (0.46 v. 0.39, p < .07). Within two short years, polarization was picking up steam. In 1993, strong Republicans were significantly more conservative than strong Democrats (0.56 v. 0.31, p < .01). After 1993, partisans polarized further.

To put it directly, in the 1980s there was no connection between party loyalties and public opinion on moral issues. Back then, if you knew someone's party ID, you could not predict where they stood on abortion and same-sex relations. But once the parties staked out diverging positions on these issues, party images and moral issues started to align in the American psyche. Today, if you know someone's party ID, you can pretty easily guess where they stand on abortion and gay rights.

The key questions this chapter seeks to answer is how and why party ID and moral issues became closely intertwined. Did people change their minds about these issues to reflect their party ID, or did they change their party to reflect their feelings about these issues? Identity-based theories hold that partisans adopt the positions endorsed by their party when they realize where the parties stand. The theory of moral power rests on a contrarian logic. We contend that the GOP's embrace of moral conservativism, combined with pushback by Democratic elites, clarified the parties' moral visions. In response, many Americans changed their party ID to reflect their visceral feelings about abortion and same-sex rights. Party ID did not shape moral issues alone, but rather, moral issues also shaped party ID.

Our theory harkens back to older theories of issue-driven party revision (Downs 1957; Franklin and Jackson 1983). These approaches have fallen out of favor because so much evidence indicates that party ID is hard to move and few people hold strong feelings about most issues. But abortion and gay rights are not like most issues. Using data from seven panel studies, we find that party ID shapes moral issues and issues shape party ID. However, the issue-to-party effect is roughly twice as large as the party-to-issue effect, suggesting that moral issues are stronger than party ties. We also show that moral issue positions predict party switching, a particularly hard test of our theory. When people are out of step with their party on abortion and gay rights, some of them exit the party. Overall, our results suggest that moral issue attitudes are central elements in the belief systems of everyday Americans. To be sure, party ID *is* important. Moral issues may be more important.

The Party ID to Issues Model

Party ID Defined

Per *The American Voter*, we define party ID as a psychological attachment to a political party (Campbell et al. 1960). This attachment reflects how we see our political selves and where our principal political loyalties lie. These ties develop during childhood, solidify by early adulthood, and hold steady as we age. We stick with our party because it represents "our kind" of people, meaning those who belong to the same social groups that we belong to (Green, Palmquist, and Schickler 2002; Mason 2018). Once in place, party ID motivates us to take a positive view of things associated with our party and a dim view of things associated with "them." We reflexively adopt the views put forward by our parties and leaders. Recommendations from the other side are dismissed with little thought (Bartels 2002; Cohen 2003).

People cling to these identities more tenaciously than they cling to other political orientations. From the seminal works in the field (Campbell et al. 1960; Converse 1964) to recent cutting-edge work (Lavine, Johnston, and Steenbergen 2012; Barber and Pope 2019), scholars have shown that the effects of party ID on political judgment are broad, deep, and largely (not completely) immune from the influence of other political attitudes and beliefs. The stability and impact of party ID explains why many analysts conclude that it is the strongest political predisposition in the minds of the American people.

Later, we examine two aspects of party ID. The first is partisan strength— that is, where someone falls along a continuum ranging from strong Democrat to strong Republican. The second thing we look at is categorical attachment—that is, whether someone thinks of herself as a Democrat, an independent, or a Republican. This two-pronged approach lets us study how the strength of party ties change and how often people leave their party.

How Partisan Identities Shape Public Opinion

Groups help people pursue their interests and achieve their goals. These interests and goals reflect a mix of instrumental benefits (e.g., material resources) and emotional benefits (i.e., solidarity and positive self-esteem). The price of group membership is conformity to group beliefs. By accepting the positions the group takes on various matters, one confirms that she is a member in good standing, that she is committed to the group, and that others in the group can count on her in competition with rival groups.

In the case of party ID, it seems likely that emotional incentives drive partisan conformity more so than self-interest. When parties do well in elections, members rejoice. When parties lose, members are upset and feel anxious. The thought of spending time with copartisans elicits warm feelings. Spending time with members from the other side does not (Green, Palmquist, and Schickler 2002; Iyengar, Sood, and Lelkes 2012; Huddy, Mason, and Aarøe 2015). By contrast, there is less evidence that self-interest motivates partisan attachment (Sears and Citrin 1985; Sears and Funk 1991). Put simply, we conform to party positions because it feels good to agree with people like us, not because conformity advances our material self-interest.

To conform, partisans need to discern where their side stands on a given issue. This is where party messaging through the information environment comes into play. One especially influential line of thinking heralds the role party leaders play in signaling where the parties come down on public controversies (Zaller 1992; Levendusky 2009; Lee 2016). In an effort to mobilize public support, party leaders and candidates take positions that they believe will help them prevail on Election Day and in the court of public opinion during the governing season. They seek to burnish the party brand and tarnish their rival's reputation. They broadcast messages in campaign contacts; in TV, print, and online media; and in other forums. Voters learn where the parties stand from these sources. They also find out from social sources, such as talk radio, friends, and social media. For this two-step flow of information to work on a large scale, a given issue must attract enough attention from the media to break through the mass public's political apathy.

Careful readers may see a paradox here. We have argued that most people do not hold genuine feelings on most issues. If this is so, why do parties bother advertising where they stand on issues? They do so for at least three reasons. First, some candidates and party leaders mistakenly believe that most people care about issues. Second, candidates may know that most people care little about most issues, but they also recognize that subsets of voters care passionately about single issues. Third, politicians try to mobilize support for their preferred policies by persuading the public to adopt the party's position. In short, the parties have good reasons to publicize where they stand even though these efforts elude many people.

When political elites clash intensely on highly charged, easily understood issues, news organizations devote a lot of attention to the conflict. The ensuing coverage activates partisan identities across large swaths of the public. When partisans in the electorate receive these messages, they take little notice of the reasons given for or against the policy. Instead, they reflexively accept the position taken by their side and reject the ideas advanced by the other side. So long as one's party backs a policy, that is reason enough to accept it. If the other side supports a policy, that is grounds to reject it.[1] When party leaders regularly deliver the same message through the media, their copartisans in the electorate learn how they should line up on the issues (Levendusky 2009).

In short, in high-intensity information environments people receive a steady dose of cues about where the parties stand. They get the cues through some mix of chronic or episodic attention to the media, discussion with family or friends, online, and other channels. The net result is that many if not most people become aware of the most intense debates. Debate details typically elude them, but no matter. As long as they know where the parties stand, they can toe the party line. Of course, we cannot presume that any given issue breaks through in this fashion. The next section explains why we think abortion and same-sex rights are an exception to the rule.

The Parties Evolving Positions on Abortion and Gay Rights

Our story begins with the political awakening of conservative Christians that we documented last chapter. The New Christian Right (NCR) aimed to build an enduring GOP majority on the votes of millions of conservative white Christians who felt threatened by an increasingly secular culture. This would entail peeling off Catholics and evangelicals from the Democratic Party. It would also require mobilizing religiously conservative people who did not vote. Religious Right leaders enthusiastically backed Ronald Reagan in 1980. He welcomed their support. Reagan's victory over Carter suggested that the NCR's political strategy could bear electoral fruit. As a result, the budding relationship between the Religious Right and the GOP grew stronger in the years to come.

Over the course of his presidency, Reagan's deft use of religious language and symbols in public speeches resonated with NCR leaders and millions of conservative Christians (Domke and Coe 2010). But while movement leaders appreciated Reagan's paeans to God, religion, and the Judeo-Christian heritage, his restraint when talking about abortion/homosexuals disappointed many in the Religious Right. A lack of policy achievements compounded their frustrations. By the end of the 1980s, more than a few movement leaders felt the GOP had taken their electoral support in exchange for nothing. Movement activists redoubled their efforts to push the party to take up the NCR's agenda (Lienesch 1993; Layman 2001).

These efforts soon bore fruit. By the early 1990s, the GOP effectively adopted key parts of the Religious Right's policy agenda. The year 1992 was a watershed moment. At the GOP convention that August, Patrick Buchanan (1992) delivered a fiery address to the delegates on the convention floor and to millions of television viewers at home. Buchanan denounced "abortion on demand" and tallied up the human cost—"25 million unborn children destroyed since *Roe v. Wade*." He attacked a "militant . . . homosexual rights movement" and condemned "the amoral idea that gay and lesbian couples should have the same standing in law as married men and women." He explicitly linked religion with conservative moral politics: "There is a religious war going on in this country. It is a cultural war, as critical to the kind of nation we shall be as was the Cold War itself, for this war is for the soul of America." Buchanan emphasized where the candidates—and by extension the parties—stood: "in that struggle for the soul of America, Clinton & Clinton are on the other side, and George Bush is on our side."

A month earlier at his party's convention, Bill Clinton had staked out clear positions on both controversies. On abortion, he said "I am not pro-abortion; I am pro-choice, strongly. I believe this difficult and painful decision should be left to the women of America." And this: "George Bush won't guarantee a woman's right to choose; I will." He also urged Americans

132   CHAPTER SEVEN

to "Look beyond the stereotypes that blind us" and denounced Republican efforts to demonize outgroups—including gays. While Clinton's words and subsequent actions were less emphatic in some respects than what Democratic candidates would say in the future, they contrasted sharply with the stances taken by President Bush and the GOP.

Given public dissatisfaction with a recession-weakened economy, the Bush campaign emphasized culture war issues in "a concerted effort by the Republican Party to win the heart and soul of middle-class white America" (Edsall 1992). The Bush team believed that campaigning on moral issues and candidate character would serve the president better than focusing on the economy. On the campaign trail, Bush and Clinton sparred over abortion. They also clashed over Clinton's proposal to allow gays to serve openly in the military. Both issues weighed heavily on voters' minds as they cast their ballots on Election Day, more so than in the past (Abramowitz 1995; Rhodebeck 2015).

From that point forward, opposition to abortion/gay rights helped define the GOP brand. In response, the Democratic Party became the party of moral tolerance, slowly at first and with greater passion over time. For GOP voters, it did not matter whether the party nominated a conspicuously devout, born-again Christian like George W. Bush or his complete antithesis in a thrice-divorced, misogynistic playboy like Donald Trump. The party's commitment to repealing *Roe. v. Wade* and resisting same-sex rights mattered more. The American public took notice and responded accordingly. Democratic identifiers became more progressive. Republicans remained firmly in the traditional camp. The sorting process moved slowly at first but grew steadily year over year (Bafumi and Shapiro 2009).

All of this suggests that party signals on abortion and gay rights were crystallizing. To bring some evidence to bear on how moral issue messaging evolved, we return to the news headlines database from chapter 3. For each headline in our sample, we looked to see if it also contained one of twenty words signaling partisan/political contestation.[2] Since health policy and tax policy are also highly contested, we included these news articles in the same analysis.

Figure 7.2 plots the percentage of newspaper headlines that reference partisan/political conflict each year from 1980 through 2022. The figure shows that moral issues became increasingly political starting in the late 1980s. Two things stand out. First, while roughly 30 percent of moral issue headlines included a political term throughout most of the 1980s, this number soared to 44 percent in 1989. Coupled with the increase in message

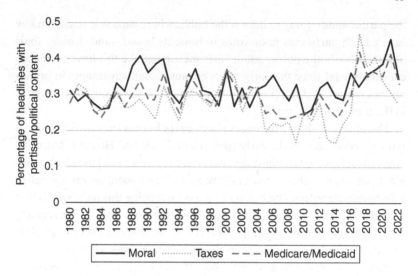

FIGURE 7.2. Headlines with political signals
Notes: Lines represent the percentage of headlines in the newspaper headline database that include a term signaling political conflict or partisanship. Moral issues include these terms 33.0 percent of the time versus 28.3 percent for taxes and 25.5 percent for healthcare. The data come from our newspaper headline database (see online chapter 3 appendix for additional details).

volume we documented in chapter 3, it is clear that starting in the late 1980s Americans found themselves immersed in a changed information environment. This new context included more coverage of moral issues (see figure 3.2) that took on a distinctly partisan/political flavor (figure 7.2). Americans started to see who belonged in each moral camp.

The second thing that stands out in figure 7.2 is that politicization is a bit more pronounced for moral issues than for either taxes or Medicare/Medicaid. To be sure, these are all intensely political topics. However, the proportion of headlines that employ conflict frames is higher for moral issues than for taxes (0.33 > 0.28, $p < .001$). This also holds true for Medicare Medicaid (0.33 > 0.26, $p < .001$). In conjunction with the chapter 3 findings, figure 7.2 implies that Americans could increasingly see which party matched their position on moral issues—more so than other prominent issues.

Our data shows that the information environment has contained numerous signals about party positions on moral issues since the late 1980s. Importantly, these signals do not merely occur at the whim of the media—they also emerge from actions taken by government leaders. Consider the voting records of members of Congress and the Senate. Floor votes give the parties another way to inform the public where each side stands on key issues. Each party uses floor votes to hone its brand—and damage their opponent's—in the public mind. Party messaging like this has become increasingly vital since the early 1990s because small advantages in branding can make the difference between who sits in the majority and who is in the minority (Lee 2016).

The ability to draw inferences about party brands from voting records requires good data. In the early 1980s, Keith Poole and Howard Rosenthal (1985) developed a technique that uses roll call votes to estimate legislators' ideal points on a liberal-conservative scale. These ideal points are called DW-Nominate scores. The key assumption underlying this technique is that a single latent dimension determines how legislators vote. By aggregating individual scores across multiple roll call votes, researchers can calculate the ideological distance between the parties in a single chamber in each Congress. Scholars can also chart how the ideological distance between the parties shrinks or grows. By taking stock of research that uses DW-Nominate scores, we gain added insight into party branding during the culture war era.

The parties have been moving further apart in ideological space since the 1980s. In both chambers, Democrats have shifted to the left, Republicans to the right (McCarty, Poole, and Rosenthal 2008; Hare and Poole 2014). Joshua Zingher (2022) reports that state legislatures have also polarized in recent decades. The GOP has stood well to the right of their Democratic rivals in every legislative chamber in every state from 1996 and 2018. As the parties have moved further apart in ideological space, the clarity of the party brands has crystallized.

Because a single left-right dimension explains most of the variation in congressional roll call voting, few works examine what goes on in specific issue areas. A reader might ask whether the polarization trend described holds with equal force for abortion and gay rights. The answer is yes. Employing a range of measures and different sets of legislators, political scientists have shown that the parties polarized on abortion from the early 1970s to the late 2000s (Adams 1997; Karol 2009; D'Antonio, Tuch, and Baker 2013). The same holds true for LGBT issues (Lindaman and Haider-Markel 2002; Bishin, Freebourn, and Teten 2021).

We can illustrate the growing clarity in partisan signaling by examining how voting on a similar piece of legislation has changed throughout the years. We use the so-called Hyde Amendment and related provisions that have passed through Congress for decades. These provisions restrict federal funding for abortions in appropriation bills. Originally introduced by Iowa GOP representative Henry J. Hyde in 1976, the Hyde Amendments have gone through different iterations down through the years (e.g., carving out exceptions in cases of rape or incest) (Liu and Shen 2022). Votes on the Hyde provisions reveal where the parties stand on abortion. These votes come up regularly in party messages, campaign ads, and other communications.

While the original Hyde vote was contentious, it was not partisan. Hyde successfully added the language "None of the funds appropriated under this Act shall be used to pay for abortions or to promote or encourage abortions" to a Department of Labor and Health, Education, and Welfare Appropriation Act. The original Hyde Amendment vote passed narrowly with support from both parties: 107 Democrats and 92 Republicans voted yea. The nays garnered 133 votes from Democrats and 32 from Republicans (67 abstained).[3] Indeed, Republican M. Caldwell Butler (VA-06) spoke in opposition to the amendment, arguing on the grounds of equality that abortion should not be denied to the poor through funding restrictions "while it remains available to the wealthy under the present state of the law" (Congressional Record House, p. 20412).

In contrast, subsequent votes on Hyde provisions have taken on an increasingly partisan character. For example, in 2017 House Republicans voted to effectively make the Hyde Amendment permanent. The legislation, which never became law, passed the House with 235 Republicans voting in favor. None opposed it. Meanwhile, 183 Democrats opposed the measure, with only 3 breaking ranks to join the GOP majority.

Joe Biden, long a Democratic supporter of the Hyde Amendment during his years as a senator from Delaware, provides a second example of how party positions on abortion evolved. Out of step with the rest of the party and anticipating a run for president, Biden declared in 2019: "If I believe health care is a right as I do, I can no longer support an amendment that makes that right dependent on someone's zip code" (Caputo 2019). The history of the Hyde amendment underscores how the parties have polarized on abortion over the course of the culture war.

As the parties and political elites became more polarized on abortion and gay rights, the public noticed. The national media yoked together moral issues and politics, providing voters with the cues they needed to gauge the party line. Research suggests that public awareness of party differences on these issues has grown. Susan Hansen (2014) used NES data to show that the public saw bigger differences between the abortion positions of presidential candidates as the culture war raged on year over year. We took a peek at NES data and found that the percentage of the public that placed the Democratic candidate to the left of the GOP candidate increased from 59 percent in 1992, to 63 percent in 2004, and to 73 percent in 2016.[4] On gay rights, the lack of data precludes a definitive statement. As far as we can tell, polls have not consistently asked about which party is more supportive of gay rights. That said, growing public awareness on abortion suggests that the same pattern likely holds for knowledge of party differences on same-sex rights.

Evidently, the increasing clarity of elite signaling and ongoing media coverage of partisan conflict did not escape the public. During the culture war, much of the American public learned where the parties stood on moral issues. Knowing this, partisans in the electorate were well-positioned to adopt the party line when asked to report where they stood on abortion and gay rights.

Expectations

We think it is fair to claim that the parties have diverged on moral issues and that much of the public knows this. The question is what happens when people find out that their views on these issues are out-of-line with their party. Standard theories hold that strong partisan identities shape weak issue attitudes. People go along with their parties on these issues. Doing so affirms one's commitment to the team and minimizes whatever cognitive dissonance they may feel upon learning that they are out of step with fellow partisans. In short, the logic of party ID to issue theories yields the following familiar hypothesis: party ID drives temporal change in moral issue positions.

The Moral Issues to Party ID Model

In this section, we reverse the typical causal sequence to theorize that feelings about moral issues induce party updating. We begin with a review of revisionist theories of party ID, which explain why it moves in response to other political attitudes and beliefs. We then argue that the growing clarity of the party brands has provided Americans with opportunities to adjust their party ties to fit their deeply held moral sensibilities.

No one believes that party ID is perfectly fixed, but scholars differ over what it takes to induce change. The standard theories set a high bar for updating. In this view, most people stick with their party through thick and thin (Campbell et al. 1960; Green, Palmquist, and Schickler 2002). Nothing short of once-in-a-lifetime calamities like the Civil War or the Great Depression fracture party bonds. Other events, such as rising unemployment or a foreign policy debacle, do not disrupt party ties. Moreover, issues do not break the bonds that bind us to parties. Instead, policy positions derive from long-standing party loyalties.

In contrast to this take, revisionist theories hold that party ID responds to the normal ebbs and flows of public life. Morris Fiorina's (1981) "running tally" model holds that new information about the state of the economy, political scandals, and foreign affairs induces periodic updating of party bonds. People render judgments about how things have gone in the country over the past year or two. These retrospective judgments feed into evaluations of the party. When things have gone well, the president's party shines. Weak partisans feel warmer toward their political compatriots. Independents and a few people from across the aisle switch to align with the president's party. When things have gone poorly, the president's copartisans push away. For some, party attachments cool. Others may leave the party. This openness to change is modest, but not negligible. In this way, party ID responds to short-term forces in public affairs.

Retrospective judgments like these may affect party ID, but since issues are central to our story we focus on issue-based models of party updating. The idea is simple. Nearly everyone accepts that party ID is stable and impactful, but some dispute the claim that policy does not govern party choice. In a classic work, Charles Franklin and John Jackson (1983) theorized that people align with the party that is closer to their views on key policies. Some people take liberal or progressive positions on issues. They identify with the Democratic Party in part because it pursues the policies they favor. Other individuals take conservative positions on these issues. By pushing such solutions, the GOP secures the backing of policy conservatives in the mass public. This logic underlies issue to party ID models (cf. Downs 1957). These models make little distinction between different subsets of issues. Instead, policy preferences in general drive party change (e.g., Abramowitz and Sanders 1998; but see Killian and Wilcox 2008 for an important exception on the abortion issue).

Although issue-proximity theories of party choice retain favor in some quarters of the field, our read of the literature is that few scholars endorse this view. A lot of evidence shows that most people do not hold genuine attitudes on enough issues for this approach to take hold. As we have noted at various points, panel data and experimental analyses support conventional party-to-issue theories. Party ID is more durable and impact-ful than most issue attitudes.[5]

Where does this leave us on the question of party ID's vulnerability to the influence of moral issues? Party ID is among the most durable psychological forces in the minds of American voters, but it is not eternal. It is hard to move, but it is not permanent. We have argued that feelings toward abortion and gay rights are stronger than feelings about other issues. People experience visceral moral reactions in response to messages about both issues. The previous section showed that as issue messaging intensified in public discourse, the parties took increasingly distinct stands on the issues. Many people learned that Democrats are pro-choice and pro-gay rights and that the GOP is pro-life and cool toward gay rights. The combination of high message intensity and instinctive emotional responding has rendered moral attitudes durable and, we think, quite impactful. The theory of moral power contends that people responded to this information by updating their party loyalties to better reflect their moral tastes on abortion and gay rights. By taking this step, they can reduce the cognitive dissonance that arises from such disconnects.

This line of reasoning yields two testable propositions. First, attitudes on moral issues will engender change in the positions people take on the seven-point party ID scale, all else equal. This test tells us whether moral issues shape the strength of party attachments. Second, moral issues will also induce party switching. This test reveals whether those who are out of step with their party on moral issues take the drastic step of ditching the party. This provides a harder test of our theory because it takes more effort to leave a party than to cool toward it.

Analysis

Continuity and Change in Party ID

To test these predictions, we use data from the three NES panels, the three GSS panels, and the PALS panel. The issue scales use multiple items about abortion and gay rights (see chapter 4 and its appendix for details). Recall that the scale ranges from 0.00 (most progressive) to 1.00 (most conservative). To tap party ID, we use the standard seven-point scale.[6] The scale runs from strong Democrat (0.00) to strong Republicans (1.00). Pure independents reside at the midpoint. To test for party switching, we use the three-point party scale (0 = Democrats, 1 = pure independents, and 2 = Republicans). Here, we code leaners as partisans.

MORAL ISSUES AND PARTY CHANGE 139

To begin, we follow the lead of Edward Dreyer (1973) and Morris Fiorina (1981) by charting how much partisan stability and change exists in our panels. We do so by cross-tabulating subjects' party ID at time 1 and time 2 in each dataset. We look at partisan stability and change on the three-point (table 7.1a) and the seven-point (table 7.1b) scales.

In table 7.1a, the top row counts "stand patters"—that is, the percentage of respondents who stuck with their party in both waves of a panel. This group includes subjects who were Democrats in both waves, those who were Republican in both waves, and the pure independents at both times. The bottom row counts the percentage of respondents who switched sides from one wave to the next. The "switchers" include Democrats who became pure independents or Republicans; pure independents who moved into a party; and Republicans who became pure independents or Democrats.

Table 7.1b does the same with the seven-point scale. Here, stand patters denote panelists who chose the same exact point on party ID in both waves. Switchers took two different points on the scale. This covers small shifts, such as a Republican moving one spot over to the strong Republican

TABLE 7.1A **Partisan stand patters and switchers: Three-point party ID scale**

	NES 1992–1996	NES 2000–2004	GSS 2006–2010	GSS 2008–2012	GSS 2010–2014	PALS 2006–2012	NES 2016–2020
% Stand patters	78	84	76	78	77	77	80
% Switchers	22	16	24	22	23	23	20
	100%	100%	100%	100%	100%	100%	100%
Number of cases	(593)	(831)	(1,260)	(1,280)	(1,291)	(1,282)	(2,824)

Notes: Cell entries are percentages. Independent leaners are treated as partisans for the category stable figure.

TABLE 7.1B **Partisan stand patters and switchers: Seven-point party ID scale**

	NES 1992–1996	NES 2000–2004	GSS 2006–2010	GSS 2008–2012	GSS 2010–2014	PALS 2006–2012	NES 2016–2020
% Stand patters	46	55	51	55	53	51	54
% Switchers	54	45	49	45	47	49	46
	100%	100%	100%	100%	100%	100%	100%
Number of cases	(593)	(831)	(1,260)	(1,280)	(1,291)	(1,282)	(2,824)

Notes: Cell entries are percentages.

category, as well as large shifts, such as a pure independent moving three spots into the strong Democrat category.

To start with the three-point scale, table 7.1a reveals that stand patters outpace switchers by a wide margin in every dataset. The percent who stand by their party varies from 76 percent in 2006–2010 to 84 percent in 2000–2004. On the flip side, the percent that switch varies from 16 to 24 percent. Some of this churn reflects movement into and out of the pure independent category. But there is some aisle-crossing too. Table 7.1b records higher levels of instability on the seven-point scale. This, of course, is no surprise given the more stringent criterion we use to identify stand patters. With that said, 46 to 55 percent of the samples selected the same exact position on the seven-point scale in both waves.

On average, 78 percent of the respondents stood pat on the three-point scale and 52 percent did the same on the seven-point scale. These data paint a portrait of substantial continuity coupled with nontrivial change. Most partisans do not switch teams, but some do. And just under half the public adjusts their level of commitment as the years roll by.

This data reveals that meaningful shifts in party ID occur over four to six years. It says nothing about why these shifts occur. Some of these changes are rooted in personal circumstances that affect a single person, such as moving from a small town in upstate New York to the metropolitan New York City area. In other cases, national forces, such as a deep recession or foreign policy fiasco, may fracture party bonds. The theory of moral power holds that some of the churn happens because voters adjust their party ties to fit their views on moral issues.[7] Let us see what the evidence says.

Party Change Results

We are now ready to estimate the dynamic relationship between moral issue opinions and party ID. We turn again to cross-lagged regressions (CLR) to unpack the relationship between these variables. First, we model moral issues$_t$ as a linear function of issue opinion$_{t-1}$, seven-point party ID$_{t-1}$, and the control variables described in the last chapter. We then model the impact that moral issues$_{t-1}$ have on party ID$_t$, controlling for party ID$_{t-1}$ and the controls. Assuming all else remains constant, CLR models can uncover evidence of two-way relationships.[8]

We again use forest plots to summarize the CLR estimates. Figure 7.3 presents the key results. The top pane reports the predicted effect party ID$_{t-1}$ has on moral issue opinions$_t$ in each panel, ceteris paribus. Each cir-

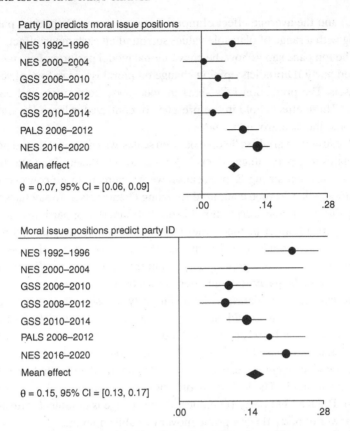

FIGURE 7.3. Forest plot summarizing the effects of party ID and moral issues on each other
Notes: Each point estimate comes from the OLS cross-lagged model results reported in tables A7.1 and A7.2. The point estimate for each study is bounded by 90 percent CIs. The mean effect θ represents the precision-weighted point estimate across all seven datasets. We also report the 95 percent CI for θ. The weight of each study is proportional to the size of the point estimate circle.

cle represents the point estimate. The lines extending out from the point are the lower and upper 90 percent confidence limits. Table A7.1 in the chapter appendix gives the complete estimates for each model. The bottom pane shows the point estimates and 90 percent confidence intervals for the issue$_{t-1}$-to-party$_t$ effect in each dataset. The full set of estimates are in appendix table A7.2. At the bottom of each plot, we report the precision-weighted mean effect across the seven studies (θ) and the 95 percent confidence interval. This tells us the average effect of party ID on issues (top pane) and the average effect of moral issues on party ID (bottom pane), along with a range of plausible values surrounding each mean effect.

The top pane shows how the conventional model performs. For starters, lagged party ID predicts opinion change on moral issues in four of seven datasets. The prediction falls short in 2000–2004, 2006–2010, and 2010–2014.[9] These effects hold in the presence of controls for lagged moral issues and the background variables.

Because the variables lie on 0.00–1.00 scales, we can translate the point estimates into percentage effects. Take the 0.07 coefficient for 1992–1996. This means that strong Republicans$_{92}$ were 7 percent more conservative on moral issues in 1996 compared to strong Democrats$_{92}$. To say the same thing differently, the gap on moral issues between strong partisans in 1992 was 7 percent larger in 1996. Another example is that the point estimate for 2016–2020 equals 0.12. This means that the gap on moral issues between strong partisans grew by 12 percent from 2016 to 2020. For the five other panels, the party-to-issue effect varies from 1 to 9 percent.

Across the seven datasets, the mean party-to-issue effect comes in at 0.07. The 95 percent confidence interval equals [0.06, 0.09]. We conclude that the distance between strong Republicans and strong Democrats on moral issues increased on average by some 6 to 9 percent. Although this effect may not seem large, it strikes us as meaningful given that moral issues are so stable. The feelings people hold on moral issues do not waver much. The fact that party ID induces some change is notable. It attests to the power of party ID as a prime mover of public opinion.

These results are consistent with the claim that party ID shaped beliefs about abortion and gay rights throughout the culture war era. The theoretical explanation is that partisans took cues from party leaders and other copartisans—and rejected cues from the other side—to deduce positions on moral issues. The ready availability of pro-life, anti-gay messages from Republican leaders nudged Republican partisans in the public to move in the conservative direction on both issues. Democratic identifiers exposed to these cues moved in the opposite direction. They also responded positively to pro-choice/pro-gay messages from Democratic leaders. In short, the bounty of party cues facilitated issue conformity among a portion of the public. This is what party-driven sorting looks like.

So, how does the theory of moral power fare? Quite well, according to the results in the bottom half of figure 7.3. In every test, the moral issue variable predicts future movement toward the GOP on the seven-point scale.[10] Moral issues predict the largest changes in party ID in 1992–1996 and 2016–2020. Again, it helps to think of these effects in terms of percentages. To take some examples, we see the biggest effect in the first NES dataset. Moral conservatives in 1992 moved 22 percent closer to the GOP by 1996 compared to moral progressives in 1992. The first GSS estimate indicates that moral conservatives in 2006 moved 10 percent closer to the GOP by 2010 relative to moral progressives. Finally, we see another large effect in the last NES dataset, which shows that moral conservatives$_{16}$ moved some 21 percent closer to the GOP by 2020 than moral progressives$_{16}$.

Across the seven panels the mean issue-to-party effect is 0.15. The 95 percent confidence interval is [0.13, 0.17], meaning that the gap on party ID between moral progressives and conservatives grew by some 13 to 17 percent. Put simply, moral issues drove partisans further apart—an example of issue-driven sorting. This evidence confirms the hypothesis that feelings about moral issues do alter long-standing partisan ties. When people experience some tension between their party ties and views of abortion/gay rights, they often adjust the former to better reflect the latter. Pro-choice/pro-gay folks move toward the Democratic side. Pro-life/anti-gay folks move in the GOP direction.

To help readers appreciate how big the respective effects are, we turn to a second set of graphics. We leverage our data to plot the predicted scores on moral issues for respondents with different partisan attachments. This tells us how much party ID drives change in moral issue opinions. We then

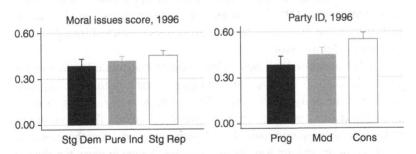

FIGURE 7.4. The relationship between party ID and moral issues, 1992–1996
Notes: Data come from the 1992–1996 regression estimates reported in tables A7.1 and A7.2. The bar graph on the left shows the predicted moral issue score in 1996 (higher scores denote more conservative positions) for strong Democrats, pure independents, and strong Republicans in 1992. The bar graph on the right shows the predicted party ID score in 1996 (higher scores denote increasing GOP affinities) for issue progressives, moderates, and conservatives in 1992. On each x-axis, the values are for respondents at the tenth, fiftieth, and ninetieth percentiles on each variable.

calculate the predicted party ID scores for persons who vary in their commitment to abortion/gay rights. This tells us the degree to which moral issue opinions generate party change.

The bar graphs in figure 7.4 summarize the results from the 1992–1996 NES. The one on the left demonstrates how party ID, measured in 1992, affects moral issues, measured in 1996, controlling for lagged issues and background factors.[11] Recall that the moral issue variable ranges from 0.00 (most pro-choice/pro-gay rights) to 1.00 (most pro-life/anti-gay). As we move from strong Democrat$_{92}$ to strong Republican$_{92}$ on the x-axis, the predicted moral conservatism score rises from 0.38 to 0.45 — a real if modest difference. This result shows the party-to-issue model in action.

Next, the bar graph on the right plots the impact that 1992 moral issues have on 1996 party ID, holding wave one party ID and all else constant. Remember that party ID ranges from 0.00 (strong Democrat) to 1.00 (strong Republican). What we see is this: moral conservatism predicts substantial movement toward the GOP over time. For moral progressives$_{92}$, the predicted party ID score equals 0.38 — essentially an independent-leaning Democrat. For morally conservative respondents who are the same on the other measured variables, their predicted party ID score is 0.54 — an independent who leans ever so slightly to the GOP side. In this example, moral issues affect the strength *and* direction of party ID.

Overall, figure 7.4 yields evidence of both party-driven and issue-driven sorting. Consistent with the party-to-issue model, as time passed in the first Clinton term Republicans took more traditional positions on moral issues than Democrats. At the same time, moral conservatives flowed more eagerly into the GOP camp than moral progressives, which affirms the issue-to-party model we favor.

Readers may wonder if these effects differ in magnitude. In other words, which variable was inducing more change? We can test this by comparing the size of the party-to-issue effect (0.07 in table A7.1) and the issue-to-party effect (0.22 in table A7.2). A formal test shows that issue-driven sorting greatly outpaced party-driven sorting ($p < .001$). In other words, at the dawn of the culture war, there was more change in party ties than in moral issue positions.

Figure 7.5 tells us what happened in 2016–2020, a quarter century later. During the Trump years, the effect of party ID on moral issue change is considerable. Indeed, it represents the biggest party effect we uncover. The bar graph on the left shows that strong Republicans$_{16}$ scored 0.12 points higher on abortion/gay rights conservatism relative to strong Democrats$_{16}$ (0.39 > 0.27). Note also that while these partisans differ significantly on

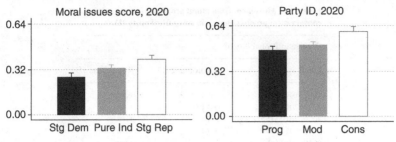

FIGURE 7.5. The relationship between party ID and moral issues, 2016–2020
Notes: Data come from the 2016–2020 regression estimates reported in tables A7.1 and A7.2. The bar graph on the left shows the predicted moral issue score in 2020 (higher scores denote more conservative positions) for strong Democrats, pure independents, and strong Republicans in 2016. The bar graph on the right shows the predicted party ID score in 2020 (higher scores denote increasing GOP affinities) for issue progressives, moderates, and conservatives in 2016. On each x-axis, the values are for respondents at the tenth, fiftieth, and ninetieth percentiles on each variable.

moral issues, both groups reside in the progressive end of the scale.[12] In any case, as called for by the conventional model, some Americans internalize the party line on abortion and same-sex rights.

The bar graph on the right hints that lagged issues had a bigger impact on party ID. The predicted party ID score in 2020 for those who opposed abortion/gay rights in 2016 equals 0.60. This corresponds to identifying as an independent-leaning Republican. The predicted score on party ID for those who strongly backed abortion and gay rights four years earlier sits at 0.46, an independent who leans ever so slightly toward the Democrats.

Which of these effects is bigger? It turns out that the effect of issues on party is again significantly larger than the effect of party on issues. A comparison of the CLR slopes from Tables A7.1 and A7.2 reveals that the former exceeds the latter well beyond chance levels ($0.21 > 0.12$, $p < .01$).[13] In plain language, the feelings people hold about abortion and gay rights predict more change in their party ties than their party ties predict in their issue opinions. Gut-level feelings about abortion and gay rights seem to be more powerful than deep-seated partisan loyalties.[14]

The Categorical Party ID Tests

We have found that the opinions Americans express about moral issues predict the direction and strength of their party ties four to six years in the future. This is, of course, vital information, but it leaves a key question unanswered. Do opinions about abortion/gay rights predict party switching?

TABLE 7.2 **Movement from moral progressivism to moral conservatism predicts change in categorical party ID**

Change in Probability of:

Panel Survey	Democratic ID	Republican ID
1992–1996 NES	−.23	+.30
2000–2004 NES	−.14	+.10
2006–2010 GSS	−.14	+.17
2008–2012 GSS	−.10	+.10
2010–2014 GSS	−.17	+.19
2006–2012 PALS	−.12	+.12
2016–2020 NES	−.23	+.21
(Unweighted) Mean	−.16	+.17

Note: Party ID is measured using the three-point scale, with independent leaners coded as partisans. For the Democratic ID column, the cell entries represent the predicted difference between the probability a morally conservative Democrat$_{t-1}$ identifies as a Democrat$_t$ versus the probability a morally progressive Democrat$_{t-1}$ identifies as a Democrat$_t$. For the Republican ID column, the cell entries represent the predicted difference between the probability a morally conservative Republican$_{t-1}$ identifies as a Republican$_t$ versus the probability a morally progressive Republican$_{t-1}$ identifies as a Republican$_t$. Morally progressive respondents are in the tenth percentile on the moral issues scale. These respondents are strongly pro-choice and pro-gay rights. Morally conservative respondents are in the ninetieth percentile on the moral issues scale. These respondents are strongly pro-life and anti-gay rights. Full model estimates appear in table A7.5 (all effects significant at p < .05).

As we saw in table 7.1a, anywhere from 16 to 24 percent of respondents in the panel surveys exit their party. Switchers include partisans who become pure independents, pure independents who become partisans, and apostates who join the other side. In this section, we look at whether some moral progressives left the GOP to become an independent or a Democrat. We also ask whether some moral conservatives abandoned the Democratic Party for either the independent or GOP camp.

To answer these questions, we model the relationship between lagged issue opinions and the three-point party ID scale. The Democratic category includes strong Democrats, Democrats, and leaners. The pure independent group contains people who answered "independent" or "something else" to the root party question and said they were not closer to either party in the follow up. The GOP category includes strong, not strong, and leaning partisans.

We use ordered logistic regression to capture the effects that moral issues$_{t-1}$ have on the probability of sticking with one's party at time t, controlling for initial party ID and the demographics. To keep things simple,

MORAL ISSUES AND PARTY CHANGE 147

table 7.2 reports predicted probabilities for Democratic and Republican ID. Readers can view the full set of estimates in appendix table A7.5.

In the Democratic column, each cell tells us how variation in moral issues in the first wave affects the probability of remaining a Democrat in the second wave. For example, the probability that a morally conservative Democrat$_{92}$ remains a Democrat$_{96}$ is 0.72. The probability that a progressive Democrat$_{92}$ was still a Democrat$_{96}$ was 0.95.[15] The difference equals −0.23 — the value in table 7.2. The difference confirms that anti-abortion/anti-gay Democrats were more likely to leave the party than pro-choice/pro-gay Democrats. Another example: conservative Democrats$_{08}$ were 0.10 less likely to stay with the party than progressive Democrats$_{08}$. This pattern shows up in every sample. The mean change is −0.16. These results suggest that pro-life/anti-gay feelings drove some Democrats away from the party. The chances of leaving were not high, but they were not trivial either.

In the Republican column, we report how variation in moral issue positions affects the probability that Republicans in wave one remained party members in wave two. To illustrate, the probability a pro-life/anti-gay Republican in 1992 remained in the fold in 1996 was 0.93. The probability a pro-choice/pro-gay Republican in 1992 stuck with the GOP was 0.63. The difference equals 0.30. This change suggests that morally progressive Republicans found it harder to remain in the GOP fold than their more conservative copartisans. This is the strongest effect we observe. One of the weakest effects is in 2008–2012. There, the estimated likelihood that pro-life/anti-gay Republicans remained with their party stood at 0.88. The corresponding estimate for pro-choice/pro-gay Republicans was 0.78, which yields a difference of 0.10. Again, morally progressive Republicans were more apt to split than those who were conservative on culture war issues. The mean predicted change comes out to 0.17. Hence, as called for by our theory, pro-choice/pro-gay views prompted a number of Republicans to exit.

Overall, we conclude that the positions people take on moral issues lead to party exit and switching. To be clear, we are not talking about widespread change in the public. Far more often than not partisans stand pat. Among those who experience dissonance between their party ties and policy views, the likelihood of sticking with the party outweighs the likelihood of leaving it. But when people do leave, morally infused feelings about abortion/same-sex rights sometimes force that choice. The conservative disgust that some Democrats harbor toward abortion and gays motivates their exit from the party. The progressive anger and revulsion that some Republicans feel in response to attacks on reproductive rights and gays drives them away from the Grand Old Party.

What about Random Measurement Error?

As noted earlier in our book, we use multiple indicator scales to produce valid and reliable measures of moral issue attitudes. We have not relied on advanced statistical estimators to further correct for random measurement error (RME) in these variables because we are sensitive to concerns about artificially inflating the stability estimates to the point that nothing changes. Having said that, we suspect some readers do not share our reservations and are curious about what happens when we correct for RME in the statistical models. Prior work shows that the failure to account for measurement error in the seven-point party ID item may overstate its susceptibility to the influence of other factors (Green and Palmquist 1990). Of course, the same thing holds for measures of issue attitudes. So, let's see what happens when we purge RME from the party ID and moral issue variables. (Readers who do not share these concerns or who want to skip over the technical details can jump ahead to the next section with no loss of continuity because the results we report lend additional support to the theory of moral power.)

We do so by using the errors-in-variables (EIV) estimator. The EIV estimator uses reliability estimates for the independent variables to generate error corrected CLR coefficients. To estimate the reliability of party ID, we turned to the work of Phil Chen and Paul Goren (2016). They estimated three-wave Wiley-Wiley models (1970) to produce reliability estimates for NES and GSS panel data. For our moral issue scales, we used the alpha reliabilities reported in the chapter 4 appendix.

Here are the key takeaways. (Table A7.6 in the appendix reports the EIV estimates.) When we take RME into account at the estimation stage, support for the party-to-issue model evaporates. In the CLR findings presented earlier in the chapter, the party-to-issue coefficient is significant in four of seven tests (see figure 7.3). In the EIV models, GOP partisanship never predicts moral conservatism. In fact, the mean EIV effect of party ID on issues is −0.03 with a 95 percent confidence interval of [−0.04, −0.01]. The interpretation here is that strong Republicans take slightly more progressive positions on moral issues down the line than strong Democrats. Given the minuscule size of the coefficient, we do not make too much of this

MORAL ISSUES AND PARTY CHANGE 149

unexpected finding. The CLR estimates from figure 7.3 strike us as more plausible ($\theta = 0.07$, 95 percent CI = [0.06, 0.09]).

For the theory of moral power, we are pleased to report that it performs as expected. Recall that the issue-to-party effect proved significant in all seven OLS CLR models, as seen in Figure 7.3. It fares well in the EIV models, reaching significance in five of seven tests. Here, the mean effect of issues on party ID comes in at 0.11 with a 95 percent confidence interval of [0.08, 0.13]. These values are smaller than the OLS estimates ($\theta = 0.15$, 95 percent CI = [0.13, 0.17]). As one might expect when we correct for RME in party ID, it proves less open to the influence of other forces. But the key point is that party ID is not immune to the power of moral issues even under this more stringent test.

All told, when we remove measurement error from the key variables in the analysis stage, moral issues continue to predict significant temporal change in party ID—just like we saw in the OLS CLR models. The EIV estimates provide another confirmation for the theory of moral power and fail to provide any support for the standard theory. Moral conservatives sort into the Republican Party. Moral progressives move into the Democratic camp. For those who prefer the EIV estimates, these results provide very strong support for the theory of moral power and no support at all for the standard partisan influence theory. For those who prefer the OLS estimates and remain sensitive to the charge that the EIV estimates overcorrect for RME, we simply say that the EIV estimates show that the issue-to-party effect is robust to different sets of assumptions about the data.

A Final Test

The CLR estimates confirm that moral issues predict change in party ID in a consistent and robust way. This provides strong correlational support for our theory. But recall the limits of the CLR method. It tells us whether differences between people at one point in time predict between-person differences at a later point in time. It tells us nothing directly about within-person change. To gain insight into that process, we come back to the fixed effects (FE) estimator that we deployed in the last chapter.

To remind readers, this method uses difference scores so each person can serve as their own control for all covariates (observed and unobserved) that do not vary over time. Because of this, FE models provide a stronger, but not definitive, basis for causal inference (Allison 2009). We used the FE estimator to see if within-person change in moral issues predicts within-person change in party ID, measured using the seven-point scale.[16] We controlled for changes in liberal-conservative ID and religious ID strength.

Here, we summarize the take-home points (the unstandardized regression estimates appear in table A7.7 at the end of the appendix). As expected, moral issue change predicts party change in all three datasets, accounting for whatever portion of party change depends on ideological- and religious-driven change. Take the 2006–2010 GSS panel. People that moved one point—a large change given the coding of this variable—in the conservative direction on abortion/gay rights between 2006 and 2010 shifted 0.08 points in the GOP direction ($p < .05$, one-tailed test). The 2008–2012 GSS similarly show that a right-wing shift on issues predicts a 0.14 point move toward the GOP ($p < .01$). For 2010–2014, the moral issue change coefficient is 0.16 ($p < .01$). The standardized coefficients vary from 0.07 to 0.14, suggesting more modest effects.

The takeaway point is good news for the theory of moral power. The FE estimates bolster our CLR findings. Within-person change on key cultural issues predicts within-person change in party ID, controlling for change in ideological and religious ID and all time-invariant factors. Since we have not controlled for factors that vary over time, we must concede that the FE results are suggestive, not definitive. With that said, the full suite of analyses carried out in this chapter is consistent with the hypothesis that feelings toward moral issues catalyze partisan change.

Chapter Summary

Decades of research show that standing partisan loyalties structure the positions people take on the defining social and political issues of the times. We do not identify with a party because it represents our views on tax cuts or gun control or climate change or most other issues. Instead, attachments to a party—and the desire to remain in the good graces of fellow partisans—motivate us to endorse party positions on these and other issues. When parties lead, partisans follow.

We have shown that abortion and gay rights are critical exceptions to the party-over-issue model that constitutes the conventional wisdom. Armed with data from seven panel studies, we pitted the partisan influence hypothesis against the moral power hypothesis. We found some evidence that people bring moral issues into closer alignment with their party. We found more evidence—and stronger evidence at that—that people update their party loyalties to reflect their feelings about abortion and gay rights. Our findings suggest that while reciprocal relations exist, the influence of moral issues is likely stronger than that of party ID.

This brings our main empirical analysis to a close. The final chapter summarizes what we have discovered, the limits of what we can claim, suggestions for future work, and what it all means for understanding American religion and politics.

CHAPTER EIGHT

Abortion, Gay Rights, and American Politics

In a well-publicized chat in 2010, *Americablog* deputy editor Joe Sudbay (2012) pressed President Obama on his beliefs about same-sex marriage. At that time, neither the president nor his party had endorsed gay marriage. Obama responded, "I have been to this point unwilling to sign on to same-sex marriage primarily because of my understandings of the traditional definitions of marriage. But I also think you're right that attitudes evolve, including mine." Obama's position continued to evolve in the lead up to his reelection bid. In a 2012 interview with ABC News, President Obama declared, "At a certain point I've just concluded that for me, personally, it is important for me to go ahead and affirm that I think same-sex couples should be able to get married" (Gast 2012). This marked the first time a US president publicly supported gay marriage.

It was natural to wonder if Obama had privately backed gay marriage before doing so publicly was politically feasible. Democratic strategist David Axelrod (2015, 447) has claimed that Obama supported same-sex marriage as early as 1996. However, Obama "knew that his view was way out in front of the public's. Opposition to gay marriage was particularly strong in the Black church, and as he ran for higher office, he grudgingly accepted the counsel of more pragmatic folks like me, and modified his position to support civil unions rather than marriage."

Like Billy Graham and Donald Trump, Barack Obama feared backlash if he broke with his supporters on key moral issues. In private settings, the pro-life Graham counseled women against abortion, but he avoided the issue in public. Even when Reverend Graham spoke to church groups, who, presumably, were already "in the fold," he avoided those issues be-

ABORTION, GAY RIGHTS, AND AMERICAN POLITICS

cause he considered them matters for theological debate and not appropriate for the pulpit.[1] And while Trump demonized many groups on the campaign trail in 2015–2016, he did not go after gays. Never known for restraint, Trump treaded cautiously here. Their fears underscore our book's key contention. Like Autumn and Dawn, many Americans have made up their minds about abortion and gays. Most Americans are so dug in on these issues that charismatic leaders make no effort to change their hearts and minds. If they make such an effort, the blowback will be swift, fierce, and politically damaging.

Our book sheds new light on the power of moral issues. We have shown that gut-level feelings about abortion and gay rights are strong enough to alter the trajectory of American religion and politics. In this last chapter, we review the key findings, discuss a number of lingering questions, and take up the implications our work has for the decline of religion, moral sorting, citizen competence, and the future of the culture war.

Summary

Principal Findings

To recap, the theory of moral power rests on four propositions. (1) The information environment has supplied Americans with plenty of chances to evaluate abortion and gay rights over the three-decade history of the culture war. (2) The visceral moral emotions people experience in response to issue messages have rendered moral issue attitudes durable and impactful. (3) People sometimes update core identities when these conflict with other strong psychological dispositions. (4) People bring their religious and partisan identities into alignment with their feelings about abortion and gay rights.

Let's review how our theory has fared. To begin with the information environment, chapter 3 confirmed that the volume of messages on abortion and same-sex rights rose sharply starting in the late 1980s. It has remained high ever since. This pattern emerged in the usual political places: party platforms, newspapers, congressional campaigns, and the halls of governance. Moral issue messages also spilled over into areas far removed from politics, such as popular TV shows, roadside billboards, and Sunday sermons. Moreover, message sources framed the issues using the language of moral anger and disgust. The spread of moral issue messages through political, entertainment, and other apolitical venues, combined with distinctive emotive framing, rendered abortion and gay rights accessible in the minds of voters.

In response, huge swaths of the public now hold viscerally charged attitudes on moral issues that have endured for many years. Chapter 4 showed that people socialized to feel conservative moral disgust oppose abortion and gays. At the same time, we argued that those socialized to feel progressive anger and disgust in response to attacks on women, same-sex-individuals, and their respective rights respond by doubling down on pro-choice, pro-gay sympathies. The evidence we presented and reviewed implies that moral emotions stabilize these attitudes.

Multiple pieces of evidence attest to this stability. The continuity correlations in chapter 4, the stand patter results from chapter 5, and the ability of moral issues to repel the influence of party ID in chapter 7 confirmed that the positions people take on moral issues persist for long periods of time. All that said, moral issues do not endure indefinitely. Fairly high levels of continuity coexist with some change.

We then explored whether moral issues predict identity change. As called for by canonical theories of public opinion, Americans do update their positions on moral issues to conform to some of their bedrock identities. But, as predicted by our rival theory, Americans also adjust their religious and party ties to fit their views of moral issues. People sometimes leave religion or parties when their ties to these groups clash with their feelings about these issues. Moral progressives exit organized religion and the GOP, while moral conservatives embrace religion and the Republican Party. Finally, the issue-to-identity effects usually matched and often eclipsed the identity-to-issue effects. The latter result was especially true in the case of party ID.

In sum, the results of multiple tests confirm our theory's key predictions. In a high intensity information environment, attitudes toward abortion and gay rights take root in automatic moral emotions, hold steady for extended periods of time, and induce identity change. Moral issue attitudes predict religious change. Political identities do not. Likewise, moral issue attitudes predict partisan change to a much greater extent than attachments to organized religion. Our evidence suggests that feelings about abortion and same-sex individuals and rights are stronger than religious and partisan identities, and thus, occupy more central positions in the belief systems of everyday Americans.

We are confident that feelings about abortion and gay rights are durable. We are also comfortable concluding that these feelings shape identities.

ABORTION, GAY RIGHTS, AND AMERICAN POLITICS   155

The same results emerged time and again in different datasets; in different time periods; with different measures of moral issues; across a range of statistical methods; and across a range of alternative model specifications. While this rich body of observational evidence supports the inference that these attitudes affect identities, it does not justify definitive causal inferences. The theory of moral power provides a plausible explanation for what sets attitudes toward abortion and gay rights apart from other issues, but it should be very clear that more work is necessary to build the causal case. We believe a combination of experimental methods (e.g., multiple lab, survey, and field experiments) and tests of heterogeneous treatment effects would serve this goal. Experiments would also help us disentangle moral emotions from other potential causal mechanisms, such as issue-based identities, as the basis of attitude strength (Mason 2015).

Remaining Questions

This book aims to launch a conversation about the role moral issues play in public opinion, American religion, and American politics. It has raised far more questions than it has answered. Here, we share our thoughts on some future avenues of research.

First, we have argued that moral issues are different from *most* issues, not *all* issues. We have theorized that the instinctual emotions people experience when they process messages about abortion and gays fortify their underlying attitudes, rendering them durable and impactful. What other issues fit this profile? Most obviously, feelings about transgender rights seem likely to fit the bill. We have more to say on this in the last section of the chapter.

Another issue that springs to mind is immigration. This issue has been salient in the information environment since the mid-2000s. Immigration attitudes are rooted in moral disgust, endure, and impact short-term judgments (Aarøe, Petersen, and Arceneaux 2017; Sides, Tesler and Vavreck 2018; Kustov, Laaker, and Reller 2021). Marisa Abrajano and Zoltan Hajnal (2015) make a strong case that immigration attitudes generate change in party ID over time. Given this profile, immigration attitudes seem a fair bet to alter other group ties such as American national identity. We also wonder how much moral issues and immigration work in tandem to shape party ID. Conflict over abortion, gay rights, and immigration provide a plausible policy-based account of growing partisan polarization in the mass public.

Second, future work should test if attitudes toward moral issues affect other social and political identities. In the field of religion, researchers might study denomination switching, such as moving from mainline to evangelical Protestant. Researchers might also study those who, like Autumn and Dawn from chapter 2, moved between liberal, moderate, and conservative Christian churches (Braunstein 2022 provides an excellent framework for thinking about other forms of religious backlash and movement). In the field of politics, the next move is to take up liberal-conservative identities. Although similar to party ID in some respects, ideological labels do not resonate with the public as much as party labels do (Kinder and Kalmoe 2017). As such, the search for conditional effects makes sense.

This idea points to a third area worth a close look: subgroup effects. Researchers frequently take subgroup differences into account when thinking about the relationship between identities and issues. The idea is that these links are stronger in some populations relative to others. It is easy to identify a number of theoretical candidates that might condition the effects we saw in chapters 6-7. These include political awareness (Zaller 1992), issue importance (Carsey and Layman 2006), social group ties (Patrikios 2008; Achen and Bartels 2016), and age (Margolis 2018). Our simple models surely misses some heterogeneity in the mass public. Another idea worth a close look: to what extent do attitude properties, such as moral conviction or ambivalence, condition the relationships described here (Lavine, Johnston, and Steenbergen 2012; Ryan 2014, 2017).

Fourth, our results suggest that moral issue attitudes may be stronger psychological forces in the American public mind than party ID and religious ID. Several pieces of evidence sustain this conclusion. The effects of moral issues on party change are stronger than the effects of party ID on issue change. Moral issue attitudes predict religious exit, party ID does not. Likewise, the effects of issue attitudes on religious change are somewhat larger than the reverse effects. Moral issues also predict partisan updating, religious ID does not. All of this suggests that moral issues are more important than core identities in the political belief systems of the American voter.

With that said, we acknowledge that the matter is far from settled in at least two key respects. On the one hand, we need research on how other aspects of religion (e.g., religious belief) and other issues (e.g., immigration) fit into the picture. On the other hand, as noted, we need experimental evidence in general and on heterogeneous treatment effects in particular to sort out for whom these issues matter the most. The work done here leads us to believe that future research will sustain the conclusion that moral issues are strong. But it remains to be seen for whom this holds true and under what conditions it holds true.

To conclude, the theory of moral power sheds new light on the dynamic relationship between public opinion on moral issues and core identities. Clearly, more work is necessary to strengthen the case for the causal effects of issues and to nail down the theory's boundary conditions. That said, we remain convinced that the feelings people hold about abortion and gays play a major role in shaping religion and politics in the contemporary United States. In this spirit, we now pivot to the broader implications our work has for the rise of the religious nones, moral sorting in the political parties, citizen competence, and the future of America's culture war.

Implications

The Rise of the "Nones"

As we reviewed in chapter 6, the Religious Right has long aimed to restore religion's place in American public life. These efforts have produced the opposite effect. As the Religious Right plunged deeper into public affairs, more and more Americans left organized religion. Joseph Baker and Buster Smith (2015, 87) put it like this: "In an ironic self-fulfilling prophecy, the religious Right decried America's purported secularity, ultimately leading to an increase in the number of Americans who were secular, and diminishing organized religion's standing among large segments of the public." The rise of the nones is exhibit A in the case of religious decline.

One leading explanation for this trend centers on political backlash against organized religion. As we noted in earlier chapters, Michael Hout and Claude Fischer (2002) have argued that as the Religious Right drew closer to the GOP, many liberals and moderates in the mass public, alarmed by the symbolic connection between conservative politics and religion, fled religion. In this account, political identities drive religious exodus. Cultural issues do not play a role. "The divisive issues themselves, for example, abortion and gay rights, could be the link . . . but we do not include them in our analysis because we think they are more likely the consequence of changed religious identity than a cause of it" (ibid., 185).

We concur that political backlash plays an important role in the rise of the nones, but in lieu of political identities we found that feelings about abortion and gay rights motivate religious exit. Our analyses revealed that moral issues predict religious updating, that these effects hold in the presence of political identities; and that the effects of political identities no longer hold in the presence of moral issues.

To see how the rise of the nones evolved among different moral camps, we turn to some simple charts. We use 1977–2021 GSS data to trace the rise of the nones in three different moral camps. Like in chapter 5, we demarcate these groups with the yes/no question that gauges respondent support for abortion for any reason and the dichotomized measure of whether respondents think that same-sex relations are wrong. Moral progressives back abortion and same-sex relations. Moral conservatives reject these. Moderates take the liberal position on one issue and a conservative position on the other.

Figure 8.1 plots the percentage of each moral faction that identified as none in a given survey. In 1977, 15 percent of progressives identified as none versus 7 percent of moderates and 2 percent of conservatives. Over the next four decades, the share of nones climbed in each group. The share of nones rose the most among pro-choice, pro-gay respondents. By 2021, over 40 percent of moral progressives had no connection to organized religion. The comparable figures are 20 percent for moderates and 8 per-

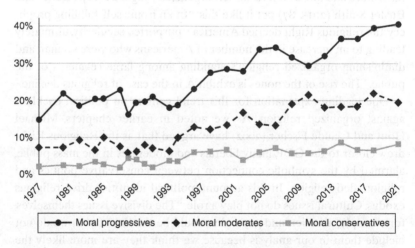

FIGURE 8.1. The rise of the nones within different moral camps, 1977–2021
Notes: The figure plots the percentage of respondents who did not identify with any religious tradition in a given survey for moral progressives, moderates, and conservatives. The data come from the GSS Cumulative Data File.

cent for moral conservatives. Thus, the thirteen-point difference between the progressive and conservative camps in 1977 more than doubled to 33 percent by 2021.

Figure 8.1 suggests that while people of all cultural issue tastes were leaving religion over time, the most progressive proved the most eager to leave. Moving forward, we expect that the replacement of older generations with younger voters will intensify the rise of the nones. We also think that the Supreme Court's 2022 *Dobbs* ruling, which nullified the constitutional right to an abortion, will push the share of the nones even higher. It would not surprise us if the number of moral moderates who abandon organized religion accelerates as well. Moral progressives and moderates are losing their religion at unprecedented rates.

The Moral Sort

Evidence that party ID and issue opinions have aligned over the past few decades is indisputable (Bafumi and Shapiro 2009; Levendusky 2009). The key question is which factor drives this sorting process. One school of thought maintains that the growing clarity of elite signals in political debate led many voters to adopt their party's positions. When people receive unambiguous signals from party sources, they update their positions on the issues to conform to what their copartisans believe. This is party-driven sorting. It obviously follows from the standard identity-to-issue model and fits well with findings that most people hold weak attitudes on most policy issues. By contrast, the theory of moral power contends that voters respond to moral messages in a different way. As message volume and clarity on abortion and gay rights ramps up, many people find out that they are out of step with their party on these issues. They respond by bringing their party ID in line with their views of moral issues. This is issue-driven sorting.

Chapter 7 showed that issue-driven sorting was more pervasive than party-driven sorting. As this moral sort played out, the party coalitions changed. Democrats became the pro-choice/pro-gay rights party. The GOP became a sanctuary for pro-life/anti-gay rights constituents. To see how the moral sort has unfolded during the history of the culture war, figure 8.2 presents nine histograms. Each histogram displays the size of three moral factions in the Democratic, pure independent, and Republican camps at three points in time. The 1977 data provides a snapshot of public opinion before the culture war began. The 1993 data show us where the

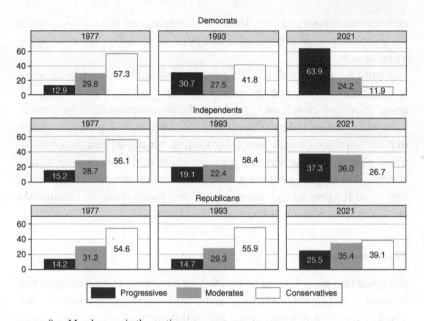

FIGURE 8.2. Moral camps in the parties, 1977–2021
Notes: The figure plots the percentage of moral progressives, moderates, and conservatives among Democrats, pure independents, and Republicans in 1977, 1993, and 2021. The data come from the GSS Cumulative Data File.

public stood at a critical inflection point a few months after the 1992 battle for the soul of America; 2021 is the most recent year for which we have data. As we did previously, we use the "abortion under any circumstances" and "same-sex relations are wrong" items to pin down the moral factions.

Let us begin in the top left corner. In 1977, 57 percent of Democrats opposed abortion and disapproved of same-sex relations. A mere 13 percent approved of both. The second row reveals a nearly identical pattern for 1977 independents. The third row shows the same for the GOP. Moral conservatives made up 55 percent of the party. Only 14 percent of Republicans approved of abortion and same-sex intimacy. In 1977, then, moral conservatives were ascendant to the same high degree in each party. Moral sorting did not exist in year one of Jimmy Carter's presidency. This is why Jimmy Carter could call abortion wrong on the campaign trail and the congressional parties contained a mix of pro-choice and pro-life members. The moral angst bubbling up in some parts of the country had yet to penetrate the public mind.

The second column in figure 8.2 shows that the moral sort was underway by 1993. The rise of the New Christian Right attracted the media's gaze in the late 1980s. The 1992 election clarified better than any prior contest

ABORTION, GAY RIGHTS, AND AMERICAN POLITICS 161

where the parties stood on abortion and gay rights. The American people responded. A progressive shift in the Democratic Party was now evident. The share of conservative Democrats fell from 57 percent in 1977 to 42 percent by 1993. At the same time, the share of progressives shot up from 13 percent to 31 percent. By contrast, moral conservatives remained the dominant faction in the independent and Republican camps in 1993. In fact, the GOP coalition did not change at all over the previous sixteen years.

By 2021, things were drastically different. On the Democratic side, moral progressives took over. They surged past moderates and conservatives by huge margins (64 percent versus 24 percent versus 12 percent). Pure independents had also liberalized. Moral progressives (37 percent) and moderates (36 percent) were at parity. Conservatives brought up the rear (27 percent). In the GOP, moral conservatives remained the largest faction at 39 percent, but their majority was gone. After exceeding the liberal camp by some 40 percent in both 1977 and 1993, their margin had dropped all the way down to 14 percent in 2021.[2]

Figure 8.2's lessons could not be any clearer. The Democratic coalition has radically changed. In 1977, moral conservatives outnumbered progressives 57 to 13 percent. By 2021, the pattern reversed: moral progressives now held a decisive 64 to 12 percent lead. The GOP has also liberalized but at a much slower pace and more on same-sex relations than on abortion. In 1977, conservatives trounced progressives 55 versus 14 percent. By 2021, the conservative majority had shrunk to a precarious plurality (39 percent). Nevertheless, the GOP remains the political home for the dwindling number of Americans who hold traditional views on abortion and gays. To sum up, the parties in the electorate differed little on abortion and gay rights in the 1970s. Today, the parties are comprised of distinct moral factions that share little common ground. Public opinion on moral issues has driven change in party coalitions. The moral issue substrates of public opinion have deep ramifications, including presidential approval and the vote choice (Tesler 2015).

Citizen Competence

In this section, we reflect on what our results mean for assessing citizen competence. Experts and laypersons alike believe that voters should hold meaningful preferences on the issues of the day and back parties and candidates who share these preferences. The parties and leaders in turn work to deliver what the voters want in order to secure enough electoral support to win and retain office (Downs 1957). This is how representative democracy should work.

Studies reviewed in chapters 1 and 2 conclude that most voters have failed this test. This has been a consistent theme in decades of research. The most forceful articulation of this skepticism comes from Christopher Achen and Larry Bartels. Their 2016 book *Democracy for Realists* summarizes large bodies of literature from disparate fields that converge on the simple and dispiriting conclusion that voters do not—indeed they cannot—meet the standards imposed on them by naive "folk theories" of democracy. Achen and Bartels urge us to take group memberships and social identities seriously as we imagine what American democracy can and should be.

We concur that most people do not have stable views on most issues, do not choose parties that reflect these views, and do not vote for candidates on policy grounds.[3] Views on abortion and LGBT rights represent a rare exception. These views are more stable and consequential than the feelings people hold on most other issues. Moral issue attitudes motivate some people to cast aside groups that no longer reflect their views about the core culture war issues. To the credit of voters, some issues matter.

But is the power of moral issues to disrupt group ties enough to redeem folk theories of democracy? The answer is no. No pair of issues can bear that weight. Moreover, moral issue attitudes do not reflect the kinds of principled and ethical judgments called for by folk theories of democracy. We cannot presume that the positions people take on these issues reflect what Robert Dahl (1989) has called "enlightened" preferences. Instead, the positions we take on abortion and same-sex issues reflect automatic, visceral emotions that we experience in response to messages we see in the information environment. Lurking beneath the surface, moral anger and disgust guide political choices in secret ways. Most people take the positions they do on abortion and gay rights because these positions feel right, not because these positions reflect careful or principled thought.[4]

The Culture War Rages On and On

When we started work on this book in 2016, we naively believed that abortion politics had stabilized for the foreseeable future. With conservatives on the Supreme Court holding a 5–4 majority and the pragmatic John Roberts as the median justice, the constitutional right to abortion seemed secure. We thought further restrictions were likely but that the federal right to choose would remain in some form. Six years later, the

ABORTION, GAY RIGHTS, AND AMERICAN POLITICS   163

2022 *Dobbs v. Jackson* verdict eliminated that right. Privately, GOP politicians were elated. Publicly, they were subdued. Many feared backlash in the upcoming midterm elections, so they said little about abortion on the campaign trail or anywhere else for that matter (Weisman 2022). Donald Trump remained quiet as well, stating privately that the decision was "bad for Republicans" (Haberman and Bender 2022). Though we were wrong about the stability of abortion politics in 2016, the palpable fear felt by Republican leaders and candidates in 2022 did not surprise us in the least. Those who remained silent on *Dobbs* behaved like Billy Graham, Barack Obama, and Donald Trump before them. This is exactly what the theory of moral power calls for.

Republican politicians were right to be afraid. In August, Kansas voters soundly rejected an anti-abortion amendment to the state constitution. Then on Election Day 2022, Democrats performed far better than anyone could have imagined before the *Dobbs* decision came down. Although the party lost its House majority, the thirteen-seat swing was much closer than the typical midterm outcome in a new president's first term—and far closer than professional prognosticators expected in the pre-*Dobbs* world. Democrats also picked up one seat in the Senate to move from a 50–50 to 51–49 margin. Voters in three states (California, Michigan, and Vermont) enshrined abortion protections in their state constitutions. Voters in two red states (Kentucky and Montana) rejected amendments that would have limited abortion rights (Stracqualursi, Cole, and LeBanc 2022).

Varied state laws and a slew of court challenges have rendered abortion access unpredictable. None of this has escaped the voting public. Consider the 2023 Supreme Court election in Wisconsin. Liberal Janet Protasiewicz signaled a desire to overturn an 1849 abortion ban. She soundly defeated conservative Daniel Kelly, who, like many in the GOP in the post-*Dobbs* world, remained silent on the issue. Despite this silence, Wisconsin voters saw the election as a referendum on abortion rights (Epstein 2023). Interest groups like NARAL described Kelly as "a Federalist Society justice endorsed by numerous anti-choice extremist groups, who has written extensively about his opposition to reproductive freedom." Invoking the language of moral disgust, the conservative "Women Speak Out PAC" ran an ad stating that "Janet Protasiewicz and her bloodthirsty comrades don't care about Wisconsin's values. They care about making money killing babies." The race brought over 1.8 million voters to the polls. Turnout stood at 1.2 million in the last off-cycle Wisconsin Supreme Court race in 2019. Events like this leave little doubt that the GOP will be on the defensive for some time. Anti-*Dobbs* backlash has rocked American politics (Radcliffe and Thomas-DeVeaux 2022). Like the NCR in the 1990s, pro-life forces are learning about the power of moral backlash firsthand.

In our judgment, the politics of gay rights remain fluid as well. Consider religious exemption laws. These laws let individuals, religious institutions, nonprofits, businesses, and corporations opt out of providing services to same-sex individuals. In its 2018 *Masterpiece Cakeshop v. Colorado Civil Rights* decision, the Supreme Court ruled in favor of the cake shop's owner, who had refused on religious grounds to bake a wedding cake for a same-sex couple. Gay rights have spilled over into conflicts in education. Florida's GOP governor Ron DeSantis signed the "Don't Say Gay" bill in the spring of 2022. The law bans teaching students about gender identity before the fourth grade. Books that address sexual identity have been banned from the shelves of public libraries and schools across the nation. Clarence Thomas's concurring opinion in *Dobbs v. Jackson* invited challenges to the constitutionality of same-sex marriage.

The GOP must proceed cautiously on gay rights. Given the rise in acceptance of same-sex relations and support for gay marriage in recent years, GOP candidates who disparage same-sex individuals and push to roll back marriage equality court electoral disaster. In light of this, they have sought new moral issues to exploit for political gain. Enter transgender rights.

Transgender rights represent a new front in America's culture war. Consider the uproar surrounding Bud Light beer (Stewart 2023). In an attempt to market its beer to an emerging demographic, Bud Light signed a sponsorship deal with transgender social media influencer Dylan Mulvaney. Mulvaney, dressed like Holly Golightly from *Breakfast at Tiffany's*, posted a video of herself drinking Bud Light to celebrate March Madness and her first year of womanhood. Within days, all hell broke loose. The musicians Travis Tritt and Kid Rock denounced Bud Light. Kid Rock posted an online video of himself shooting cans of Bud Light with an assault-style rifle and declaring "F**k Bud Light and f**k Anheuser-Busch." Politicians got involved too. Representative Ted Lieu tweeted a photograph of himself drinking Bud Light with his Democratic colleagues. GOP leaders like Florida governor Ron DeSantis and Texas representative Dan Crenshaw urged beer drinkers to boycott Bud Light (Telford 2023). As we write this, Modelo has overtaken Bud Light as America's best-selling beer, two Bud Light marketing executives associated with the campaign are on leave, and Mulvaney has fled to Peru (Holpuch and Creswell 2023; Valinsky 2023).

The Bud Light ruckus recalls other controversies that we described earlier in the book, such as the Hallmark Channel ad that included two brides kissing at the altar; Jerry Falwell's attack on the purple Teletubby Tinky Winky; the long-running battle between the NCR and the Disney Company; abortion plot lines in popular TV shows like *Seinfeld*, *House*, and *Friday Night Lights*; anti-gay sermons in the pews; and tweets from Rick Warren, Franklin Graham, and Taylor Swift. The culture war rages on and on. Issues like these will shape American politics and society for years to come.

Acknowledgments

Moral Issues is the second book each of us has written. It has taken a long time to complete. Sometime in 2014, Chapp approached Goren with the idea of doing a paper on the relationship between moral issues and religious orientations. Over the next two years, we developed the initial version of our theory and tested some of its empirical implications. Scholars have long noted that public opinion on issues like abortion and gay rights differed in important ways from opinions on other issues. Our theory explained what, in our view, made "moral issues" different. Our data showed that moral issues were stronger than either of us had initially expected. This first cut appeared in the *American Political Science Review* in 2017. This convinced us the idea had legs, meriting a full book treatment. At the time, we thought, foolishly, that since we had both published a book previously, things would proceed somewhat smoothly. They did not. Goren spent six years as department chair at Minnesota. Chapp served a three-year chair term at St. Olaf before taking on other administrative responsibilities. Then COVID-19 hit, followed by the shutdown, economic disruption, the murder of George Floyd, mass protests in the Twin Cities and across the nation, a 2020 presidential campaign unlike any other, and a failed insurrection. While there is no doubt that the state of the world and our administrative responsibilities delayed our progress, some of the early choices we made about what to put in the book and how to frame it really slowed us down. The initial drafts had too many analyses, too much empirical minutia, and not nearly enough on the big picture, on what our results meant for understanding American religion and politics. To use a (dated) musical analogy, the book was too much like Yes's *Tales from Topographic Oceans*, dense and self-indulgent, and not enough like Lou Reed's *New York*, taut and focused. Somehow we had missed the forest for the trees. Luckily, the feedback and support we received from colleagues and friends over the years has improved the manuscript immeasurably.

We must begin by acknowledging our debt to the first-rate team at the University of Chicago Press. During the early stages of the project, Chuck Myers's enthusiasm for the project convinced us we might be on to something. After Chuck retired, Sara Doskow handled the transition seamlessly. Her astute advice and patience, along with the tough but fair feedback we received from the two anonymous reviewers, helped us rediscover the forest. Our debt of gratitude on this score is beyond measure. Rosemary Frehe and Erika Barrios provided clear editorial guidance when the book moved into production.

Our debts extend to many, many individuals in the profession and beyond. David Campbell, Howie Lavine, Geoff Layman, Lily Mason, and Michael Tesler provided cogent feedback on the first draft of what became our *APSR* paper. For help on the project at various stages, we thank Anat Bardi, Larry Bartels, Dawn Baunach, Martin Bisgaard, Amber Boydstun, Drew Brown, Penny Edgell, Chris Federico, Booth Fowler, Elsie Goren, Indi Goren, Lisa Goren, Jonathan Haidt, Marc Hetherington, Dan Hofrenning, James Hollyer, Larry Jacobs, Andy Karch, Lasse Lausten, Howie Lavine, Matt Luttig, Valerie Martinez-Ebers, Michael Minta, Matt Motta, Dan Myers, Kathryn Pearson, Michael Bang Petersen, Andrew Proctor, Phil Shively, Gretchen Sisson, Rune Slothuus, Amy Smith, Paul Sniderman, Jane Sumner, and Grant Wacker. Colin Harris, Cindy Kam, Kathryn Pearson, and Anne Thompson graciously shared data we used in our content analysis work. Thanks to Ceci Chapp for dutifully taking photographs of billboards along rural highways. We also received some useful feedback from copanelists and audience members at the 2019 APSA and 2015 MWPS conferences. The Departments of Political Science at Aarhus University and the University of Wisconsin gave us a chance to present this and related work in the early stages of development. We appreciate the opportunity and hospitality. Comments from the four reviewers on the *APSR* piece proved to be a big help.

This project would not have been possible without the insights and hard work from a team of dedicated undergraduate research assistants. At the University of Minnesota, Caitlyn Barrett, Cassie Varrige, and Maren Viker all provided valuable research assistance. At St. Olaf College, Mari Arneson, Tyler Benning, India Bock, My Khe Nguyen, Caroline Pippert, Evie Slater, and Addison Tryon helped advance the project. Cali Goulet

ACKNOWLEDGMENTS

and Matthew Blake's data science work assisted in generating many of the figures displayed throughout the book. Andrew Myers deserves special recognition for helping build the content analysis datasets used in chapter 3.

Our personal debts run deeper. Paul thanks his felines, Bambi and Big Zoof, and some of his favorite bands and musicians — Aretha Franklin, Les Rallizes Dénudés, the Stones, Stereolab, and the Velvet Underground — for getting him through some difficult days. Even more critical was the love and support of his children: Nurullah, Elsie, and Indigo. Most importantly, he thanks his wife, Lisa, for all her love, support, patience, and good cheer over the years. Paul dedicates this book to the memory of his father, Nurullah, who passed away in 1992, and his mother, Elaine, who passed away in 2020.

Chris thanks his canine, Lily, and acknowledges Rancid, Frank Turner, Sam Cooke, The Clash, and Tommy Guerrero for providing a soundtrack during the writing process. Children Sam and Ceci are a constant source of inspiration who have been asking probing and imaginative questions about politics since they were five or six, if not younger. Chris is especially thankful to his wife, Jolene, who has been a beacon of unending love and support during the somewhat isolating process of research and writing. Chris dedicates this book to his family, who have never wavered in their passion for politics and commitment to inquiry.

Appendixes

Chapter 4 Appendix

Question Wording for Moral Issue Attitudes

1992–1996 NES

1. "There has been some discussion about abortion during recent years. Which one of the opinions on this page best agrees with your view? You can just tell me the number of the opinion you choose. (1) By law, abortion should never be permitted. (2) The law should permit abortion only in case of rape, incest, or when the woman's life is in danger. (3) The law should permit abortion for reasons other than rape, incest, or danger to the woman's life, but only after the need for the abortion has been clearly established. (4) By law, a woman should always be able to obtain an abortion as a matter of personal choice" (four-point scale).

2. 101-point feeling thermometer: "Gay men and lesbians; that is, homosexuals."

3. "Do you favor or oppose laws to protect homosexuals against job discrimination?" Follow up probe gauges support as "Strongly or not strongly?" (four-point scale).

4. "Do you think homosexuals should be allowed to serve in the United States Armed Forces or don't you think so?" Follow up probe gauges support as "Strongly or not strongly?" (four-point A follow scale).

2000–2004 NES

1. Same wording as 1992–1996 abortion question.

2. Same wording as 1992–1996 point feeling thermometer:

3. Same wording as 1992–1996 "protect homosexuals against job discrimination" item.

172 APPENDIXES

2016–2020 NES

1. Same wording as 1992–1996 abortion question.
2. "Do you favor or oppose laws to protect gays and lesbians against job discrimination?" Follow up probe gauges support as "Strongly or not strongly?" (four-point scale).
3. "Which comes closest to your views? Gay and lesbian couples should be allowed to legally marry. Gay and lesbian couples should be allowed to form civil unions but not legally marry. There should be no legal recognition of a gay or lesbian couple's relationship" (three-point scale).
4. "Do you think business owners who provide wedding-related services should be allowed to refuse services to same-sex couples if same-sex marriage violates their religious beliefs, or do you think business owners should be required to provide services regardless of a couple's sexual orientation?" (six-point scale).

2006–2010, 2008–2012, AND 2010–2014 GSS

1. "Please tell me whether or not you think it should be possible for a pregnant woman to obtain a legal abortion if . . . the woman wants it for any reason?" (E)
2. ". . . there is a strong chance of serious defect in the baby?" (T)
3. ". . . the woman's own health is seriously endangered by the pregnancy?" (T)
4. ". . . she is married and does not want any more children?" (E)
5. ". . . the family has a very low income and cannot afford any more children?" (E)
6. ". . . she became pregnant as a result of rape?" (T)
7. ". . . she is not married and does not want to marry the man?" (E)

Yes-no response options for all questions. (T) indicates item used in "traumatic" abortion mini-scale; (E) indicates items used in "elective abortion" mini-scale. These mean we use E and T additive scales in the CFA models below.

8. "What about sexual relations between two adults of the same sex—do you think it is always wrong, almost always wrong, wrong only sometimes, or not wrong at all?" (four-point scale, agree/disagree format).
9. "Do you agree or disagree with the following statement: Homosexual couples have the right to marry one another" (five-point scale, agree/disagree format).

2006–2012 PALS

1. "The only legal marriage should be a marriage between one man and one woman" (five-point scale, agree/disagree format).

APPENDIXES

2. "Do you personally believe that abortion should be legal under (1) almost all circumstances, (2) most circumstances, (3) some circumstances, (4) only extreme circumstances, (5) under no circumstances" (five-point scale).
3. "Do you believe that each of the following is morally wrong or not a moral issue? Having an abortion when the fetus is old enough to survive on its own outside the mother's womb. Would you say that is always morally wrong, usually morally wrong, sometimes morally wrong, never morally wrong, or not a moral issue?" (five-point scale).
4. "Using genetic engineering, that is changing a person's DNA or genes, to create a baby that is smarter, stronger, or better looking." Responses range from "always morally wrong" to "not a moral issue" (five-point scale).

2012 CCES

1. See 1992–1996 NES abortion item.
2. 101-point feeling thermometer: "How would you rate gay men and lesbians?"
3. "Do you favor or oppose laws to protect homosexuals against job discrimination?" (four response options ranging from "favor strongly" to "oppose strongly").
4. "Do you believe gays and lesbians should be: allowed to get legally married, allowed a legal partnership similar to but not called marriage, or given no legal recognition to gay and lesbian relationships?"

2016 CCES

1. "Do you support or oppose each of the following proposals? Always allow a woman to obtain an abortion as a matter of choice" (two-point scale).
2. "Allow employers to decline coverage of abortion in insurance plans" (two-point scale).
3. "Prohibit the expenditure of funds authorized or appropriated by federal law for any abortion (two-point scale).
4. "Make abortion illegal in all circumstances" (two-point scale).
5. "Do you favor or oppose allowing gays and lesbians to marry legally?" (two-point scale).

Question Wording for Disgust Sensitivity

2012 AND 2016 CCES

Please tell us how much you agree or disagree with each of the following statements, or how true it is about you. Strongly disagree (very untrue about me) / Mildly disagree (somewhat untrue about me) / Neither agree nor disagree / Mildly agree (somewhat true about me) / Strongly agree (very true about me)

1. I might be willing to try eating monkey meat, under some circumstances.
2. If I see someone vomit, it makes me sick to my stomach.
3. I never let any part of my body touch the toilet seat in public restrooms.
4. I probably would not go to my favorite restaurant if I found out that the cook had a cold.

How disgusting would you find each of the following experiences? Not disgusting at all / Slightly disgusting / moderately disgusting / very disgusting / extremely disgusting

1. You are about the drink a glass of milk when you smell that it is spoiled.
2. You see maggots on a piece of meat in an outdoor garbage pail.
3. A friend offers you a piece of chocolate shaped like dog doo.
4. You take a sip of soda, then realize that you drank from a glass that an acquaintance of yours had been drinking from.

TABLE A4.3 **Disgust sensitivity predicts moral issues, 2012 and 2016 CCES data**

	Moral issues$_{12}$	Moral issues$_{16}$
Age	0.002**	0.00
	(3.31)	(0.35)
Female	−0.08**	−0.03
	(−3.03)	(−0.90)
African American	−0.05*	0.01
	(−1.65)	(0.25)
College graduate	−0.08**	−0.05*
	(−3.81)	(−1.68)
Openness	−0.26**	−0.21**
	(−4.09)	(−2.72)
Consciousness	0.06	0.00
	(0.89)	(0.04)
Extraversion	−0.05	−0.02
	(−1.00)	(−0.29)
Agreeableness	−0.12*	0.06
	(−1.86)	(0.84)
Neuroticism	−0.23**	0.25**
	(−3.95)	(3.76)
Disgust sensitivity	0.30**	0.20**
	(4.64)	(2.43)
Constant	0.46**	0.21**
	(4.77)	(2.16)
R^2	.12	.06

APPENDIXES   175

TABLE A4.3 *(continued)*

	Moral issues$_{12}$	Moral issues$_{16}$
F test	11.70**	4.13**
Number of observations	1,434	798

* p < .05, ** p < .01 (one-tailed test).
Notes: These are ordinary least squares estimates. The *t*-statistics are
in parentheses. Weighted estimates. Disgust sensitivity and moral
issues coded so that higher scores reflect increasingly disgusted and
conservative responses, respectively. All variables lie on a 0–1 range
except age, which is measured in years.

Chapter 5 Appendix

TABLE A5.1 **Linear decomposition of intracohort change and cohort succession**

	Same-sex relations 1973–2021	Same-sex relations 1988–2021	Same-sex marriage 1988–2021
Constant	22.116**	30.200**	33.845**
	(0.2857)	(0.5175)	(0.653)
Year	–0.0061**	–0.0098**	–0.0122**
	(0.0002)	(0.0003)	(0.0003)
Cohort	–0.0048**	–0.0051**	–0.0045**
	(0.0001)	(0.0002)	(0.0002)
R^2	.145	.133	.166
Cases	39,972	26,563	15,888

* p < .05, ** p < .01 (two-tailed test).
Notes: Unstandardized coefficients reported with standard errors in parentheses. All data
comes from the GSS Cumulative Data File. "Year" corresponds to the year administered.
"Cohort" is the birth year of the respondent. We use these coefficients to estimate
intercohort change.

Chapter 6 Appendix

TABLE A6.1 **The impact of religious ID$_{t-1}$ on moral issues$_t$, OLS estimates**

	NES$_{1992-96}$	GSS$_{2006-10}$	GSS$_{2008-12}$	GSS$_{2010-14}$	PALS$_{2006-12}$	NES$_{2016-20}$
Moral issues$_{t-1}$	0.72**	0.81**	0.79**	0.85**	0.68**	0.69**
	(20.09)	(36.60)	(30.76)	(37.64)	(16.36)	(34.30)
Religious ID$_{t-1}$	0.05*	0.03*	0.10**	0.05*	0.07**	0.04**
	(2.05)	(1.81)	(4.32)	(2.37)	(3.33)	(3.86)
Age	0.00	0.00	0.00	–0.00	0.001*	0.001**
	(0.88)	(0.90)	(0.09)	(–0.28)	(2.36)	(3.94)

continues

TABLE A6.1 *(continued)*

	NES$_{1992-96}$	GSS$_{2006-10}$	GSS$_{2008-12}$	GSS$_{2010-14}$	PALS$_{2006-12}$	NES$_{2016-20}$
Woman	−0.03	−0.01	−0.03*	−0.02*	0.00	−0.01
	(−1.63)	(−0.92)	(-1.73)	(−1.84)	(0.20)	(−1.03)
Married	−0.01	0.02	0.03	−0.03*	0.03**	0.01
	(−0.91)	(1.65)	(1.60)	(−2.05)	(2.42)	(1.21)
African American	−0.06**	0.03	−0.03	−0.03	0.00	−0.04*
	(−3.16)	(1.39)	(-1.16)	(−1.56)	(0.14)	(−2.08)
College graduate	−0.02	−0.05**	−0.03*	−0.01	−0.05**	−0.02*
	(−1.35)	(−3.41)	(−1.98)	(−0.54)	(−3.06)	(-2.40)
South	0.03	−0.01	−0.00	0.04**	−0.01	0.02*
	(1.63)	(−0.42)	(−0.11)	(3.12)	(−0.46)	(2.07)
Constant	0.08*	0.05	0.00	0.02	0.08**	−0.00
	(2.13)	(1.67)	(0.16)	(0.74)	(2.48)	(−0.06)
R^2	.59	.69	.70	.72	.46	.58
F test	112.30**	272.79**	226.13**	426.70**	96.18**	264.84**
Number of observations	511	753	749	703	1,259	2,586

* $p < .05$, ** $p < .01$ (one-tailed test).
Notes: OLS = ordinary least squares estimates. Unstandardized coefficients reported with *t*-statistics in parentheses. Estimates adjusted to account for the complex sample design. Moral issues and religious ID are coded so that higher scores reflect increasing issue conservatism and religious identifier (0 = none, 1 = identifies with a religion), respectively. All variables lie on a 0–1 range except age, which is measured in years.

TABLE A6.2 **The impact of moral issues$_{t-1}$ on religious ID$_t$, logistic regression estimates**

	NES$_{1992-96}$	GSS$_{2006-10}$	GSS$_{2008-12}$	GSS$_{2010-14}$	PALS$_{2006-12}$	NES$_{2016-20}$
Moral issues$_{t-1}$	0.75	2.03**	2.29**	2.17**	3.43**	2.30**
	(1.17)	(5.62)	(3.75)	(4.33)	(4.24)	(6.14)
Religious ID$_{t-1}$	3.07**	2.90**	4.17**	3.74**	5.35**	2.43**
	(7.83)	(11.26)	(12.36)	(15.31)	(11.63)	(15.32)
Age	0.02	0.01*	0.02*	0.03**	0.04**	0.03**
	(1.51)	(2.00)	(2.05)	(3.11)	(3.75)	(4.78)
Woman	0.44	0.96**	0.63*	0.59*	−0.09	0.62**
	(1.14)	(3.88)	(1.82)	(2.36)	(−0.26)	(3.75)
Married	−0.03	0.08	0.47	0.28	0.30	0.20
	(−0.09)	(0.30)	(1.37)	(1.09)	(0.90)	(1.25)
African American	−0.04	−0.02	0.33	1.07**	1.68**	0.04
	(−0.06)	(−0.06)	(0.49)	(2.40)	(2.95)	(0.10)
College graduate	0.52	0.06	−0.26	−0.05	0.19	−0.33*
	(1.53)	(0.21)	(−0.76)	(−0.18)	(0.61)	(−2.11)
South	0.57	−0.21	0.37	−0.24	−0.36	−0.05
	(1.30)	(−0.65)	(1.01)	(−1.07)	(−0.97)	(−0.30)
Constant	−1.73**	−2.25**	−3.55**	−4.08**	−6.90**	−2.21**
	(−3.14)	(−5.55)	(−5.21)	(−6.43)	(−8.22)	(−7.21)
McKelvey & Zavonia R^2	.32	.42	.59	.55	.62	.44

TABLE A6.2 (*continued*)

	NES$_{1992-96}$	GSS$_{2006-10}$	GSS$_{2008-12}$	GSS$_{2010-14}$	PALS$_{2006-12}$	NES$_{2016-20}$
F test	19.24**	24.04**	22.90**	32.61**	19.19**	33.83**
Number of observations	575	805	793	746	1,303	2,582

* p < .05, ** p < .01 (one-tailed test).
Notes: Unstandardized coefficients reported with *t*-statistics in parentheses. Estimates adjusted to account for the complex sample design. Moral issues and religious ID are coded so that higher scores reflect increasing issue conservatism and religious identifier (0 = none, 1 = identifies with a religion), respectively. All variables lie on a 0–1 range except age, which is measured in years.

TABLE A6.3 **The impact of moral issues$_{t-1}$ on religious ID$_t$ with controls for party ID$_{t-1}$ and liberal-conservative ID$_{t-1}$, logistic regression estimates**

	NES$_{1992-96}$	GSS$_{2006-10}$	GSS$_{2008-12}$	GSS$_{2010-14}$	PALS$_{2006-12}$	NES$_{2016-20}$
Moral issues$_{t-1}$	0.86	2.13**	1.91**	2.04**	3.47**	2.18**
	(1.20)	(5.73)	(2.84)	(3.78)	(3.48)	(5.35)
Religious ID$_{t-1}$	3.13**	2.94**	4.24**	3.73**	5.70**	2.42**
	(7.36)	(10.99)	(12.28)	(15.01)	(8.93)	(15.34)
Age	0.01	0.02*	0.02*	0.03**	0.04**	0.03**
	(1.13)	(2.12)	(2.14)	(2.93)	(3.55)	(4.72)
Woman	0.48	0.94**	0.74*	0.62**	0.08	0.63**
	(1.20)	(3.67)	(2.08)	(2.39)	(0.20)	(3.69)
Married	0.04	0.05	0.48	0.26	0.66*	0.19*
	(0.12)	(0.18)	(1.34)	(0.99)	(1.69)	(1.19)
African American	0.01	−0.12	0.67	1.11**	2.22**	0.08
	(0.02)	(−0.25)	(0.95)	(2.56)	(3.08)	(0.22)
College graduate	0.57	0.13	−0.36	0.01	0.51	−0.31*
	(1.64)	(0.43)	(−1.01)	(0.02)	(1.49)	(−1.95)
South	0.72*	−0.25	0.31	−0.25	−0.15	−0.06
	(1.70)	(−0.81)	(0.83)	(−1.07)	(−0.33)	(−0.34)
Party ID	0.55	−0.50	0.66	0.42	0.52	0.13
	(1.18)	(−1.14)	(1.20)	(0.90)	(0.91)	(0.50)
Liberal-conservative ID	0.02	0.36	0.18	0.27	0.57	0.12
	(0.02)	(0.48)	(0.19)	(0.40)	(1.08)	(0.82)
Constant	−2.03**	−2.27**	−3.95**	−4.35**	−8.26**	−2.40**
	(−3.37)	(−4.83)	(−5.43)	(−6.55)	(−8.16)	(−6.81)
McKelvey & Zavonia R^2	.35	.43	.60	.56	.69	.44
F test	15.19**	18.93**	19.62**	23.89**	14.36**	26.18**
Number of observations	548	788	768	725	951	2,573

* p < .05, ** p < .01 (one-tailed test).
Notes: Unstandardized coefficients reported with *t*-statistics in parentheses. Estimates adjusted to account for the complex sample design. Moral issues and religious ID are coded so that higher scores reflect increasing issue conservatism and religious identifier (0 = none, 1 = identifies with a religion), respectively. All variables lie on a 0–1 range except age, which is measured in years.

TABLE A6.4 **The impact of moral issues$_{t-1}$ on religious ID$_t$ with additional controls, 2010–2014 GSS, logistic regression estimates**

	Model 1	Model 2
Moral issues$_{t-1}$	1.64*	3.11**
	(2.16)	(3.84)
Religious ID$_{t-1}$	4.03**	3.85**
	(7.84)	(10.18)
Age	0.02	0.05**
	(1.36)	(4.54)
Woman	0.81*	0.61*
	(2.02)	(1.73)
Married	0.26	0.33
	(0.67)	(0.89)
African American	2.13**	0.51
	(2.54)	(0.62)
College graduate	0.43	−0.30
	(0.98)	(−0.77)
South	−0.30	−0.32
	(−0.78)	(−0.85)
Rural resident at 16	−0.36	0.05
	(−0.57)	(0.09)
Big-city resident at 16	−0.02	0.80
	(−0.03)	(1.41)
Religious ID at 16	2.04*	0.02
	(2.30)	(0.04)
Rural resident now	1.27*	−0.21
	(2.03)	(−0.27)
Big-city resident now	−0.27	0.51
	(−0.67)	(1.19)
Children at home	0.95	−0.02
	(0.73)	(−0.02)
Close to LGB individuals	−0.39	−4.23*
	(−0.24)	(−2.01)
Autonomy over obedience	1.32	
	(1.63)	
Attitudes toward premarital sex		0.41
		(0.60)
Constant	−6.75**	−5.24**
	(−4.39)	(−5.07)
McKelvey & Zavonia R^2	.55	.61
F test	5.24**	12.61**
Number of observations	358	370

* p < .05, ** p < .01 (one-tailed test).
Notes: Unstandardized coefficients reported with t-statistics in parentheses. Estimates adjusted to account for the complex sample design. Moral issues and religious ID are coded so that higher scores reflect increasing issue conservatism and religious identifier (0 = none, 1 = identifies with a religion), respectively. All variables lie on a 0–1 range except age, which is measured in years. The results are similar in the other GSS data sets (data not shown). Premarital sex and autonomy are not available on the same GSS ballots.

TABLE A6.5 **The impact of moral issues$_{t-1}$ on religious ID$_t$ with additional controls, 2006-2012 PALS data, logistic regression estimates**

	Model 1
Moral issues$_{t-1}$	2.23**
	(2.92)
Religious ID$_{t-1}$	5.25**
	(11.95)
Age	0.05**
	(3.83)
Woman	−0.24
	(−0.63)
Married	0.36
	(1.05)
African American	1.71**
	(2.95)
College graduate	0.28
	(0.93)
South	−0.44
	(−1.15)
Support for conservative Christian groups	1.94**
	(3.34)
Support traditional sexual morality	1.10
	(1.20)
Constant	−7.50**
	(−8.91)
McKelvey & Zavonia R^2	.66
F test	19.85**
Number of observations	1,271

* $p < .05$, ** $p < .01$ (one-tailed test).
Notes: Unstandardized coefficients reported with *t*-statistics in parentheses. Estimates adjusted to account for the complex sample design. Moral issues and religious ID are coded so that higher scores reflect increasing issue conservatism and religious identifier (0 = none, 1 = identifies with a religion), respectively. All variables lie on a 0–1 range except age, which is measured in years.

TABLE A6.6 **The impact of strength of religious ID$_{t-1}$ on moral issues$_t$, OLS estimates**

	GSS$_{2006-10}$	GSS$_{2008-12}$	GSS$_{2010-14}$
Moral issues$_{t-1}$	0.77**	0.79**	0.78**
	(28.02)	(26.59)	(27.29)
Strength of religious ID$_{t-1}$	0.10**	0.09**	0.14**
	(4.43)	(2.87)	(4.46)
Age	0.00	0.00	−0.00
	(0.34)	(0.27)	(−0.54)
Woman	−0.02*	−0.03*	−0.03**
	(−2.38)	(−1.76)	(−2.46)

continues

TABLE A6.6 *(continued)*

	GSS$_{2006-10}$	GSS$_{2008-12}$	GSS$_{2010-14}$
Married	0.02	0.03*	−0.03*
	(1.58)	(1.66)	(−2.09)
African American	0.02	−0.03	−0.04*
	(1.31)	(−1.15)	(−2.13)
College graduate	−0.06**	−0.04*	−0.01
	(−3.78)	(−2.13)	(−0.97)
South	−0.00	0.01	0.04**
	(−0.27)	(0.02)	(3.09)
Constant	0.05*	0.03	0.03
	(2.06)	(0.94)	(1.01)
R^2	.70	.70	.72
F test	333.15**	196.55**	401.65**
Number of observations	745	695	673

* $p < .05$, ** $p < .01$ (one-tailed test).
Notes: OLS = ordinary least squares estimates. Unstandardized coefficients reported with t-statistics in parentheses. Estimates adjusted to account for the complex sample design. Moral issues and strength of religious ID are coded so that higher scores reflect increasing issue conservatism and stronger religious identity strength, respectively. All variables lie on a 0–1 range except age, which is measured in years.

TABLE A6.7 **The impact of moral issues$_{t-1}$ on strength of religious ID$_t$, OLS estimates**

	GSS$_{2006-10}$	GSS$_{2008-12}$	GSS$_{2010-14}$
Moral issues$_{t-1}$	0.22**	0.12**	0.09**
	(6.21)	(3.83)	(2.95)
Strength of religious ID$_{t-1}$	0.60**	0.68**	0.74**
	(14.80)	(21.86)	(25.15)
Age	0.001**	0.001**	0.001**
	(4.27)	(2.81)	(3.73)
Woman	0.07**	0.06**	0.02
	(4.20)	(3.65)	(1.64)
Married	0.03*	0.03*	0.02
	(2.30)	(1.87)	(1.18)
African American	0.04	0.05*	0.06**
	(1.47)	(2.03)	(2.66)
College graduate	0.00	−0.01	−0.00
	(0.30)	(−0.36)	(−0.20)
South	−0.00	−0.00	−0.04**
	(−0.24)	(−0.15)	(−2.47)
Constant	−0.04	−0.02	−0.03
	(−1.46)	(−0.69)	(−0.99)
R^2	.60	.69	.66
F test	192.78**	210.25**	283.61**
Number of observations	772	730	709

* $p < .05$, ** $p < .01$ (one-tailed test).
Notes: OLS = ordinary least squares estimates. Unstandardized coefficients reported with t-statistics in parentheses. Estimates adjusted to account for the complex sample design. Moral issues and strength of religious ID are coded so that higher scores reflect increasing issue conservatism and religious identity strength, respectively. All variables lie on a 0–1 range except age, which is measured in years.

APPENDIXES

TABLE A6.8 **Two-period fixed-effects model of within-person change in religious ID strength**

	GSS 2006–2010	GSS 2008–2012	GSS 2010–2014
Moral issue Δ → Religious ID Δ	0.09*	0.13**	−0.00
	(2.33)	(2.47)	(−0.14)
Party Δ → Religious ID Δ	0.03	−0.03	0.02
	(0.48)	(−0.76)	(0.56)
Ideology Δ → Religious ID Δ	0.01	−0.05	0.01
	(0.14)	(−1.13)	(0.34)
Constant	−0.01*	−0.01	−0.02
	(−1.90)	(−0.56)	(−2.16)
Number of cases	698	654	639

* p < .05, ** p < .01 (one-tailed test).
Notes: Ordinary least squares estimates applied to difference scores measures. Unstandardized coefficients reported with t-values in parentheses. Each coefficient estimates the degree to which within-person change in the independent variable predicts within-person change in religious ID strength from wave 1 to wave 2, all else equal. Estimates adjusted to account for the complex sample design.

Chapter 7 Appendix

TABLE A7.1 **The impact of seven-point party ID_{t-1} on moral issues$_t$, OLS estimates**

	$NES_{1992–96}$	$NES_{2000–4}$	$GSS_{2006–10}$	$GSS_{2008–12}$	$GSS_{2010–14}$	$PALS_{2006–12}$	$NES_{2016–20}$
Moral issues$_{t-1}$	0.71**	0.71**	0.81**	0.81**	0.86**	0.69**	0.63**
	(18.77)	(18.61)	(31.52)	(30.70)	(37.80)	(16.84)	(26.66)
Party ID_{t-1}	0.07**	0.01	0.04	0.05*	0.03	0.09**	0.12**
	(2.48)	(0.19)	(1.38)	(2.12)	(1.02)	(4.28)	(7.88)
Age	0.00	0.00	0.00	0.00	−0.00	0.002**	0.001**
	(1.03)	(1.35)	(1.09)	(0.69)	(−0.09)	(2.83)	(4.70)
Woman	−0.03	0.00	−0.01	−0.01	−0.02	0.01	−0.00
	(−1.41)	(0.08)	(−0.83)	(−0.80)	(−1.66)	(0.69)	(−0.36)
Married	−0.01	0.03*	0.02	0.03	−0.03*	0.03**	0.01
	(−0.80)	(1.69)	(1.59)	(1.63)	(−2.00)	(2.47)	(0.89)
African American	−0.04*	0.11**	0.04	−0.01	−0.03	0.03	0.00
	(−1.89)	(2.52)	(1.63)	(−0.21)	(−1.58)	(1.29)	(0.11)
College graduate	−0.03*	−0.05**	−0.05**	−0.03*	−0.00	−0.05**	−0.02*
	(−1.71)	(−3.20)	(−3.24)	(−1.86)	(−0.30)	(−3.27)	(−2.38)
South	0.03*	0.01	−0.01	0.01	0.05**	−0.01	0.02*
	(1.72)	(0.70)	(−0.43)	(0.43)	(3.44)	(−0.68)	(1.76)
Constant	0.09*	0.05	0.05*	0.03	0.04	0.07*	−0.03*
	(2.55)	(1.37)	(1.77)	(0.91)	(1.15)	(2.24)	(−1.81)
R^2	0.59	0.55	0.69	0.69	0.72	0.47	0.59
F test	131.87**	70.83**	314.47**	209.30**	403.18**	88.07**	358.34**
Number of observations	512	629	752	747	700	1,247	2,589

* p < .05, ** p < .01 (one-tailed test).
Notes: OLS = ordinary least squares estimates. Unstandardized coefficients reported with t-statistics in parentheses. Estimates adjusted to account for the complex sample design. Moral issues and party ID are coded so that higher scores reflect increasing issue conservatism and Republican partisanship, respectively. All variables lie on a 0–1 range except age, which is measured in years.

TABLE A7.2 **The impact of moral issues$_{t-1}$ on seven-point party ID$_t$, OLS estimates**

	NES$_{1992-96}$	NES$_{2000-4}$	GSS$_{2006-10}$	GSS$_{2008-12}$	GSS$_{2010-14}$	PALS$_{2006-12}$	NES$_{2016-20}$
Moral issues$_{t-1}$	0.22**	0.13*	0.10**	0.09**	0.13**	0.17**	0.21**
	(7.05)	(1.89)	(3.51)	(3.03)	(5.63)	(4.02)	(7.75)
Party ID$_{t-1}$	0.77**	0.86**	0.72**	0.78**	0.73**	0.74**	0.72**
	(20.44)	(26.83)	(28.44)	(28.67)	(24.59)	(23.60)	(37.07)
Age	−0.001*	−0.00	0.001*	−0.00	−0.00	−0.00	0.00
	(−1.73)	(−1.38)	(1.79)	(−1.24)	(−0.35)	(−0.53)	(0.89)
Woman	−0.02	0.03	−0.00	−0.00	0.00	−0.02	−0.01
	(−1.08)	(1.02)	(−0.17)	(−0.20)	(0.17)	(−0.94)	(−0.84)
Married	−0.01	0.02	0.03*	−0.00	0.01	0.04**	0.02*
	(−0.41)	(0.67)	(2.40)	(−0.18)	(0.84)	(2.64)	(1.84)
African American	−0.11**	0.06	−0.15**	−0.11**	−0.06*	−0.11**	−0.12**
	(−5.22)	(0.91)	(−7.21)	(−4.79)	(−2.73)	(−4.34)	(−5.05)
College graduate	0.04*	0.01	0.03*	0.00	0.04**	0.04*	−0.03**
	(2.09)	(0.40)	(1.94)	(0.27)	(2.42)	(2.16)	(−3.01)
South	0.02	−0.03	0.04*	0.02	0.01	0.01	0.00
	(0.82)	(−1.15)	(1.99)	(1.11)	(0.59)	(0.26)	(0.24)
Constant	0.05	0.06	0.00	0.11**	0.06*	−0.02	0.08**
	(1.47)	(0.73)	(0.01)	(3.70)	(1.82)	(−0.44)	(3.89)
R^2	0.66	0.67	0.64	0.69	0.64	0.59	0.65
F test	269.67**	206.21**	244.07**	200.82**	238.10**	225.90**	598.54**
Number of observations	580	676	804	792	741	1,276	2,607

* p < .05, ** p < .01 (one-tailed test).
Notes: OLS = ordinary least squares estimates. Unstandardized coefficients reported with *t*-statistics in parentheses. Estimates adjusted to account for the complex sample design. Moral issues and party ID are coded so that higher scores reflect increasing issue conservatism and Republican partisanship, respectively. All variables lie on a 0–1 range except age, which is measured in years.

TABLE A7.3 **The impact of moral issues$_{t-1}$ on party ID$_t$ with additional controls, GSS estimates**

	GSS$_{2006-2010}$	GSS$_{2008-2012}$	GSS$_{2010-2014}$
Moral issues$_{t-1}$	0.08**	0.06*	0.11**
	(2.59)	(1.76)	(4.08)
Party ID$_{t-1}$	0.69**	0.72**	0.70**
	(28.84)	(22.47)	(20.41)
Age	0.00*	−0.00	−0.00
	(1.85)	(−1.58)	(−0.38)
Female	−0.00	−0.02	0.00
	(−0.32)	(−0.96)	(0.12)
Married	0.03*	−0.01	0.01
	(2.05)	(−0.47)	(0.72)
African American	−0.16**	−0.13**	−0.05**
	(−8.04)	(−5.13)	(−2.32)
College graduate	0.04*	0.01	0.03*
	(2.16)	(0.31)	(2.20)

TABLE A7.3 *(continued)*

	GSS$_{2006-2010}$	GSS$_{2008-2012}$	GSS$_{2010-2014}$
South	0.03	0.01	0.01
	(1.51)	(0.54)	(0.46)
Rural resident	0.05*	−0.02	−0.01
	(2.42)	(−0.79)	(−0.27)
Big-city resident	0.00	−0.02	0.03
	(0.11)	(−0.85)	(1.57)
Religious identifier	0.02	0.05*	0.01
	(0.65)	(2.03)	(0.39)
Liberal-conservative ID	0.08**	0.13*	0.08*
	(2.69)	(2.90)	(1.73)
Close to LGB individuals			−0.18
			(−1.46)
Constant	−0.04	0.07*	0.04
	(−1.09)	(2.20)	(1.08)
R^2	.65	.71	.64
F test	154.25**	151.46**	143.43**
Number of observations	789	767	713

* p < .05, ** p < .01 (one-tailed test).
Notes: OLS = ordinary least squares estimates. Unstandardized coefficients reported with *t*-statistics in parentheses. Estimates adjusted to account for the complex sample design. Moral issues and party ID are coded so that higher scores reflect increasing issue conservatism and Republican partisanship, respectively. All variables lie on a 0–1 range except age, which is measured in years.

TABLE A7.4 **The impact of moral issues$_{t-1}$ on party ID$_t$ with additional controls, NES and PALS estimates**

	PALS$_{06-12}$	NES$_{16-20}$
Moral issues$_{t-1}$	0.16**	0.13**
	(2.64)	(4.59)
Party ID$_{t-1}$	0.68**	0.66**
	(14.26)	(25.84)
Age	−0.00	−0.00
	(−0.18)	(−0.77)
Woman	−0.02	−0.01
	(−1.03)	(−0.74)
Married	0.05**	0.02
	(2.83)	(1.61)
African American	−0.14**	−0.12**
	(−4.63)	(−4.78)
College graduate	0.03	−0.01
	(1.66)	(−1.20)
South	0.01	0.00
	(0.46)	(0.20)
Religious ID$_{t-1}$	−0.01	
	(−0.40)	
Support for conservative Christian groups	0.06	
	(1.22)	

continues

TABLE A7.4 *(continued)*

	PALS$_{06-12}$	NES$_{16-20}$
Support traditional sexual morality	−0.02	
	(−0.38)	
Liberal-conservative ID	0.13**	0.18**
	(2.40)	(5.57)
Rural resident		0.03*
		(1.94)
Big-city resident		−0.01
		(−0.60)
Knows gays		−0.01
		(−0.94)
Has gay friends		−0.01
		(−0.71)
Has gay family members		0.00
		(0.23)
Authoritarianism		0.03
		(1.64)
Openness		−0.01
		(−0.38)
Constant	−0.06	0.05
	(−1.35)	(1.15)
R^2	.63	.66
F test	172.25**	466.68**
Number of observations	928	2446

* $p < .05$, ** $p < .01$ (one-tailed test).
Notes: OLS = ordinary least squares estimates. Unstandardized coefficients reported with *t*-statistics in parentheses. Estimates adjusted to account for the complex sample design. Moral issues and party ID are coded so that higher scores reflect increasing issue conservatism and Republican partisanship, respectively. All variables lie on a 0–1 range except age, which is measured in years.

TABLE A7.5 **The impact of moral issues$_{t-1}$ on three-point party ID$_t$, ordered logistic regression estimates**

	NES$_{1992-96}$	NES$_{2000-4}$	GSS$_{2006-10}$	GSS$_{2008-12}$	GSS$_{2010-14}$	PALS$_{2006-12}$	NES$_{2016-20}$
Moral issues$_{t-1}$	2.83**	1.62*	1.18**	0.76*	1.48**	1.18**	2.26**
	(7.62)	(1.99)	(4.18)	(2.04)	(6.51)	(2.86)	(8.08)
3-pt Party ID$_{t-1}$	1.94**	2.07**	1.96**	2.20**	2.20**	1.75**	1.88**
	(13.46)	(10.76)	(16.69)	(14.31)	(12.73)	(14.14)	(18.67)
Age	−0.01	−0.01	0.00	−0.00	−0.00	−0.00	0.00
	(−0.88)	(−0.85)	(0.81)	(−0.44)	(−0.47)	(−0.55)	(1.58)
Woman	−0.37	0.19	0.00	0.06	−0.21	−0.13	−0.21
	(−1.64)	(0.57)	(0.02)	(0.27)	(−1.13)	(−0.83)	(−1.50)
Married	0.16	−0.12	0.26*	−0.19	0.09	0.24	0.32*
	(0.71)	(−0.37)	(1.96)	(−0.85)	(0.48)	(1.37)	(2.17)
African American	−2.19**	0.06	−1.61**	−1.72**	−0.82**	−1.30**	−1.24**
	(−4.07)	(0.07)	(−5.25)	(−5.05)	(−3.30)	(−4.95)	(−4.91)
College graduate	0.43*	0.31	0.51*	−0.09	0.30*	0.24	−0.21*
	(1.71)	(1.04)	(2.39)	(−0.41)	(1.71)	(1.38)	(−1.74)

TABLE A7.5 *(continued)*

	NES$_{1992-96}$	NES$_{2000-4}$	GSS$_{2006-10}$	GSS$_{2008-12}$	GSS$_{2010-14}$	PALS$_{2006-12}$	NES$_{2016-20}$
South	0.32	−0.54	0.30	0.21	0.19	0.19	0.11
	(1.55)	(−1.40)	(1.57)	(0.98)	(0.83)	(0.80)	(0.79)
Cut-point 1	2.72	1.92	2.67	1.40	2.00	2.02	2.17
Cut-point 2	3.42	2.44	3.97	2.92	3.53	3.38	3.40
McKelvey & Zavonia R^2	0.63	0.67	0.61	0.61	0.58	0.53	0.65
F test	37.11**	18.49**	51.93**	32.22**	45.19**	41.19**	77.14**
Number of observations	580	676	804	792	741	1,276	2,607

* p < .05, ** p < .01 (one-tailed test).
Notes: Unstandardized coefficients reported with *t*-statistics in parentheses. Estimates adjusted to account for the complex sample design. Moral issues and party ID are coded so that higher scores reflect increasing issue conservatism and Republican partisanship, respectively. All variables lie on a 0–1 range except age, which is measured in years, and three-point party ID, which is coded 0 = Democrat, 1 = pure independent, and 2 = Republican.

TABLE A7.6 **EIV estimates predicting party-driven/issue-driven change in moral issue positions/party ID**

	NES$_{1992-96}$	NES$_{2000-4}$	GSS$_{2006-10}$	GSS$_{2008-12}$	GSS$_{2010-14}$	PALS$_{2006-12}$	NES$_{2016-20}$
DV = Moral issues$_t$:							
Moral issue positions$_{t-1}$	1.03**	1.51**	0.92**	0.97**	1.00**	1.33**	1.08**
	(19.29)	(12.59)	(33.46)	(34.71)	(37.08)	(22.40)	(34.72)
Party ID$_{t-1}$	−0.00	−0.24**	0.02	−0.02	−0.03	−0.01	−0.04*
	(−0.12)	(−3.73)	(0.66)	(−0.70)	(−1.19)	(−0.21)	(−2.15)
Number of observations	512	629	752	747	700	1,247	2,745
DV = Party ID$_t$:							
Moral issue positions$_{t-1}$	0.24**	0.06	0.04	0.07**	0.09**	0.18**	0.18**
	(4.19)	(0.61)	(1.16)	(2.44)	(2.72)	(2.97)	(5.41)
Party ID$_{t-1}$	0.90**	1.06**	0.86**	0.89**	0.85**	0.84**	0.88**
	(24.84)	(25.64)	(27.80)	(34.43)	(23.14)	(28.75)	(38.95)
Number of observations	580	676	804	792	741	1,276	2,768

* p < .05, ** p < .01 (one-tailed test).
Notes: EIV = errors in variables regression estimates. Control variables have been omitted to preserve clarity. Unstandardized coefficients reported with *t*-statistics in parentheses. Moral issues and party ID are coded so that higher scores reflect increasing cultural conservative and Republican partisanship, respectively. Both variables lie on a 0–1 range.

TABLE A7.7 **Two-period fixed-effects model of within-person change in party ID strength**

	GSS 2006–2010	GSS 2008–2012	GSS 2010–2014
Moral issue Δ → Party ID Δ	0.08*	0.14**	0.16**
	(1.90)	(2.49)	(2.36)
Religious Δ → Party ID Δ	0.02	−0.04	0.02
	(0.48)	(−0.78)	(0.56)
Ideology Δ → Party ID Δ	0.21**	0.06	0.09
	(3.56)	(1.41)	(2.58)
Constant	−0.02**	0.03**	0.00
	(−2.37)	(3.36)	(0.22)
Number of cases	698	654	639

* p < .05, ** p < .01 (one-tailed test).
Notes: Ordinary least squares estimates applied to difference scores measures. Unstandardized coefficients reported with *t*-values in parentheses. Each coefficient estimates the degree to which within-person change in religious commitment from time 1 to time 2 predicts within-person change in moral issues over time, all else equal. Estimates adjusted to account for the complex sample design.

Notes

Chapter One

1. This account draws on his *New York Times* obituary (Goodstein 2018) and Grant Wacker's (2014, 1–4, 13–19, 23; 2018, 4–7) biographical works.

2. During the 1970s, Graham faced criticism over his stance on the Vietnam War and his defense of Richard Nixon during the Watergate scandal, so he likely had several issues in mind when he said this.

3. We use the terms *gay rights*, *same-sex rights*, and *LGBT rights* interchangeably. Since the survey questions we rely on later on in the book do not ask about transgender rights, we make greater use of the phrases *gay rights* and *same-sex rights* throughout these pages.

4. Respondents had five response options to choose from.

5. To be clear, we believe that many Americans held fairly strong views about abortion and gays/lesbians prior to this time frame. Our presumption is that the number of Americans holding strong views has increased since the 1980s and that many of those who already held fairly strong feelings saw those feelings intensify as issue salience grew.

Chapter Two

1. We changed the names to guarantee anonymity. These in-person interviews lasted seventy-five minutes.

2. These analyses build on and go beyond our initial work on the moral issues–party ID link (Goren and Chapp 2017).

3. Other factors, such as family structure, peers, schools, and so on, impact what children learn. Parental influence remains robust when researchers take these factors into account (Jennings, Stoker, and Bowers 2009; Carlson and Knoester 2011; Pacheco and Kreitzer 2016; Bengston et al 2018).

4. Automatic responses are spontaneous, subconscious, uncontrollable, and

188   NOTES TO CHAPTER 4

consume few cognitive resources (Lodge and Taber 2013). When people respond to moral issue messages, the emotional responses they feel often go undetected.

5. Abortion comes up twice more in the episode, giving viewers even more chances to encounter the issue. After Elaine tells Jerry how well a first date went, he taunts her with "what is his stand on abortion?" When Elaine mentions abortion to her date later on, he responds "You know, someday we're gonna get enough people on the Supreme Court to change that law." Elaine, crushed, ends the relationship.

Chapter Three

1. In practice, most articles focused on politics in the lesbian and gay community. Very few articles focused on the transgender community.

2. We are indebted to the Oberlin College and Northwestern University Congressional Candidate Website Project (n.d.). This project helped us grab website text in cases where the Library of Congress archive contained dead links.

3. The Sermon Central database only includes broad descriptors of religious tradition. For instance, we were unable to distinguish between different Lutheran synods in our weighting process. The denominational weights help correct for a large undercount of Catholics in the sample, but it is still far from a representative cross-section of American Sunday mornings.

4. Daniel Williams (2010) notes that in 1976, First Lady Betty Ford, Republican National Committee chair Mary Smith, and Vice President Nelson Rockefeller were all vocally pro-choice.

5. Supreme Court politics likely affects this pattern in other ways. Michael Evans and Shanna Pearson-Merkowitz (2012) found that coverage of Supreme Court judicial appointments focuses disproportionately on moral issues, abortion most notably. We agree. 1986–1987 saw four nominees: Rehnquist, Scalia, Bork, and Kennedy. Media attention often focused on how they would rule on moral issues. Headlines like "Abortion Rights Group Plans All-Out Attack on Bork Nomination" (Beamish 1987) were commonplace during this period.

6. For example, abortion and gay rights were often minor subplots on the *West Wing* but were not scored as "moral issues" in our dataset.

7. The difference between weighted and unweighted numbers merits some discussion. Catholic homilies are underrepresented on Sermon Central but tend to make frequent mention of abortion. For this reason, when we weight the numbers in figure 3.7 to account for an undercount of Catholics, the abortion estimate goes up.

Chapter Four

1. As we point out in chapter 1, we think that many people already held fairly strong views about abortion, gays, and same-sex rights prior to the 1980s. As moral

NOTES TO CHAPTER 4   189

messages multiplied, the number of people holding strong attitudes increased. And
some of those saw their already strong views grow even stronger.

2. The answers people give may change even though their underlying "true" attitudes have remained stable, suggesting that answers vary from one reading to the
next due to random measurement error (RME). The next section and the online
measurement appendix discuss why we use multiple indicator scales, but not error
correction estimators, to account for RME in our data. We make an exception in
chapter 7, where we use both standard and error correction estimators to model
the relationship between party ID and moral issue attitudes.

3. One of the questions asks about "having an abortion when the fetus is old
enough to survive on its own outside the mother's womb." The other question asks
about approving the use of "genetic engineering, that is changing a person's DNA
or genes, to create a baby that is smarter, stronger, or better looking."

4. We thank Cindy Kam for sharing the 2016 data with us.

5. We expect older people, women, Blacks, and non–college graduates to hold
more conservative views than younger people, men, non-Blacks, and college grads.
As well, since open personality types seek out and embrace novel experiences,
they may be less fearful of all kinds of threats—including moral threats. We predict
that openness will be negatively associated with cultural conservatism. We also
control for other personality traits (conscientiousness, extraversion, agreeableness,
and neuroticism).

6. These correspond to respondent scores at the tenth, fiftieth, and ninetieth
percentile in the disgust distribution.

7. Correlations reflect relative stability within a distribution (i.e., interrespon-
dent stability) rather than absolute stability for a given individual (i.e., intrare-
spondent stability). We examine both types of stability throughout the book.

8. We tap religious ID strength using two items. The first item reads, "Would
you call yourself a strong (tradition) or not very strong (tradition)." Here, tradition
indicates the answer respondents gave to the denomination question (e.g., Protestant, Catholic, etc.). The response options are "strong," "somewhat strong" (volunteered), "not very strong," and "no religion." The second item reads, "To what extent do you consider yourself a religious person?" The response options are "very
religious," "moderately religious," "slightly religious," or "not religious." We prefer
this measure over the dichotomous ID measure (1 = affiliated, 0 = "none") because
the former is based on two measures and evinces more variability than the latter.
Note the mean continuity correlation for our dichotomous measure is 0.63 across
the datasets.

9. We use the standard party ID variable that appears on the NES and GSS
surveys. Here is the NES wording: "Generally speaking, do you usually think of
yourself as a Republican, a Democrat, an Independent, or what?" Those who answered "Republican" or "Democrat" received this probe: "Would you call yourself a strong Republican/Democrat or a not very strong Republican/Democrat?"
Those who did not answer "Republican" or "Democrat" in the root question

received this probe: "Do you think of yourself as closer to the Republican Party or the Democratic Party?"

10. Since the sampling distribution of Pearson's r is not normally distributed, we use Fisher's z-transformation to estimate the confidence intervals.

Chapter Five

1. "What about sexual relations between two adults of the same sex—do you think it is always wrong, almost always wrong, wrong only sometimes, or not wrong at all?" Figure 5.1 displays the percentage of respondents who answered "only sometimes" or "not at all." The marriage question provides five agree/disagree options to the prompt "Homosexual couples should have the right to marry one another." Figure 5.1 displays the percentage of respondents who "agreed" or "strongly agreed." The correlation between these trends is 0.72 ($p < .001$).

2. We rely on the broadest measure of abortion support in the GSS: "Please tell me whether or not you think it should be possible for a pregnant woman to obtain a legal abortion if the woman wants it for any reason?" Figure 5.1 displays the percentage of respondents who answered "yes."

3. The problem is that age is a linear combination of period and cohort. It is impossible to estimate linear effects for all three dynamics at once, even when we think all three are generating change (Fosse and Winship 2019).

4. This approach omits a variable like age and estimates linear effects for the other factors (Firebaugh 1989; Firebaugh and Harley 1991). One can then use regression coefficients to estimate what proportion of the variance is due to (say) period versus cohort effects. This technique produces interpretable linear decompositions. However, by omitting a variable this technique makes strong assumptions about what is—and is not—responsible for opinion change. In response, scholars have developed alternative approaches for estimating age, period, and cohort influences (e.g., Fosse and Winship 2019).

5. Table A5.1 in the appendix reports the estimation details.

6. The frequency with which members of different cohorts appear in the GSS data varies by year. Figures 5.3 and 5.4 begin tracking a cohort when at least 100 members are consistently present in the data.

7. The available panels do not stretch back into the 1970s, so it is impossible to look at changing patterns over the decades. Moreover, panel studies cannot detect cohort replacement, because they only include respondents eighteen or older on the first wave and those still alive on the second wave.

8. If we pool the three panels, the difference between abortion stability and gay rights stability is significant at $p < .001$.

9. The difference in movement to the left is significantly greater in the case of gay rights than abortion in the pooled data ($p < .05$, one-tailed).

NOTES TO CHAPTER 6

10. Other polls have shown less change on abortion (Pew 2022c).

11. In the pooled data, the difference between the proportion of mismatched respondents in both waves is not statistically significant (p = .52, two-tailed).

12. The decrease in the proportion of consistent traditionalists between pooled panel waves is statistically significant, as is the increase in consistent progressives (both p < .01, two-tailed).

Chapter Six

1. Research shows that politics shapes other aspects of religion, such as church attendance (Patrikios 2008; Margolis 2018).

2. We are not the first to advance the case that moral issue attitudes shape religious ID. Robert Putnam and David Campbell (2010, 626n26) report the results of such tests in a footnote in their book *American Grace*. David Campbell, Geoffrey Layman, and John Green (2021) report that attitudes toward gay marriage predict secular orientations (i.e., a mix of identity, belief, and behavior).

3. We provide a broad sketch of this history. Our aim is to highlight aspects that are most relevant to unpacking the logic of the religious ID to issues model. To inform our review, we draw on the work of Robert Wuthnow (1988), James Hunter (1992), David Leege and Lyman Kellstedt (1993), Michael Lienesch (1993), Geoffrey Layman (2001), Lisa McGirr (2001), David Domke and Kevin Coe (2010), Robert Putnam and David Campbell (2010), Lydia Bean (2014), and Robert Jones (2016).

4. For example, on the GSS questionnaires we recode all respondents who expressed a preference on relig_1 for one of the traditions (e.g., Protestant, Catholic, Jewish, Muslim/Islam, Hindu, etc.) as 1. Respondents who chose "none" were coded as 0.

5. The first is age, measured in years. The second is gender ID, coded 1 for woman and 0 for man. The third control is for marital status (1 = married, 0 = otherwise). Fourth, we code Black 1 for African American and 0 otherwise. Fifth, college graduate equals 1; non–college graduate equals 0. Finally, we distinguish between southerners (coded 1) and non-southerners (coded 0). We expect that age, gender, Black, marital status, and South will covary positively with religious ID and moral issues. College graduate should covary negatively with religion and issues. In the interest of moving quickly to the key quantities of interest, we do not discuss the control variable results (see appendix tables A6.1–A6.2 for the details).

6. Given a number of small samples, we use 90 percent CIs.

7. Since we are pooling the data across multiples studies, we switch to 95 percent CIs for these means.

8. We use the tenth, fiftieth, and ninetieth percentile scores to denote progressives, moderates, and conservatives, respectively.

NOTES TO CHAPTER 7

9. To probe the robustness of moral issues on religious exit, we took advantage of an extensive set of variables on the GSS panels to estimate more models. We controlled for preadult socialization (i.e., whether respondents lived in rural, suburban, or urban locales at age sixteen; whether they were a "none" at sixteen); contemporary background factors (i.e., whether respondents currently lived in rural, suburban, or urban locales; the number of nonadult children they have; whether they were close to LGB individuals); and psychological variables (i.e., relative preference for autonomy over obedience in child-rearing values; attitudes toward premarital sex). The effect of issues on religious ID held (see appendix table A6.4 for an illustration with 2010–2014 GSS data).

We also used the PALS data to assess the robustness of the moral issue effect controlling for views of the Christian Right and sexual morality. Since opinions about these things correlate with religious ties and moral issues, models that do not control for them may overestimate the power of issues to predict religious withdrawal. We measured support for the Christian Right with a five-point question that asked, "Do you support or oppose conservative Christian groups active in politics, such as the Christian Coalition, American Family Association, or Focus on the Family?" We created a simple additive scale that uses two five-point agree/disagree items to tap opinion on traditional sexual morality (alpha = 0.53). The items assess agreement with these statements: (1) "Sexual intercourse before marriage is wrong." (2) "It is usually a good idea for a couple to live together before marriage." Once again, the moral issue effect held (see table A6.5 in the appendix).

10. The models include controls for the six social demographic variables employed earlier. The results do not change when we add political identities.

11. We chose this dataset because it comes closest to the average effect of ID strength/issues on issues/ID strength in the datasets. We use scores at the tenth, fiftieth, and ninetieth percentile for each predictor in the bar graph. We controlled for the lagged dependent variable and six social demographics in generating these predicted values.

12. A formal test reveals that this difference is not significant. The same holds for 2008–2012. By contrast, in 2006–2010, the issues-to-religion effect is larger than the religion-to-issues effect (0.22 > 0.10, p < .01).

13. In what follows, we control for within-person change in party ID and ideological ID.

14. The null effect in 2010–2014 is puzzling in light of the heated debate over same-sex marriage from 2010–2015. We could offer various substantive or methodological explanations, but these would be purely speculative.

Chapter Seven

1. Michael Barber and Jeremy Pope (2019) recently provided a compelling demonstration of the partisan cue-taking process. They exploited Donald Trump's

NOTES TO CHAPTER 7

penchant for taking liberal and conservative positions on the same issues (at different points in time) to test whether Republican identifiers changed their policy views in the presence of Trump cues. Their survey experiment showed that many (not all) Republicans altered their positions on salient issues to match whatever Trump said. If he said he wanted to increase the minimum wage, many Republicans went along with this. If he favored a cut in the minimum wage, many Republicans followed suit. If people held strong attitudes on these issues, their opinions did not bend so easily in the face of elite cues. Evidence like this suggests that partisans readily conform (also see Cohen 2003).

2. We coded articles for the words *Republican(s)*, *Democrat(s)*, *GOP*, *party*, *partisan*, *bill*, *legislation* (*legislate*), *Congress*, *capital*, *court*, *president*, *protest(s)*, *activist(s)*, *debate(s)*, *campaign(s)*, *candidate(s)*, *rally*, *referendum*, *vote(s)*, and *law(s)*.

3. After the Democratic Congress passed the bill, GOP president Ford vetoed it. A bipartisan supermajority overrode the veto by a count of 312–93.

4. We believe these data understate public awareness. Given the somewhat convoluted wording of the NES item (see the measurement appendix for chapter 4), it seems to us that a measure along the lines of "which party backs abortion rights" would do a better job tapping knowledge of party differences.

5. Issue attitudes are usually too weak to affect much in the way of party change. However, *usually* does not mean *always*. Some studies report that policy attitudes perform as advertised by issue-proximity models, but only under limited conditions. In one exemplary work, Thomas Carsey and Geoffrey Layman (2006) found that issue-based party change is confined to isolated issue publics on a trio of issues, including abortion. Among respondents who cared about abortion and knew the party positions, the relationship was bidirectional. That is, party ID and abortion opinion shaped one another to a similar degree. Among people who knew where the parties stood but did not care about abortion, party ID shaped issues. Thus, while support for the issue-proximity hypothesis emerged in select issue publics, the classic model applied more broadly. As Carsey and Layman (2006, 474) noted, "party identification is a 'moving force in politics' that tends to be moved itself *only in special circumstances*" (emphasis added). To conclude, revisionist models define the scope conditions of the classic model. In so doing, they qualify that model. They do not fundamentally alter it (Chen and Goren 2016).

6. Here is the NES wording: "Generally speaking, do you usually think of yourself as a Republican, a Democrat, an independent, or what?" Democratic and Republican respondents receive this follow-up question: "Would you call yourself a strong Republican/Democrat or a not very strong Republican/Democrat?" Non-partisan respondents get this follow-up: "Do you think of yourself as closer to the Republican Party or the Democratic Party?" Wording on the other surveys is similar.

7. Another view holds that the observed changes in party ID reflect random measurement error. When analysts employ techniques to correct for this error, party ID proves more stable and less vulnerable to the effects of other psychological

forces than revisionists report (Green and Palmquist 1990). We return to this point later on.

8. Since we cannot account for all possible confounders, our estimates do not give dispositive evidence about causality. Subsequent tests buttress the CLR-based claims we go on to make, but again, even these results do not prove we have identified causal effects.

9. In these datasets, the 90 percent CI crosses the 0.00 reference, meaning that we cannot infer with confidence that party ID predicts opinion change. In the four other datasets, the CIs fall to the right of the 0.00 reference line, which lets us conclude that party ID predicts opinion change.

10. In every dataset, the 90 percent CI does not contain 0.00. Hence, we can conclude with a high degree of confidence that feelings about abortion/same-sex rights forecast party updating.

11. In figures 7.4 and 7.5, we use the scores for respondents at the tenth, fiftieth, and ninetieth percentile of party ID/moral issues to predict moral issues/party ID.

12. GOP liberalism on moral issues may seem odd to readers. This reflects their acceptance of same-sex marriage and support for laws to shield gays and lesbians from job discrimination in the survey. It also reflects the fact that the issue scale contains only one abortion item. If more such items appeared on the NES instrument, we think Republicans' issue score would be more conservative.

13. For the other datasets, the estimated issue-to-party effect always exceeds the estimated party-to-issue effect in magnitude, and these differences usually approach and occasionally reach statistical significance. Here are the results, along with the associated p-values for each difference-of-slopes test: (1) 2000–2004: 0.13 v. 0.01, $p < .15$; (2) 2006–2010: 0.10 v. 0.04, $p < .10$; (3) 2008–2012: 0.09 v. 0.05, $p < .25$; (4) 2010–2014: 0.13 v. 0.03, $p < .01$; and (5) 2006–2012: 0.17 v. 0.09, $p < .06$.

14. Readers may wonder about the robustness of the issue-to-party effect if we control for other variables. To address this concern, we ran a series of new models with additional covariates. In the GSS panels, we added dummy variables for rural resident and big-city resident (suburbanites are the excluded category); the dichotomous measure of religious ID from chapter 6; the seven-point liberal-conservative self-placement scale; and whether respondents reported that they were close to any nonstraight individuals. The issue-to-party effect weakens by 15 to 33 percent in the GSS models but remains significant at conventional levels (see appendix table A7.3). We then turned to the PALS and 2016–2020 NES to run further tests. For the PALS model, we added religious ID, support for Christian conservative groups, support for traditional sexual morality, and liberal-conservative ID. The issue coefficient effect dipped from 0.17 in the original model to 0.16 in the more fully specified model and remained highly significant. The NES model controls for liberal-conservative ID, dummy variables for rural and big-city residents, knowing gays, having gay friends, having gay family members, authoritarianism, and the openness personality trait. Once again, the issue-to-party

NOTES TO CHAPTER 8

effect declined in magnitude (from 0.21 to 0.13) but held (p < .01). Appendix table A7.4 lists the PALS and NES estimates. In short, while the inclusion of more demographic and psychological variables diminishes the issue-to-party effect in the CLR models, the effect remains statistically and substantively potent in every case.

15. We define progressives as subjects in the tenth percentile on moral issues. These folks hold strong pro-choice, pro-gay sentiments. Moral conservatives are in the ninetieth percentile. They are staunchly pro-life and reject same-sex rights.

16. To measure within-person change in our GSS datasets, we subtract the moral issue score at $time_1$ from its $time_2$ value. This new variable ranges from −1.00 to 1.00. A score of −1.00 means that a person with the most conservative position on abortion/gay rights in $wave_1$ took the most progressive position on social issues at $wave_2$. Contrariwise, a score of 1.00 indicates the most avid supporter of abortion/gay rights in $wave_1$ switched to the most extreme anti-abortion/anti-gay stances in $wave_2$. A score of 0.00 means someone held identical positions in both waves. We also create a party difference score. Here, −1.00 denotes complete movement in the Democratic direction while 1.00 denotes full movement toward the GOP. We use the GSS data to regress the party change score on the issue change score, controlling for changes in liberal-conservative ID and religious identity strength (see chapter 6).

Chapter Eight

1. We thank Grant Wacker for sharing his insights on this point with us.

2. The *tau b* measure of association shows the variables were unrelated in 1977 (−0.02). *Tau b* rose to 0.14 in 1993 and 0.37 in 2021.

3. Voters may draw on general principles, but specific issues hardly matter (Goren 2013).

4. A counterargument is that the positions people take on these issues reflect a mix of gut-level emotions and normative beliefs about the good and just society (i.e., values). To the extent that values shape moral issue attitudes, the conclusion that these attitudes are bereft of cognition is overblown. To this we respond (1) the theory of moral power holds that moral issues likely shape values much in the same way they shape identities; and (2) some empirical work finds that core values are endogenous to political attitudes (e.g., McCann 1997). This is an area ripe for future research.

Bibliography

Aarøe, Lene, Michael Bang Petersen, and Kevin Arceneaux. 2017. "The Behavioral Immune System Shapes Political Intuitions: Why and How Individual Differences in Disgust Sensitivity Underlie Opposition to Immigration." *American Political Science Review* 111 (2): 277–94.

Abrajano, Marisa, and Zoltan L. Hajnal. 2015. *White Backlash: Immigration, Race, and American Politics*. Princeton: Princeton University Press.

Abramowitz, Alan I. 1995. "It's Abortion, Stupid: Policy Voting in the 1992 Presidential Election." *Journal of Politics* 57 (1): 176–86.

Abramowitz, Alan I., and Kyle L. Saunders. 1998. "Ideological Realignment in the US Electorate. "*Journal of Politics* 60 (3): 634–52.

Achen, Christopher H. 1975. "Mass Political Attitudes and the Survey Response." *American Political Science Review* 69 (4): 1218–31.

Achen, Christopher H., and Larry M. Bartels. 2016. *Democracy for Realists: Why Elections Do Not Produce Responsive Government*. Princeton: Princeton University Press.

Adams, Greg D. 1997. "Abortion: Evidence of an Issue Evolution." *American Journal of Political Science* 41 (3): 718–37.

Allison, Paul D. 2009. *Fixed Effects Regression Models*. Los Angeles: Sage.

Allport, Gordon W. 1954. *The Nature of Prejudice*. Reading, MA: Addison-Wesley.

Alphonso, Gwendoline. 2015. "From Need to Hope: The American Family and Poverty in Partisan Discourse, 1900–2012." *Journal of Policy History* 27 (4): 592–635.

Althaus, Scott L., Jill A. Edy, and Patricia F. Phalen. 2001. "Using Substitutes for Full-Text News Stories in Content Analysis: Which Text is Best?" *American Journal of Political Science* 45 (3): 707–23.

American Presidency Project. n.d. "Documents." Accessed October 17, 2022. https://www.presidency.ucsb.edu/documents.

Ansolabehere, Stephen, Jonathan Rodden, and James M. Snyder Jr. 2008. "The Strength of Issues: Using Multiple Measures to Gauge Preference Stability,

Ideological Constraint, and Issue Voting." *American Political Science Review* 102 (2): 215–32.

Applebome, Peter. 2007. "Jerry Falwell, Moral Majority Founder, Dies at 73." *New York Times*, May 16, 2007. https://www.nytimes.com/2007/05/16/obituaries/16 falwell.html.

Arnett, Jeffrey Jensen. 2000. "Emerging Adulthood: A Theory of Development from the Late Teens Through the Twenties." *American Psychologist* 55 (5): 469–80.

Asch, Solomon E. 1951. "Effects of Group Pressure upon the Modification and Distortion of Judgments." In *Groups, Leadership, and Men: Research in Human Relations*, edited by Harold Guetzkow, 177–90. Pittsburgh: Carnegie Press.

Associated Press. 1991. "Keeping Borders Closed to AIDS Sufferers Decried by Gay Groups." May 28, 1991.

Aviles, Gwen. 2019. "Inclusive or Hypocritical? Mixed Reviews for Trump Campaign's LGBTQ Merchandise." *NBC News*, December 6, 2019. https://www .nbcnews.com/feature/nbc-out/inclusive-or-hypocritical-mixed-reviews-trump -campaign-s-lgbtq-merchandise-n1097326.

Axelrod, David. 2015. *Believer: My Forty Years in Politics*. New York: Penguin.

Bafumi, Joseph, and Robert Y. Shapiro. 2009. "A New Partisan Voter." *Journal of Politics* 71 (1): 1–24.

Baker, Joseph O., and Buster G. Smith. 2015. *American Secularism: Cultural Contours of Nonreligious Belief Systems*. New York: New York University Press.

Bakker, Bert N., and Yphtach Lelkes. 2018. "Selling Ourselves Short? How Abbreviated Measures of Personality Change What We Think about Personality and Politics." *Journal of Politics* 80 (4): 1311–25.

Barber, Michael, and Jeremy C. Pope. 2019. "Does Party Trump Ideology? Disentangling Party and Ideology in America." *American Political Science Review* 113 (1): 38–54.

Barringer, M. N., J. E. Sumerau, and David A. Gay. 2020. "Generational Variation in Young Adults' Attitudes toward Legal Abortion: Contextualizing the Role of Religion." *Social Currents* 7 (3): 279–96.

Bartels, Larry M. 2000. "Partisanship and Voting Behavior, 1952–1996." *American Journal of Political Science* 44 (1): 35–50.

Bartels, Larry M. 2002. "Beyond the Running Tally: Partisan Bias in Political Perceptions." *Political Behavior* 24 (2): 117–50.

Baunach, Dawn Michelle. 2011. "Decomposing Trends in Attitudes Toward Gay Marriage, 1988–2006." *Social Science Quarterly* 92 (2): 346–63.

Baunach, Dawn Michelle. 2012. "Changing Same-Sex Marriage Attitudes in America from 1988 Through 2010." *Public Opinion Quarterly* 76 (2): 364–78.

Beale, Lewis. 1992. "An Abortion That Shook Prime Time: Television: Twenty Years Ago This Week, Maude Faced the Dilemma of an Unplanned Pregnancy—And an Estimated 65 Million People Tuned In." *Los Angeles Times*, November 10, 1992. https://www.latimes.com/archives/la-xpm-1992-11-10-ca-175-story.html.

BIBLIOGRAPHY

Beamish, Rita. 1987. "Abortion Rights Group Plans All-Out Attack on Bork Nomination." Associated Press, July 11, 1987.

Bean, Lydia. 2014. *The Politics of Evangelical Identity: Local Churches and Partisan Divides in the United States and Canada*. Princeton, NJ: Princeton University Press.

Belluck, Pam. 2004. "Massachusetts Gives New Push to Gay Marriage." *New York Times*, February 5, 2004. https://www.nytimes.com/2004/02/05/us/massachusetts-gives-new-push-to-gay-marriage.html.

Bengston, Vern L., R. David Hayward, Phil Zuckerman, and Merril Silverstein. 2018. "Bringing Up Nones: Intergenerational Influences and Cohort Trends." *Journal for the Scientific Study of Religion* 57 (2): 258–75.

Bennett, Lisa. 1998. "The Perpetuation of Prejudice in Reporting on Gays and Lesbians—*Time* and *Newsweek*: The First Fifty Years." The Joan Shorenstein Center on the Press, Politics, and Public Policy. Research Paper R-21.

Bennett, W. Lance. 2005. *News: The Politics of Illusion*. 6th ed. Chicago: University of Chicago Press.

Billy Graham Library. 2013. "Crusade City Spotlight: New York, NY." *Blog from the Bill Graham Library*, January 8, 2013. https://billygrahamlibrary.org/crusade-city-spotlight-new-york-ny/.

Bishin, Benjamin G., Justin Freebourn, and Paul Teten. 2021. "The Power of Equality? Polarization and Collective Mis-representation on Gay Rights, 1989–2019." *Political Research Quarterly* 74 (4): 1009–23.

Boey, Valerie. 2022. "'Please Don't Mess with Our Children': Christian Conservatives Protest Outside Disney World." Associated Press, May 16, 2022. https://www.fox35orlando.com/news/christian-conservatives-protest-outside-disney-world.

Bos, Angela L., Jill S. Greenlee, Mirya R. Holman, Zoe M. Oxley, and J. Celeste Lay. 2022. "This One's for the Boys: How Gendered Political Socialization Limits Girls' Political Ambition and Interest." *American Political Science Review* 116 (2): 484–501.

Boydstun, Amber E. 2013. *Making the News: Politics, the Media, and Agenda Setting*. Chicago: University of Chicago Press.

Brader, Ted. 2006. *Campaigning for Hearts and Minds: How Emotional Appeals in Political Ads Work*. Chicago: University of Chicago Press.

Braunstein, Ruth. 2022. "A Theory of Political Backlash: Assessing the Religious Right's Effects on the Religious Field." *Sociology of Religion* 83 (3): 293–323.

Brewer, Paul R. 2003. "The Shifting Foundations of Public Opinion about Gay Rights." *Journal of Politics* 65 (4): 1208–20.

Buchanan, Patrick J. 1992. "Culture War Speech: Address to the Republican National Convention (18 August 1992)." https://voicesofdemocracy.umd.edu/buchanan-culture-war-speech-speech-text/.

Burge, Ryan P. 2021. *The Nones: Where They Came from, Who They Are, and Where They Are Going*. Minneapolis: Fortress Press.

Cahill, Courtney Megan. 2005. "Same-Sex Marriage, Slippery Slope Rhetoric, and the Politics of Disgust: A Critical Perspective on Contemporary Family Discourse and the Incest Taboo." *Northwestern University Law Review* 99 (4): 1543–1611.

Cahill, Courtney Megan. 2013. "Abortion and Disgust." *Harvard Civil Rights-Civil Liberties Law Review* 48 (2): 409–56.

Campbell, Angus, Philip E. Converse, Warren E. Miller, and Donald E. Stokes. 1960. *The American Voter.* New York: Wiley.

Campbell, David E., Geoffrey C. Layman, and John C. Green. 2021. *Secular Surge: A New Fault Line in American Politics.* Cambridge: Cambridge University Press.

Caplan, Arthur. 2015. "Ten Years After Terri Schiavo, Death Debates Still Divide Us: Bioethicist." *NBC News,* March 31, 2015. https://www.nbcnews.com/health /health-news/bioethicist-tk-n333536.

Caputo, Marc. 2019. "Biden Reverses Abortion Funding Stand." *Politico,* June 6, 2019. https://www.politico.com/story/2019/06/06/biden-abortion-2020-reverse-13 56593.

Carlson, Daniel L., and Chris Knoester. 2011. "Family Structure and the Intergenerational Transmission of Gender Ideology." *Journal of Family Issues* 32 (6): 709–34.

Carmines, Edward G., Jessica C. Gerrity, and Michael W. Wagner. 2010. "How Abortion Became a Partisan Issue: Media Coverage of the Interest Group-Political Party Connection." *Politics & Party* 38 (6): 1135–58.

Carmines, Edward G., and James A. Stimson. 1980. "The Two Faces of Issue Voting." *American Political Science Review* 74 (1): 78–91.

Carmines, Edward G., and James A. Stimson. 1989. *Issue Evolution: Race and the Transformation of American Politics.* Princeton: Princeton University Press.

Carsey, Thomas M., and Geoffrey C. Layman. 2006. "Changing Sides or Changing Minds? Party Identification and Policy Preferences in the American Electorate." *American Journal of Political Science* 50 (2): 464–77.

Casey, Logan. 2016. "The Politics of Disgust: Public Opinion Toward LGBTQ People & Policies." PhD dissertation, University of Michigan.

Chapman, Hanah A., and Adam K. Anderson. 2013. "Things Rank and Gross in Nature: A Review and Synthesis of Moral Disgust." *Psychological Bulletin* 139 (2): 300–327.

Chapman, Hanah A., D. A. Kim, Josuha M. Susskind, and Adam K. Anderson. 2009. "In Bad Taste: Evidence for the Oral Origins of Moral Disgust." *Science* 323:1222–26.

Chapp, Christopher. 2012. *Religious Rhetoric and American Politics: The Endurance of Civil Religion in Electoral Campaigns.* Ithaca, NY: Cornell University Press.

Chapp, Christopher. 2019. "Resource Mobilization among Religious Activists." In *The Oxford Encyclopedia of Politics and Religion,* edited by Paul A. Djupe, Mark J. Rozell, and Ted G. Jelen. Oxford: Oxford University Press.

Chapp, Christopher, Paul Roback, Kendra Johnson-Tesch, Adrian Rossing, and Jack Werner. 2019. "Going Vague: Ambiguity and Avoidance in Online Political Messaging." *Social Science Computer Review* 37 (5): 591–610.

Chasmar, Jessica, and Kelly Laco. 2022. "DeSantis Slams 'Woke' Disney after CEO Condemns Parents' Rights Bill." *Fox News*, March 10, 2022. https://www.fox news.com/politics/desantis-woke-disney-ceo-parents-rights-bill.

Chen, Philip G., and Paul N. Goren. 2016. "Operational Ideology and Party Identification: A Dynamic Model of Individual-Level Change in Partisan and Ideological Predispositions." *Political Research Quarterly* 69 (4): 703–15.

Chomsky, Daniel, and Scott Barclay. 2010. "The Mass Media, Public Opinion, and Lesbian and Gay Rights." *Annual Review of Law and Social Science* 6:387–403.

Clark, Cory J., Brittany S. Liu, Bo M. Winegard, and Peter H. Ditto. 2019. "Tribalism is Human Nature." *Current Directions in Psychological Science* 28 (6): 587–92.

Cohen, Geoffrey L. 2003. "Party over Policy: The Dominating Impact of Group Influence on Political Beliefs." *Journal of Personality and Social Psychology* 85 (5): 808–22.

Cole, Elizabeth R., Lanice R. Avery, Catherine Dodson, and Kevin D. Goodman. 2012. "Against Nature: How Arguments about the Naturalness of Marriage Privilege Heterosexuality." *Journal of Social Issues* 68 (1): 46–62.

Coombs, Alexa Moutevelis. 2015. "SICK: ABC's 'Scandal' Sets Main Character's Abortion to 'Silent Night.'" Accessed December 6, 2021. https://www.newsbust ers.org/blogs/culture/alexa-moutevelis/2015/11/19/sick-abcs-scandal-sets-main -characters-abortion-silent.

Conover, Pamela Johnston. 1988. "The Role of Social Groups in Political Thinking." *British Journal of Political Science* 18 (1): 51–76.

Converse, Philip E. 1964. "The Nature of Belief Systems in Mass Publics." In *Ideology and Discontent*, edited by David E. Apter, 206–61. New York: The Free Press.

Converse, Philip E. 1969. "Of Time and Partisan Stability." *Comparative Political Studies* 2 (2): 139–71.

Converse, Philip E. 1970. "Attitudes and Non-Attitudes: Continuation of a Dialogue." In *The Quantitative Analysis of Social Problems*, edited by E. R. Tufte, 168–89. Reading, MA: Addison-Wesley.

Converse, Philip E., and Gregory B. Markus. 1979. "Plus ça change . . . : The New CPS Election Study Panel." *American Political Science Review* 73 (1): 32–49.

Cook, Elizabeth Adell, Ted G. Jelen, and Clyde Wilcox. 1992. *Between Two Absolutes; Public Opinion and the Politics of Abortion*. Boulder: Westview Press.

Curtis, Valerie. 2011. "Why Disgust Matters." *Philosophical Transactions B* 366 (1583): 3478–90.

Dancey, Logan, and Paul Goren. 2010. "Party Identification, Issue Attitudes, and the Dynamics of Political Debate." *American Journal of Political Science* 54 (3): 686–99.

D'Antonio, William V., Steven A. Tuch, and Josiah R. Baker. 2013. *Religion, Politics, and Polarization: How Religiopolitical Conflict is Changing Congress and American Democracy*. Lanham, MD: Rowman and Littlefield.

Dahl, Robert A. 1989. *Democracy and Its Critics*. New Haven: Yale University Press.

Delli Carpini, Michael X., and Scott Keeter. 1996. *What Americans Know about Politics and Why It Matters*. New Haven: Yale University Press.

Dickson, Brian. 2002. "The Couch." Transcript of episode of *Seinfeld*, written by Larry David. Accessed August 1, 2023. https://www.seinfeldscripts.com/TheCouch.html.

Djupe, Paul A., and Christopher P. Gilbert. 2009. *The Political Influence of Churches*. Cambridge: Cambridge University Press.

Domke, David, and Kevin Coe. 2010. *The God Strategy: How Religion Became a Political Weapon in America*, updated ed. New York: Oxford University Press.

Downs, Anthony. 1957. *An Economic Theory of Democracy*. New York: Harper.

Downs, Anthony. 1972. "The Issue-Attention Cycle and the Political Economy of Improving Our Environment." *The Political Economy of Environmental Control*, edited by Anthony Downs, Joe S. Bain, and Warren Frederick Ilchman, 9–34. Berkeley: University of California Press.

Dreyer, Edward C. 1973. "Change and Stability in Party Identifications." *Journal of Politics* 35 (3): 712–22.

Druckman, James N. 2001. "The Implications of Framing Effects for Citizen Competence." *Political Behavior* 23 (3): 225–56.

Druckman, James N., Martin J. Kifer, and Michael Parkin. 2014. "US Congressional Campaign Communications in an Internet Age." *Journal of Elections, Public Opinion and Parties* 24 (1): 20–44.

Druckman, James N., Martin J. Kifer, Michael Parkin, and Ivonne Montes. 2018. "An Inside View of Congressional Campaigning on the Web." *Journal of Political Marketing* 17 (4): 442–75.

Durkee, Alison. 2022. "Disney Says Striking Down 'Don't Say Gay' Law Is Company's Goal After DeSantis Signs Bill." *Forbes*, March 28, 2022. https://www.forbes.com/sites/alisondurkee/2022/03/28/disney-says-striking-down-dont-say-gay-law-is-companys-goal-after-desantis-signs-bill/.

Eagly, Alice H., and Shelly Chaiken. 2007. "The Advantages of an Inclusive Definition of Attitude." *Social Cognition* 25 (5): 582–602.

Edsall, Thomas B. 1992. "GOP Plans a 'Family Values' Offensive." *Washington Post*, August 19, 1992. https://www.washingtonpost.com/archive/politics/1992/08/19/gop-plans-a-family-values-offensive/7a30850d-4d5f-4894-8c55-4da684bfd326/.

Egan, Patrick J. 2020. "Identity as a Dependent Variable: How Americans Shift Their Identities to Align with Their Politics." *American Journal of Political Science* 64 (3): 699–716.

Ekman, Paul. 1992. "An Argument for Basic Emotions." *Cognition and Emotion* 6 (3/4): 169–200.

Engle, Stephen M. 2013. "Frame Spillover: Media Framing and Public Opinion of a Multifaceted LGBT Rights Agenda." *Law & Social Inquiry* 38 (2): 403–41.

BIBLIOGRAPHY

Entman, Robert M. 1993. "Framing: Toward Clarification of a Fractured Paradigm." *Journal of Communication* 43 (4): 51–58.

Epstein, Reid J. 2023. "Liberal Wins Wisconsin Court Race, in Victory for Abortion Rights Backers." *New York Times*, April 4, 2023. https://www.nytimes.com/2023/04/04/us/politics/wisconsin-supreme-court-protasiewicz.html.

Evans, Michael, and Shanna Pearson-Merkowitz. 2012. "Perpetuating the Myth of the Culture War Court? Issue Attention in Newspaper Coverage of US Supreme Court Nominations." *American Politics Research* 40 (6): 1026–66.

Fazio, Russell H. 2007. "Attitudes as Object–Evaluation Associations of Varying Strength." *Social Cognition* 25 (5): 603–37.

Festinger, Leon. 1957. *A Theory of Cognitive Dissonance*. Evanston, IL: Row, Peterson.

Finkel, Stephen E. 1995. *Causal Analysis with Panel Data*. Thousand Oaks, CA: Sage.

Fiorina, Morris P. 1981. *Retrospective Voting in American National Elections*. New Haven: Yale University Press.

Firebaugh, Glenn. 1989. "Methods for Estimating Cohort Replacement Effects." *Sociological Methodology* 19: 243–62.

Firebaugh, Glenn, and Brian Harley. 1991. "Trends in US Church Attendance: Secularization and Revival, or Merely Lifecycle Effects?" *Journal for the Scientific Study of Religion* 30 (4): 487–500.

Fosse, Ethan, and Christopher Winship. 2019. "Analyzing Age-Period-Cohort Data: A Review and Critique." *Annual Review of Sociology* 45: 467–92.

Franklin, Charles H., and John E. Jackson. 1983. "The Dynamics of Party Identification." *American Political Science Review* 77 (4): 957–73.

Freeder, Sean, Gabriel S. Lenz, and Shad Turney. 2019. "The Importance of Knowing 'What Goes with What': Reinterpreting the Evidence on Policy Attitude Stability." *Journal of Politics* 81 (1): 274–90.

Freedman, Samuel G. 1987. "Abortion Bombings Suspect: A Portrait of Piety and Rage." *New York Times*, May 7, 1987.

Froese, Paul, and Christopher Bader. 2010. *America's Four Gods: What We Say About God–and What That Says About Us*. New York: Oxford University Press.

Gadarian, Shana Kushner, and Eric Van der Vort. 2018. "The Gag Reflex: Disgust Rhetoric and Gay Rights in American Politics." *Political Behavior* 40 (2): 521–43.

Galuppo, Mia, Lacey Rose, Mikey O'Connell, and Jackie Strause. 2022. "13 Hollywood Storytellers on Bringing Abortion to the Screen, Then and Now." *The Hollywood Reporter*, July 11, 2022.

Gamson, William A., and Andre Modigliani. 1989. "Media Discourse and Public Opinion on Nuclear Power: A Constructionist Approach." *American Journal of Sociology* 95 (1): 1–37.

Gast, Phil. 2012. "Obama Announces He Supports Same-Sex Marriage." *CNN Politics*, May 9, 2012. https://www.cnn.com/2012/05/09/politics/obama-same-sex-marriage/index.html.

Gerber, Alan, and Gregory Huber. 2010. "Partisanship, Political Control, and Economic Assessments." *American Journal of Political Science* 54 (1): 153–73.

Gibson, Rhona. 2004. "Coverage of Gay Males, Lesbians in Newspaper Lifestyle Sections." *Newspaper Research Journal* 25 (3): 90–95.

GLAAD. n.d. "Pat Robertson." Accessed December 23, 2022. https://glaad.org/gap/pat-robertson/.

GLAAD. 2022. "GLAAD'S 2021–2022 Where We Are on TV Report: LGBTQ Representation Reaches New Record Highs." February 16, 2022. https://glaad.org/glaads-2021-2022-where-we-are-tv-report-lgbtq-representation-reaches-new-record-highs/.

Golan, Guy. 2006. "Inter-Media Agenda Setting and Global News Coverage: Assessing the Influence of the *New York Times* on Three Network Television Evening News Programs." *Journalism Studies* 7 (2): 323–33.

Goodstein, Laurie. 2018. "Billy Graham, 99, Dies; Pastor Filled Stadiums and Counseled Presidents." *New York Times*, February 21, 2018. https://www.nytimes.com/2018/02/21/obituaries/billy-graham-dead.html.

Goren, Paul. 2013. *On Voter Competence*. New York: Oxford University Press.

Goren, Paul, and Christopher Chapp. 2017. "Moral Power: How Public Opinion on Culture War Issues Shapes Partisan Predispositions and Religious Orientations." *American Political Science Review* 111 (1): 110–28.

Goren, Paul, Christopher M. Federico, and Miki Caul Kittilson. 2009. "Source Cues, Partisan Identities, and Political Value Expression." *American Journal of Political Science* 53 (4): 805–20.

Graham, Jesse, Jonathan Haidt, Sena Koleva, Matt Motyl, Ravi Iyer, Sean P. Wojcik, and Peter H. Ditto. 2013. "Moral Foundations Theory: The Pragmatic Validity of Moral Pluralism." *Advances in Experimental Social Psychology* 47:55–130.

Green, Donald Philip, and Bradley Palmquist. 1990. "Of Artifacts and Partisan Instability." *American Journal of Political Science* 34 (3): 872–902.

Green, Donald, Bradley Palmquist, and Eric Schickler. 2002. *Partisan Hearts and Minds*. New Haven: Yale University Press.

Gross, Kimberly. 2008. "Framing Persuasive Appeals: Episodic and Thematic Framing, Emotional Response, and Policy Opinion." *Political Psychology* 29 (2): 169–92.

Guilford, Gwynn. 2016. "Donald Trump's 'Support' of LGBT Communities in One Image." *Quartz*, October 31, 2016. https://qz.com/823649/donald-trump-unfurled-a-rainbow-flag-with-lgbt-written-on-it-at-a-rally-in-greeley-colorado-to-express-his-so-called-support.

Guth, James L., John C. Green, Corwin E. Smidt, Lyman A. Kellstedt, and Margaret M. Poloma. 1997. *The Bully Pulpit: The Politics of Protestant Clergy*. Lawrence: University Press of Kansas.

Haberman, Maggie. 2016. "Donald Trump's More Accepting Views on Gay Issues Set Him Apart in GOP." *New York Times*, April 22, 2016. https://www.nytimes.com/2016/04/23/us/politics/donald-trump-gay-rights.html.

BIBLIOGRAPHY

Haberman, Maggie, and Michael C. Bender. 2022. "The Man Most Responsible for Ending *Roe* Worries That It Could Hurt His Party." *New York Times*, June 24, 2022. https://www.nytimes.com/2022/06/24/us/politics/abortion-ruling-trump.html.

Haidt, Jonathan. 2001. "The Emotional Dog and Its Rational Tail: A Social Intuitionist Approach to Moral Judgment." *Psychological Review* 108 (4): 814–34.

Haidt, Jonathan, Clark McCauley, and Paul Rozin. 1994. "Individual Differences in Sensitivity to Disgust: A Scale Sampling Seven Domains of Disgust Elicitors." *Personality and Individual Differences* 16 (5): 701–13.

Haidt, Jonathan, Paul Rozin, Clark McCauley, and Sumio Imada. 1997. "Body, Psyche, and Culture: The Relationship Between Disgust and Morality." *Psychology and Developing Societies* 9 (1): 107–31.

Hansen, Susan. 2014. *The Politics of Sex: Public Opinion, Parties, and Presidential Elections*. New York: Routledge.

Harding, Susan Friend. 2000. *The Book of Jerry Falwell: Fundamentalist Language and Politics*. Princeton: Princeton University Press.

Hare, Christopher, and Keith T. Poole. 2014. "The Polarization of Contemporary American Politics." *Polity* 46 (3): 411–29.

Harvey, Linda. 2019. "Resolution: Stand Up to 'LGBT' Bullies in 2020." *American Family Association*. Accessed December 6, 2021. https://afa.net/the-stand/culture/2019/12/resolution-stand-up-to-lgbt-bullies-in-2020.

Herek, Gregory M., and John P. Capitanio. 1993. "Public Reactions to AIDS in the United States: A Second Decade of Stigma." *American Journal of Public Health* 83 (4): 574–77.

Hetherington, Marc J., and Jonathan D. Weiler. 2009. *Authoritarianism and Polarization in American Politics*. New York: Cambridge University Press.

Hobolt, Sara B., Thomas J. Leeper, and James Tilley. 2021. "Divided by the Vote: Affective Polarization in the Wake of the Brexit Referendum." *British Journal of Political Science* 51 (4): 1476–93.

Hogg, Michael A. 2002. "Social Categorization, Depersonalization, and Group Behavior." In *Blackwell Handbook of Social Psychology: Group Processes*, edited by Michael A. Hogg and Scott Tindale, 56–85. New York: John Wiley & Sons.

Holpuch, Amanda, and Julie Creswell. 2023. "2 Executives Are on Leave After Bud Light Promotion with Transgender Influences." *New York Times*, April 25, 2023. https://www.nytimes.com/2023/04/25/business/bud-light-dylan-mulvaney.html.

Holt-Lunstad, Julianne, Timothy B. Smith, and J. Bradley Layton. 2010. "Social Relationships and Mortality Risk: A Meta-analytic Review." *PLoS Medicine* 7 (7): e1000316. doi:10.1371/journal.pmed.1000316.

House, J. S., K. R. Landis, and D. Umberson. 1988. "Social Relationships and Health." *Science* 241 (4865): 540–45.

Hout, Michael, and Claude S. Fischer. 2002. "Why More Americans Have No Religious Preference: Politics and Generations." *American Sociological Review* 67 (2): 165–90.

Hout, Michael, and Claude S. Fischer. 2014. "Explaining Why More Americans Have No Religious Preference: Political Backlash and Generational Succession, 1987–2014." *Sociological Science* 1: 423–47.

Huddy, Leonie, Lilliana Mason, and Lene Aarøe. 2015. "Expressive Partisanship: Campaign Involvement, Political Emotion, and Partisan Identity." *American Political Science Review* 109 (1): 1–17.

Hunter, James Davison. 1992. *Culture Wars: The Struggle to Control the Family, Art, Education, Law, and Politics in America*. New York: Basic Books.

Hyman, Herbert. 1959. *Political Socialization: A Study in the Psychology of Political Behavior*. New York: Free Press.

Inbar, Yoel, David A. Pizarro, Joshua Knobe, and Paul Bloom. 2009. "Disgust Sensitivity Predicts Intuitive Disapproval of Gays." *Emotion* 9 (3): 435–39.

Iveson, Kurt. 2011. "Branded Cities: Outdoor Advertising, Urban Governance, and the Outdoor Media Landscape." *Antipode* 44 (1): 151–74.

Iyengar, Shanto, and Donald R. Kinder. 1987. *News That Matters: Television and American Opinion*. Chicago: University of Chicago Press.

Iyengar, Shanto, Gaurav Sood, and Yphtach Lelkes. 2012. "Affect, Not Ideology: A Social Identity Perspective on Polarization." *Public Opinion Quarterly* 76 (3): 405–31.

Jacobson, Gary C. 2019. *Presidents and Parties in the Public Mind*. Chicago: University of Chicago Press.

Jelen, Ted G. 2009. "Religion and American Public Opinion: Social Issues." In *The Oxford Handbook of Religion and American Politics*, edited by Corwin Smidt, Lyman Kellstedt, and James L. Guth, 217–42. New York: Oxford University Press.

Jelen, Ted G., and Clyde Wilcox. 2003. "Causes and Consequences of Public Attitudes toward Abortion: A Review and Research Agenda." *Political Research Quarterly* 56 (4): 489–500.

Jennings, M. Kent, and Richard G. Niemi. 1974. *Political Character of Adolescence: The Influence of Families and Schools*. Princeton: Princeton University Press.

Jennings, M. Kent, and Richard A. Niemi. 1981. *Generations and Politics: A Panel Study of Young Adults and Their Parents*. Princeton: Princeton University Press.

Jennings, M. Kent, Laura Stoker, and Jake Bowers. 2009. "Politics across Generations: Family Transmission Reconsidered." *Journal of Politics* 71 (3): 782–99.

Jetten, Jolanda, Nyla R. Branscombe, S. Alexander Haslam, Catherine Haslam, Tegan Cruwys, Janelle M. Jones, Lijuan Cui, Genevieve Dingle, James Liu, Sean Murphy, Anh Thai, Zoe Walter, and Airong Zhang. 2015. "Having a Lot of a Good Thing: Multiple Important Group Memberships as a Source of Self-Esteem." *PloS One* 10 (5): e0124609.

Johnson, Victoria E. 2008. *Heartland TV: Primetime Television and the Struggle for US Identity*. New York: New York University Press.

Johnston, Richard G. 2006. "Party Identification: Unmoved Mover or Sum of Preferences?" *Annual Review of Political Science* 9:329–51.

Jones, Jim. 1997. "SBC Approves Disney Boycott." *Christianity Today*, July 14, 1997.

Jones, Philip E., Paul R. Brewer, Dannagal G. Young, Jennifer L. Lambe, and Lindsay H. Hoffman. 2018. "Explaining Public Opinion toward Transgender People, Rights, and Candidates." *Public Opinion Quarterly* 82 (2): 252–78.

Jones, Robert P. 2016. *The End of White Christian America*. New York: Simon & Schuster.

Kam, Cindy D., and Beth A. Estes. 2016. "Disgust Sensitivity and Public Demand for Protection." *Journal of Politics* 78 (2): 481–96.

Kane, John V., Lilliana Mason, and Julie Wronski. 2021. "Who's at the Party? Group Sentiments, Knowledge, and Partisan Identity." *Journal of Politics* 83 (4): 1783–99.

Karol, David. 2009. *Party Position Change in American Politics: Coalition Management*. New York: Cambridge University Press.

Katz, Elihu, and Paul F Lazarsfeld. 1955. *Personal Influence: The Part Played by People in the Flow of Mass Communications*. New York: Free Press.

Kennedy, Dana. 1990. "Gay Literature Comes Out of Closet as AIDS Memoirs Proliferate." Associated Press, February 15, 1990.

Kerr, Peter A. 2003. "The Framing of Fundamentalist Christians: Network Television News, 1980–2000." *Journal of Media and Religion* 2 (4): 203–35.

Kerr, Peter A., and Patrica Moy. 2002. "Newspaper Coverage of Fundamentalist Christians, 1980–2000." *Journalism and Mass Communication Quarterly* 79 (1): 54–72.

Key, V. O. 1966. *The Responsible Electorate: Rationality in Presidential Voting, 1936–1960*. Cambridge: Belknap Press.

Killian, Mitchell, and Clyde Wilcox. 2008. "Do Abortion Attitudes Lead to Party Switching?" *Political Research Quarterly* 61 (4): 561–73.

Kinder, Donald R. 1998. "Opinion and Action in the Realm of Politics." In *Handbook of Social Psychology*, 4th ed., edited by Anthony R. Pratkanis, Stephen J. Breckler, and Anthony G. Greenwald, 778–867. Hillsdale, NJ: Lawrence Erlbaum Press.

Kinder, Donald R., and Allison Dale-Riddle. 2012. *The End of Race? Obama, 2008, and Racial Politics in America*. New Haven: Yale University Press.

Kinder, Donald R., and Cindy D. Kam. 2011. *Us Against Them: Ethnocentric Foundations of American Opinion*. Chicago: University of Chicago Press.

Kinder, Donald R., and Nathan P. Kalmoe. 2017. *Neither Liberal nor Conservative: Ideological Innocence in the American Public*. Chicago: University of Chicago Press.

Koleva, Spassena P., Jesse Graham, Ravi Iyer, Petter H. Ditto, and Jonathan Haidt. 2012. "Tracing the Threads: How Five Moral Concerns (Especially Purity) Help Explain Culture War Attitudes." *Journal of Research in Personality* 46 (2): 184–94.

Krosnick, Jon A., and Donald R. Kinder. 1990. "Altering the Foundations of Support for the President Through Priming." *American Political Science Review* 84 (2): 497–512.

Krosnick, Jon A., and Richard E. Petty. 1995. "Attitude Strength: An Overview."

In *Attitude Strength: Antecedents and Consequences*, edited by Richard E. Petty and Jon A. Krosnick, 1–24. Hillsdale, NJ: Lawrence Erlbaum.

Kumar, Anuradha. 2018. "Disgust, Stigma, and the Politics of Abortion." *Feminism and Psychology* 28 (4): 530–38.

Kustov, Alexander, Dillon Laaker, and Cassidy Reller. 2021. "The Stability of Immigration Attitudes: Evidence and Implications." *Journal of Politics* 83 (4): 1478–94.

Lavine, Howard G., Christopher D. Johnston, and Marco R. Steenbergen. 2012. *The Ambivalent Partisan: How Critical Loyalty Promotes Democracy*. New York: Oxford University Press.

Layman, Geoffrey. 2001. *The Great Divide: Religious and Cultural Conflict in American Party Politics*. New York: Columbia University Press.

Lee, Frances E. 2016. *Insecure Majorities: Congress and the Perpetual Campaign*. Chicago: University of Chicago Press.

Lee, Tien-Tsung, and Gary R. Hicks. 2011. "An Analysis of Factors Affecting Attitudes Toward Same-Sex Marriage: Do the Media Matter?" *Journal of Homosexuality* 58 (10): 1391–1408.

Leege, David C., and Lyman A. Kellstedt, eds. 1993. *Rediscovering the Religious Factor in American Politics*. Armonk, NY: M. E. Sharpe.

Lienesch, Michael. 1993. *Redeeming America: Piety and Politics in the New Christian Right*. Chapel Hill: University of North Carolina Press.

Lenz, Gabriel S. 2012. *Follow the Leader: How Voters Respond to Politicians' Policies and Performance*. Chicago: University of Chicago Press.

Levendusky, Matthew. 2009. *The Partisan Sort: How Liberals Became Democrats and Conservatives Became Republicans*. Chicago: University of Chicago Press.

Lindaman, Kara, and Donald P. Haider-Markel. 2002. "Issue Evolution, Political Parties, and the Culture Wars." *Political Research Quarterly* 55 (1): 91–110.

Liu, Edward C., and Wen W. Shen. 2022. "The Hyde Amendment: An Overview." *Congressional Research Service Reports*. https://crsreports.congress.gov/product/pdf/IF/IF12167.

Lodge, Milton, and Charles S. Taber. 2013. *The Rationalizing Voter*. New York: Cambridge University Press.

Love, Robert. 2015. "Bob Dylan Uncut: The Legendary Singer-Songwriter Opens Up about His Creative Process and His Latest Disc." *AARP the Magazine*, February 2, 2015. https://www.aarp.org/entertainment/celebrities/info-2015/bob-dylan-magazine-interview-fans.html.

Luker, Kristin. 1984. *Abortion and the Politics of Motherhood*. Berkeley: University of California Press.

Lutheran Congregations in Mission for Christ. 2020. "LCMC History." Accessed January 4, 2022. https://www.lcmc.net/history.

Mares, Courtney. 2021. "Respect Life: Pope Francis's 8 Strongest Statements Against Abortion." *Catholic News Agency*, October 4, 2021. https://www.catholicnewsagency.com/news/249172/pope-francis-abortion-statements.

Margolis, Michele F. 2018. *From Politics to the Pews: How Partisanship and the Political Environment Shape Religious Identity*. Chicago: University of Chicago Press.

Mason, Lilliana. 2015. "Distinguishing the Polarizing Effects of Ideology as Identity, Issue Positions, and Issue-Based Identity." Paper presented at the Center for the Study of Democratic Politics conference on "Political Polarization: Media and Communication Influences," Princeton University.

Mason, Lilliana. 2018. *Uncivil Agreement: How Politics Became Our Identity*. Chicago: University of Chicago Press.

McCaffrey, Dawn, and Jennifer Keys. 2000. "Competitive Framing Processes in the Abortion Debate: Polarization-Vilification, Frame Saving, and Frame Debunking." *Sociological Quarterly* 41 (1): 41–61.

McCammon, Sarah. 2018. "Looking Back on President George H. W. Bush's Legacy on Abortion." Interview by Mary Louise Kelly. *NPR*, December 4, 2018.

McCann, James A. 1997. "Electoral Choices and Core Value Change: The 1992 Presidential Campaign." *American Journal of Political Science* 41 (2): 545–63.

McCarty, Nolan, Keith T. Poole, and Howard Rosenthal. 2008. *Polarized America: The Dance of Political Ideology and Unequal Riches*. Cambridge: MIT Press.

McGirr, Lisa. 2001. *Suburban Warriors: The Origins of the New American Right*. Princeton: Princeton University Press.

Mifflin, Lawrie. 1999. "Media Talk; Falwell Takes on the Teletubbies." *New York Times*, February 15, 1999. https://www.nytimes.com/1999/02/15/business/media-talk-falwell-takes-on-the-teletubbies.html.

Mirkinson. Jack. 2023. "Homophobia and Transphobia at *The New York Times*." Interview by Jeet Heer. *The Time of Monsters*, March 1, 2023. https://www.thenation.com/podcast/society/tom-mirkinson-nyt/.

Mohammed, Saif M., and Peter D. Turney. 2013. "Crowdsourcing a Word-Emotion Association Lexicon." *Computational Intelligence* 29 (3) 436–65.

Moscowitz, Leigh M. 2010. "Gay Marriage in Television News: Voice and Visual Representation in the Same-Sex Marriage Debate." *Journal of Broadcasting and Electronic Media* 54 (1): 24–39.

Myerson, Allen R. 1997. "Southern Baptist Convention Calls for Boycott of Disney." *New York Times*, June 19, 1997. https://www.nytimes.com/1997/06/19/us/southern-baptist-convention-calls-for-boycott-of-disney.html.

NBC News. 1976. "Flashback: Jimmy Carter Called Abortion 'Wrong' and a 'Failure of Contraceptive Techniques.'" Accessed August 24, 2023. https://www.nbcnews.com/meet-the-press/video/flashback-jimmy-carter-called-abortions-wrong-and-a-failure-of-contraceptive-techniques-143526981824.

New York Times. 2005. "The Words of a Preacher: Billy Graham on His Life, the Pope's Death, and Politics in Religion." *New York Times*, June 12, 2005. https://www.nytimes.com/2005/06/12/us/the-words-of-a-preacher-billy-graham-on-his-life-the-popes-death-and.html.

Nicholson, Stephen P. 2012. "Polarizing Cues." *American Journal of Political Science* 56 (1): 52–66.

Nicholson, Stephen P., Chelsea M. Coe, Jason Emory, and Anna V. Song. 2016. "The Politics of Beauty: The Effect of Partisan Bias on Physical Attractiveness." *Political Behavior* 38 (4): 883–98.

Nielsen. 2016. "Television Is Still Top Brass, but Viewing Differences Vary with Age." Accessed January 6, 2022. https://www.nielsen.com/insights/2016/television -is-still-top-brass-but-viewing-differences-vary-with-age/.

Nielsen. 2019. "Out of Home Advertising Study." Accessed January 3, 2022. https:// www.nielsen.com/news-center/2019/out-of-home-media-as-marketing-strategy/.

Navarro, Mireya. 1995. "Disney's Health Policy for Gay Employees Angers Religious Right in Florida." *New York Times*, November 29, 1995. https://www .nytimes.com/1995/11/29/us/disney-s-health-policy-for-gay-employees-angers -religious-right-inflorida.html.

Oberlin College & Northwestern University. n.d. "Archive It." Accessed January 8, 2022. https://www.archive-it.org/organizations/316.

Olatunji, Bunmi O., Nathan L. Williams, David F. Tolin, Jonathan S. Abramowitz, Craig N. Sawchuk, Jeffrey M. Lohr, and Lisa S. Elwood. 2007. "The Disgust Scale: Item Analysis, Factor Structure, and Suggestions for Refinement." *Psychological Assessment* 19 (3): 281–97.

Olsen, Ted. 2008. "Where Jim Wallis Stands." *Christianity Today*. Accessed April 24, 2023. https://www.christianitytoday.com/ct/2008/may/9.52.html.

Pacheco, Julianna, and Rebecca Kreitzer. 2016. "Adolescent Determinants of Abortion Attitudes: Evidence from the Children of the National Longitudinal Survey of Youth." *Public Opinion Quarterly* 80 (1): 66–89.

Page, Benjamin I., and Robert Y. Shapiro. 1992. *The Rational Public: Fifty Years of Trends in Americans' Policy Preferences*. Chicago: University of Chicago Press.

Patrikios, Stratos. 2008. "American Republican Religion? Disentangling the Causal Link between Religion and Politics in the US." *Political Behavior* 30 (3): 367–89.

Paul Ekman Group. n.d. "Basic Emotions." Accessed August 3, 2023. https://www .paulekman.com/universal-emotions/what-is-disgust/.

Payne, Lee W. 2013. "'If Elected, I [Still] Promise': American Party Platforms— 1980–2008." *Journal of Political Science* 41 (1): 35–62.

Pearson, Kathryn, and Logan Dancey. 2011. "Elevating Women's Voices in Congress: Speech Participation in the House of Representatives." *Political Research Quarterly* 64 (4): 910–23.

Perse, Elizabeth M., Douglas M. McLeod, Nancy Signorielli, and Juliet Dee. 1997. "News Coverage of Abortion Between *Roe* and *Webster*: Public Opinion and Real-World Events." *Communication Research Reports* 14 (1): 97–105.

Pew Research Center. 2016. "Many Americans Hear Politics from the Pulpit." Accessed January 2, 2022. https://www.pewforum.org/2016/08/08/many-americans -hear-politics-from-the-pulpit/.

Pew Research Center. 2019. "Attitudes on Same-Sex Marriage." Accessed January 6, 2022. https://www.pewforum.org/fact-sheet/changing-attitudes-on-gay-marriage/.

Pew Research Center. 2022a. "America's Abortion Quandary." Accessed April 2, 2023. https://www.pewresearch.org/religion/2022/05/06/americas-abortion-quandary/.

Pew Research Center. 2022b. "Majority of Public Disapproves of Supreme Court's Decision to Overturn *Roe v. Wade.*" Accessed July 23, 2023. https://www.pew research.org/politics/2022/07/06/majority-of-public-disapproves-of-supreme -courts-decision-to-overturn-roe-v-wade/#americans-views-of-abortion.

Pew Research Center 2022c. "Public Opinion on Abortion." Accessed January 19, 2024. https://www.pewresearch.org/religion/fact-sheet/public-opinion-on-abortion/.

Politico Magazine. 2016. "The 155 Craziest Things Trump Said This Election." *Politico*, November 5, 2016. https://www.politico.com/magazine/story/2016/11/the -155-craziest-things-trump-said-this-cycle-214420/.

Poole, Keith T., and Howard Rosenthal. 1985. "A Spatial Model for Legislative Roll Call Analysis." *American Journal of Political Science* 29 (2): 357–84.

Price, Vincent, Lilach Nir, and Joseph N. Cappella. 2005. "Framing Public Discussion of Gay Civil Unions." *Public Opinion Quarterly* 69 (2): 179–212.

Prior, Markus. 2019. *Hooked: How Politics Captures People's Interest.* New York: Cambridge University Press.

Putnam, Robert D. 2000. *Bowling Alone: The Collapse and Revival of American Community.* New York: Simon & Schuster.

Putnam, Robert D., and David E. Campbell. 2010. *American Grace: How Religion Divides and Unites Us.* New York: Simon and Schuster.

Radcliffe, Mary, and Amelia Thomson-DeVeaux. 2022. "Abortion Was Always Going to Impact the Midterms." *FiveThirtyEight*, November 17, 2022. https://five thirtyeight.com/features/abortion-was-always-going-to-impact-the-midterms/.

Rhodebeck, Laurie A. 2015. "Another Issue Comes Out: Gay Rights Policy Voting in Recent US Presidential Elections." *Journal of Homosexuality* 62 (6): 701–34.

Richardson, Bradford. 2015. "Planned Parenthood Praises 'Scandal' for Controversial Abortion Episode." *The Hill*, November 20, 2015. https://thehill.com /policy/healthcare/260908-planned-parenthood-praises-scandal-for-controversial -abortion-episode.

Rideout, Victoria. 2008. "Television as a Health Educator: A Case Study of *Grey's Anatomy.*" *Kaiser Family Foundation.* Accessed December 6, 2021. https://www .kff.org/other/television-as-a-health-educator-a-case/.

Rohlinger, Deana A. 2002. "Framing the Abortion Debate: Organizational Resources, Media Strategies, and Movement-Countermovement Dynamics." *Sociological Quarterly* 43 (4): 479–507.

Rozin, Paul, Jonathan Haidt, and Clark R. McCauley. 2008. "Disgust." In *Handbook of Emotions*, edited by Michael Lewis, Jeannette M. Haviland-Jones, and Lisa Feldman Barrett, 757–76. New York: Guilford Press.

Rozin, Paul, Laura Lowery, Sumio Imada, and Jonathan Haidt. 1999. "The CAD

Triad Hypothesis: A Mapping Between Three Moral Emotions (Contempt, Anger, Disgust) and Three Moral Codes (Community, Autonomy, Divinity)." *Journal of Personality and Social Psychology* 76 (4): 574–86.

Rozsa, Matthew. 2019. "Hallmark's Decision to Accept Inclusive LGBTQ Ad 'Further Delegitimizes One Million Moms': GLAAD." *Salon*, December 16, 2019. https://www.salon.com/2019/12/16/hallmarks-decision-to-accept-inclusive-lgbtq-ad-further-delegitimizes-one-million-moms-glaad/.

Ryan, Timothy J. 2014. "Reconsidering Moral Issues in Politics." *Journal of Politics* 76 (2): 380–97.

Ryan, Timothy J. 2017. "No Compromise: Political Consequences of Moralized Attitudes." *American Journal of Political Science* 61 (2): 409–23.

Saperstein, Aliya, and Andrew M. Penner. 2010. "The Race of a Criminal Record: How Incarceration Colors Racial Perceptions." *Social Problems* 57 (1): 92–113.

Saperstein, Aliya, and Andrew M. Penner. 2012. "Racial Fluidity and Inequality in the United States." *American Journal of Sociology* 118 (3): 676–727.

Santoscoy, Carlos. 2015. "Thousands Quit Mormon Church to Protest Anti-Gay Policy." *On Top Magazine*, November 16, 2015. http://www.ontopmag.com/article/21859/Thousands_Quit_Mormon_Church_To_Protest_Anti_Gay_Policy.

Schaller, Mark. 2006. "Parasites, Behavioral Defenses, and the Social Psychological Mechanisms Through Which Cultures Are Evoked." *Psychological Inquiry* 17 (2): 96–137.

Schiappa, Edward, Peter B. Gregg, and Dean E. Hewes. 2006. "Can One TV Show Make a Difference? *Will & Grace* and the Parasocial Contact Hypothesis." *Journal of Homosexuality* 51 (4): 15–37.

Schwadel, Philip. 2010. "Period and Cohort Effects on Religious Nonaffiliation and Religious Disaffiliation: A Research Note." *Journal for the Scientific Study of Religion* 49 (2): 311–19.

Schwadel, Philip, and Christopher R. H. Garneau. 2014. "An Age–Period–Cohort Analysis of Political Tolerance in the United States." *The Sociological Quarterly* 55 (2): 421–52.

Sears, David O. 1983. "The Persistence of Early Political Predispositions: The Roles of Attitude Object and Life Stage." In *Review of Personality and Social Psychology*, vol. 4, edited by L. Wheeler and P. Shaver, 79–116. Beverly Hills, CA: Sage.

Sears, David O., and Christia Brown. 2013. "Childhood and Adult Political Development." In *The Oxford Handbook of Political Psychology*, 2nd ed., edited by Leonie Huddy, David O. Sears, and Jack S. Levy, 59–95. New York: Oxford University Press.

Sears, David O., and Jack Citrin. 1985. *Tax Revolt: Something for Nothing in California*. Enlarged ed. Cambridge: Harvard University Press.

Sears, David O., and Carolyn L. Funk. 1991. "The Role of Self-interest in Social and Political Attitudes." *Advances in Experimental Social Psychology* 24:1–91.

Sears, David O., and Nicholas A. Valentino. 1997. "Politics Matters: Political Events as Catalysts for Preadult Socialization." *American Political Science Review* 91 (1): 45–65.

Sermon Central. 2004. "The Abortion Controversy." Accessed April 5, 2021. https://sermoncentral.com/sermons/the-abortion-controversy-carl-kolb-sermon-on-abortion-65430%20.

Sermon Central. 2008. "A Womb with a View." Accessed April 5, 2021. https://sermoncentral.com/sermons/a-womb-with-a-view-brian-bill-sermon-on-abortion-117481?page=2&wc=800.

Sermon Central. 2015. "The Harm in Same Sex Marriage." Accessed April 5, 2021. https://sermoncentral.com/sermons/the-harm-in-same-sex-marriage-davon-huss-sermon-on-same-sex-marriage-192218?page=1&wc=800.

Sermon Central. 2017. "Homosexuality and the Christian." Accessed April 5, 2021. https://sermoncentral.com/sermons/homosexuality-and-the-christian-sam-mccormick-sermon-on-homosexuality-210716.

Sherkat, Darren E., Melissa Powell-Williams, Gregory Maddox, and Kylan Mattias de Vries. 2011. "Religion, Politics, and Support for Same-Sex Marriage in the United States, 1988–2008." *Social Science Research* 40 (1): 167–80.

Sides, John, Michael Tesler, and Lynn Vavreck. 2018. *Identity Crisis: The 2016 Presidential Campaign and the Battle for the Meaning of America.* Princeton: Princeton University Press.

Simas, Elizabeth N., and Kevin A. Evans. 2011. "Linking Party Platforms to Perceptions of Presidential Candidates' Policy Positions, 1972–2000." *Political Research Quarterly* 64 (4): 831–39.

Sisson, Gretchen, and Katrina Kimport. 2014. "Telling Stories about Abortion: Abortion-Related Plots in American Film and Television, 1916–2013." *Contraception* 89 (5): 413–18.

Sisson, Gretchen, and Katrina Kimport. 2017. "Depicting Abortion Access on American Television, 2005–2015." *Feminism & Psychology* 27 (1): 56–71.

Smith, Kevin B., Douglas Oxley, Matthew V. Hibbing, John R. Alford, and John R. Hibbing. 2011. "Disgust Sensitivity and the Neurophysiology of Left-Right Political Orientations." *PLOS One* 6 (10): e25552.

Smith, Mark A. 2015. *Secular Faith: How Culture Has Trumped Religion in American Politics.* Chicago: University of Chicago Press.

Soroka, Stuart, Lori Young, and Meital Balmas. 2015. "Bad News or Mad News? Sentiment Scoring of Negativity, Fear, and Anger in News Content." *Annals of the American Academy of Political and Social Science* 659 (1): 108–21.

Stark, Rodney, and Charles Y. Glock. 1968. *American Piety: The Nature of Religious Commitment.* Berkeley: University of California Press.

Steensland, Brian, Jerry Z. Park, Mark D. Regnerus, Lynn D. Robinson, W. Bradford Wilcox, and Robert D. Woodberry. 2000. "The Measure of American Religion: Toward Improving the State of the Art." *Social Forces* 79 (1): 291–318.

Stewart, Emily. 2023. "The Bud Light Boycott Explained as Much as Is Possible."

Vox, April 18, 2023. https://www.vox.com/money/2023/4/12/23680135/bud-light-boycott-dylan-mulvaney-travis-tritt-trans.

Stout, David. 2004. "San Francisco City Officials Perform Gay Marriages." *New York Times*, February 12, 2004. https://www.nytimes.com/2004/02/12/national/san-francisco-city-officials-perform-gay-marriages.html.

Stracqualursi, Veronica, Devan Cole, and Paul LeBlanc. 2022. "Voters Deliver Ringing Endorsement of Abortion Rights on Midterm Ballot Initiatives Across the US." *CNN*, November 9, 2022. https://www.cnn.com/2022/11/09/politics/abortion-rights-2022-midterms/index.html.

Sudbay, Joe. 2012. "BREAKING: Barack Obama Supports Marriage Equality." May 9, 2012. Accessed January 12, 2022. https://americablog.com/2012/05/breaking-barack-obama-supports-marriage-equality.html.

Tajfel, Henri. 1970. "Experiments in Intergroup Discrimination." *Scientific American* 223 (5): 96–103.

Tajfel, Henri, M. G. Billig, R. P. Bundy, and Claude Flament. 1971. "Social Categorization and Intergroup Behaviour." *European Journal of Social Psychology* 1 (2): 149–78.

Telford, Taylor. 2023. "Bud Light's Attempt to Market to New Customers Alienated Old Ones." *Washington Post*, April 22, 2023. https://www.washingtonpost.com/business/2023/04/22/bud-light-brand-identity-dylan-mulvaney/.

Terkildsen, Nayda, Frauke I. Schnell, and Cristina Ling. 1998. "Interest Groups, the Media, and Policy Debate Formation: An Analysis of Message Structure, Rhetoric, and Source Cues." *Political Communication* 15 (1): 45–61.

Terrizzi, John A., Natalie J. Shook, and W. Larry Ventis. 2010. "Disgust: A Predictor of Social Conservatism and Prejudicial Attitudes Toward Homosexuals." *Personality and Individual Differences* 49 (6): 587–92.

Tesler, Michael. 2015. "Priming Predispositions and Changing Policy Positions: An Account of When Mass Opinion is Primed or Changed." *American Journal of Political Science* 59 (4): 806–24.

Toff, Benjamin, Ibrahim Abuelyaman, Stephen Anderson, Emma Thompson, and Michaele D. Myers. n.d. "Prime Time Television in Red and Blue: Partisan Divisions in Entertainment." Accessed December 6, 2021. www.benjamintoff.com/prime-time-television-in-red-and-blue/. No longer available.

Tucker, Patrick D., Jacob M. Montgomery, and Steven S. Smith. 2019. "Party Identification in the Age of Obama: Evidence on the Sources of Stability and Systematic Change in Party Identification from a Long-Term Panel Survey." *Political Research Quarterly* 72 (2): 309–28.

Twenge, Jean M., and Andrew B. Blake. 2021. "Increased Support for Same-Sex Marriage in the US: Disentangling Age, Period, and Cohort Effects." *Journal of Homosexuality* 68 (11): 1774–84.

UNT Digital Library. n.d. "Letter from Jerry Falwell on Keeping *Old Time Gospel Hour* on Air." Accessed May 2, 2022. https://digital.library.unt.edu/ark:/67531/metadc177440/.

BIBLIOGRAPHY

U.S. Congress. 1976. *Congressional Record*. 94th Congress, 2nd session. Page 20412.

Valinsky, Jordan. 2023. "More Bad News for Bud Light as Modelo Soars in Sales." *CNN*, August 22, 2023. https://www.cnn.com/2023/08/22/business/bud-light-modelo-2023-sales/index.html.

Verba, Sidney, Kay Lehman Schlozman, and Henry E. Brady. 1995. *Voice and Equality: Civic Voluntarism in American Politics*. Cambridge: Harvard University Press.

Victor, Jennifer Nicoll, and Gina Yannitell Reinhardt. 2018. "Competing for the Platform: How Organized Interests Affect Party Positioning in the United States." *Party Politics* 24 (3): 265–77.

Voss, Brandon. 2019. "Hallmark Pulls Gay Wedding Ads under Pressure from Christian Moms." *Logo*. Accessed January 3, 2022. http://www.newnownext.com/hallmark-gay-lesbian-wedding-one-million-moms-zola/12/2019/.

Wacker, Grant. 2014. *America's Pastor: Billy Graham and the Shaping of a Nation*. Cambridge: Harvard University Press.

Wacker, Grant. 2018. "Introduction." In *American Pilgrim*, edited by Andrew Finstuen, Anne Blue Wills, and Grant Wacker, 1–22. New York: Oxford University Press.

Wald, Kenneth D, Adam L. Silverman, and Kevin S. Fridy. 2005. "Making Sense of Religion in Political Life." *Annual Review of Political Science* 8:121–43.

Weaver, Hilary. 2017. "Ellen DeGeneres's Groundbreaking Coming Out: 20 Years Later." *Vanity Fair*, April 28, 2017. https://www.vanityfair.com/style/2017/04/20th-anniversary-of-ellen-degeneres-coming-out.

Weber, Max. 1930 [2001]. *The Protestant Ethic and the Spirit of Capitalism*. Trans. Talcott Parsons. New York: Routledge Classics.

Weisman, Jonathan. 2022. "GOP Lawmakers Recast Abortion Stance, Wary of Voter Backlash." *New York Times*, May 6, 2022. https://www.nytimes.com/2022/05/06/us/politics/republicans-abortion.html.

Wilcox, Clyde, and Carin Robinson. 2011. *Onward Christian Soldiers? The Religious Right in American Politics*, 4th ed. New York: Routledge.

Wiley, David E., and James A. Wiley. 1970. "The Estimation of Measurement Error in Panel Data." *American Sociological Review* 35 (1): 112–17.

Williams, Daniel K. 2010. *God's Own Party: The Making of the Christian Right*. New York: Oxford University Press.

Winfield, Nicole. 2019. "Pope: Abortion Is Never OK, Equates It to 'Hiring a Hitman.'" Associated Press, May 25, 2019. https://apnews.com/article/pope-francis-europe-ap-top-news-health-religion-5137019e19c5410aa7e2c2b68f21824f.

Winfield, Nicole. 2023. "The AP Interview: Pope Says Homosexuality Not a Crime." Associated Press, January 25, 2023. https://apnews.com/article/pope-francis-gay-rights-ap-interview-1359756ae22f27f87c1d4d6b9c8ce212.

Wolak, Jennifer. 2009. "Explaining Change in Party Identification in Adolescence." *Electoral Studies* 28 (4): 573–83.

Woodruff, Katie. 2019. "Coverage of Abortion in Select US Newspapers." *Women's Health Issues* 29 (1): 80–86.

BIBLIOGRAPHY

Wuthnow, Robert. 1988. *The Restructuring of American Religion: Society*. Princeton: Princeton University Press.

Zaller, John R. 1992. *The Nature and Origins of Mass Opinion*. New York: Cambridge University Press.

Zaller, John, and Stanley Feldman. 1992. "A Simple Theory of the Survey Response: Answering Questions versus Revealing Preferences." *American Journal of Political Science* 36 (3): 579–616.

Zingher, Joshua N. 2022. *Political Choice in a Polarized America*. New York: Oxford University Press.

Index

Page numbers in italics refer to figures.

abortion: changes in collective opinion and, 85–86, *88*, *92*, 93, 190n2; early media coverage of, 41; as a high profile issue, 4; media "framing" and, 42–43; moral emotions related to, 31–33, 75–80; political parties and, 49–51, *50*; survey questions focusing on, 71–72, 171–73, 189n3, 190n2. *See also* moral issues
Abortion Onscreen Database, 56
Abrajano, Marisa, 12, 155
Achen, Christopher, 6, 26, 162
Advancing New Standards in Reproductive Health (ANSIRH), *55*, 56
"age-period-cohort" problem, 88–89
Alphonson, Gwendoline, 41
Americablog, 152
American Family Association, 40
American Grace (Putnam and Campbell), 191n2
American Presidency Project, 45
American Voter, The (Campbell et al.), 128
Associated Press, 45
attitudes. *See* issue/policy attitudes; moral issues; stable attitudes; strong attitudes; weak attitudes
automatic emotional reactions, 9–10, 30–31, 70, 75, 162, 187–88n4. *See also* moral disgust/anger
Axelrod, David, 152

Baker, Joseph, 157
Barber, Michael, 192n1

Barclay, Scott, 41, 54
Bartels, Larry, 26, 162
Baunach, Dawn, 89
beachhead studies, 11
Bean, Lydia, 107
Bennett, Lisa, 41
Bennett, W. L., 53
Biden, Joe, 100, 135
billboards: as a data source, 44–47; moral issues on, 59, *60*. *See also* information environment
bottom-line judgments, 18, 22, 30–31, 40
Boydstun, Amber, 41
Braunstein, Ruth, 99
Breakfast at Tiffany's, 164
Buchanan, Patrick, 131
Bud Light beer, 164
Bush, George H. W., 125, 131–32
Bush, George W., 7, 24, 51
Butler, M. Caldwell, 135

Cahill, Courtney Megan, 43
campaign communications: congressional campaign issues, 46; "family," use of word in, 42; party platforms, 45, 49, *50*, 65; religion and, 108; speeches, 46, *66*; websites, 46, 57–59, *58*, *64*. *See also* information environment
Campbell, Angus, 3, 128
Campbell, David E., 100–101, 191n2
Carsey, Thomas, 193n5
Carter, Jimmy, 125, 131, 160
Chomsky, Daniel, 41, 54

Christian Coalition, 105
Christian sermons, 47, 60–62, *61*, *67*, 68
citizen competence, 161–62
Clinton, Bill, 131–32, 144
Coe, Kevin, 104
cohort replacement: and abortion issues, 87, *88*, *92*, 93; and collective opinion, 86; and gay rights support, 86–92, *88*, 89, *90–91*; measurement strategies for, 190n4, 190n7. *See also* collective opinion
collective opinion: on moral issues, 85–86; "stand patters" vs. "switchers," 93–95, *94*, *175*. *See also* cohort replacement; stability
communication frames: conflict frames, 53, 133; emotive frames, 62–68, *63–67*; use of, 42–43. *See also* media communication
conservative moral disgust: as an automatic emotional response, 9–10, 75; core disgust elicitors and, 75–76; examples of, 33; measurement of, 76, *77*; and party switching, 145–48, *146*; as predictor of moral issue conservatism, 77, 78; socialization and, 30–31, 75–76. *See also* moral disgust/anger
Converse, Phillip, 3, 6, 37–38, 128
Cooperative Congressional Election Studies (CCES) 2012, 2016, 71, 76, 77, 173–74, *174–75*
core identities: changes within, 5, 10, 35–37, 111–13; conflicts with moral issues and, 17–19, 35–37; development of, 25–26, 187n3; moral issues and, 4; stability of, 5; standard social science claim of, 4, 16–18; theory of moral power and, 18, 28–29, 111–13. *See also* identity-to-issue theories
Cottrell, Dana, 59
Crenshaw, Dan, 164
crystallized attitudes. *See* strong attitudes
cultural conservatism: electronic and social media and, 106; other religious figures and, 106; personality traits and, 189n5; religion and, 104–6; testing of, 195n15. *See also* moral issues; Republican Party (GOP)
culture war politics: future of, 162–65; polarization of parties and, 125–28, *126*, 130–36, *133*; rise of, 48–49
Curtis, Valarie, 75

Dahl, Robert, 162
data sources: cross-sectional surveys, 70; panel data, 71; used to test claims, 44–47. *See also* measurement strategy
Daughters of Bilitis, 48
DeGeneres, Ellen, 55
Democracy for Realists (Achen and Bartels), 162
Democratic Party: abortion and, 49–51, *50*; gay rights and, *50*, 51; moral messaging on campaign websites, *58*, 59; moral sorting and, 159–61, *160*; "New Left" platform and, 49; religion and, 8–9
DeSantis, Ron, 164
Disney, 33–34, 56
Dobbs v. Jackson Women's Health Organization, 53, 57–58, 85, *126*, 159, 163–64
Dobson, James, 105
Domke, David, 104
"Don't Say Gay" bill, 164
Dreyer, Edward, 139
Druckman, James, 57
DW-Nominate scores, 134
Dylan, Bob, 1–2

Eilish, Billie, 69
Ellen, 46, 55–56
"enlightened" preferences, 162
entertainment forums (popular film and TV): communication frames in, 43; political rhetoric and, 67; religion and, 108–9; rise of moral issues messaging in, 42; TV plotlines about abortion/gay rights, 31–32, 46, 54–57, *55*, 188n5; TV shows as a data source, 45. *See also* information environment
ER, 54
Estes, Beth, 76, 78
Evangelical Lutheran Church, 111
Evans, Michael, 188n5

Falwell, Jerry, 49, 101, 104–5
Family Ties, 54
Federal Marriage Amendment, 51
Fiorina, Morris, 137, 139
Firebaugh, Glenn, 89
Fischer, Claude, 100–101, 112
Florida Department of Transportation, 46–47
Focus on the Family, 105

INDEX

folk theories of democracy, 11, 13, 162
Follow the Leader (Lenz), 24
Franklin, Charles, 137
Freeder, Sean, 6
Friday Night Lights, 55, 110

Gadarian, Shana Kushner, 78
Garneau, Christopher, 89
Gay & Lesbian Alliance against Defamation (GLAAD), 57
gay rights: changes in collective opinion and, 85–92, *88*, 89, *90–91*, 190n1; early media coverage of, 41; Hallmark channel and, 39; as a high-profile issue, 4; media "framing" and, 42–43; moral emotions related to, 33–35, 75–80; political parties and, *50*, 51; president evaluation and, 7; survey questions focusing on, 72, 171–73, 190n1; terminology and, 187n3; Walt Disney Company and, 33–34. *See also* moral issues
General Social Survey (GSS): 2006–2010, 71, 172; 2008–2012, 5–6, 71, 172; 2010–2014, 71, 172
GOP. *See* Republican Party (GOP)
Gore, Al, 24
Graham, Billy, 1–2, 4, 99, 187n2
Graham, Franklin, 99
Green, John C., 100–101, 191n2
Gregg, Peter, 43
group-centric theories. *See* group identity; theory of moral power
group identity: abortion and gay rights, 8–9; conflict of moral issues and, 17–18; group conflict and, 27; group membership and, 27; group positions and, 8, 10, 26–27; influence on core identity, 26–28; policy positions and, 27–28; theory of moral power and, 12. *See also* identity-to-issue theories

Haberman, Maggie, 3
Hajnal, Zoltan, 12, 155
Hallmark Channel, 39–40
Hansen, Susan, 134–35
Hetherington, Marc, 41
Hewes, Dean, 43
Higgens, Clay, 65
Hill Street Blues, 46
Hout, Michael, 100–101, 112

Human Rights Campaign, 40
Hyde Amendment, 134–35

identities, 4–5. *See also* core identities; group identity; issue/policy attitudes
identity revision, 10. *See also* core identities
identity-to-issue theories: core identities and, 6, 25–26; group positions and, 26–28; party-driven sorting and, 159–61, *160*; public opinion and, 28; theory of moral power and, 12
immigration, 12, 29, 155
information environment: abortion and gay rights messages within, 9, 29–30, 40–41; framing effect in, 42, 62–68, *63–67*; group identity and, 28; moral emotions (disgust/anger) and, 31–35, 39, 62–69; rise of moral issue coverage in, 41, 43–44, 48–62, 70; theory of moral power and, 29–30, 111. *See also* billboards; campaign communications; entertainment forums (popular film and TV); media communication; message volume
Internet Movie Database (IMDb), 45
issue-driven sorting, 15, 143–44, 159–61, *160*
issue/policy attitudes: development of, 8; vs. moral attitudes, 35; voters and, 24; weakness of, 5–6, 193n5
issue-voting theories, 24

Jackson, John, 137
Jelen, Ted, 2

Kalmoe, Nathan P., 38
Kam, Cindy, 76, 78
Kelly, Daniel, 163
Kerr, Peter, 107
"keywords": as a data source, 44–45, 47; word-emotion lexicon as, 48, 63–64
Kid Rock, 164
Kimport, Katrina, 42, 57
Kinder, Donald R., 38

Layman, Geoffrey, 49, 100–101, 191n2, 193n5
Lenz, Gabriel, 6, 24
Library of Congress campaign website archive, 46
Lieu, Ted, 164
Ling, Cristina, 41

220 INDEX

Linguistic Inquiry and Word Count, 108
Lummis, Cynthia, 59
Lutheran Congregations in Mission for Christ, 111

Mason, Lilliana, 35
Masterpiece Cakeshop v. Colorado Civil Rights, 164
Mattachine Society, 48
Maude, 54
McClain, Lisa, 59
McGovern, George, 49
measurement strategy: on attitudes toward abortion/gay rights, 71–72; categorical party ID tests, 145–48, *146*; for continuity and change in party ID, 138–48, *139*, *141*, *143*, *145–46*, *186*, 193–94n7; controls for demographic variables, 113, 190n4, 191n5; definition of progressive vs. moral conservatives, 195n15; disgust sensitivity measure, 76–78, 77; for issue-to party effect, 194–95n14, 194n13; minimizing random measurement error (RME), 71, 148–49, 189n2, 193–94n7; for moral issues on TV shows, 56; of moral issues stability, 80–84, *82*, 189n7; multi-item scales as a, 71, 113; for party ID, 134, *181–86*, 189–90n9, 193n6; for religious ID, 113, *175–81*, 189n8; survey questions focusing on abortion, 71–72, 171–73, 189n3, 190n2; survey questions focusing on gay rights, 72, 171–73, 190n1; use of cross-lagged regression (CLR) models, 113–14, 140–45, *141*, 149–50; use of fixed effects (FE) estimator, 149–50. *See also* data sources
media communication: coverage of HIV/ AIDS crisis, 48, 53–54; emotive language in news coverage, 62–64, *63*; identity-to-issue model and, 28; newspaper articles about moral issues, 45, 51–54, *52*, 132–33, *133*; religion and, 107–8; social media, 69; streaming services and cable, 56; US Supreme Court cases, 53. *See also* information environment
Media Research Center, 55
Meet the Press, 125
message reception: evaluations of, 22–23; about moral issues, 9–10, 29–30, 39;

about political subjects, 22; responses to, 30. *See also* moral disgust/anger
messages. *See* information environment
message volume: on abortion/gay rights issues from political parties, 28, 49–51, *50*, 68, 159; on abortion/gay rights issues in media, 41–42, *133*, 153; religion and, 103–4, 108. *See also* information environment
Miller, Warren, 128
Mirkenson, Jack, 54
Mohammed, Saif, 48
moral disgust/anger: as distinctive to abortion/gay rights, 19–20; and "enlightened" preferences, 162; media "framing" and, 42–43, 62–68, *63–67*; in moral issues messaging, 39–40, 42–43; question wording for measuring, 173–74; scales to measure data about, 70–71; socialization process of, 30–31. *See also* conservative moral disgust; message reception; progressive anger and disgust
moral emotions: in response to moral issues, 19–20. *See also* moral disgust/anger
moral issues: attitudes about, 7, 18, 22, 187n5; changes in public opinion, 95–98, *97*, 101–2; core identities and, 4; cultural conservatism and, 77, 77–78, 104–9; data to measure scales of, 70–71; definition of, 19–20; early advocacy groups for, 48–49; emotions about, 19–20; and "enlightened" preferences, 162; group-based approach and, 8–9; justification of focus on, 19; messages and, 35, 40, 43–44; nonreligious people and, 109–10; vs. other issue attitudes, 11, 35; partisan supporters and, 2–3; party ID and, 140–48, *141*, *143*, *145–46*, *181–86*; in party platforms, 49–51, *50*, 125–28, *126*; political evaluation of, 40; public opinion on, *73–74*, 188–89n1; question wording for measurement of, 171–73; stability of, 80–84, *82*. *See also* abortion; gay rights; religion
Moral Majority, 104–5
Mormon Church, 112
Moy, Patricia, 107
Mulvaney, Dylan, 164

National Abortion Rights Action League, 48
National Association for the Repeal of Abortion Laws (NARAL), 163

INDEX

National Conference of Catholic Bishops, 48

National Election Study (NES): 1992–1996, 71, 171; 2000–2004, 71, 171; 2016–2020, 71, 172

National Organization for Women, 42, 110

National Research Council (NRC), 48, 63–67

New Christian Right (NCR), 130, 160–61. *See* Religious Right

newspaper articles. *See* media communication

Newsweek, 41

New York Times, 41, 45, 54

Nielsen ratings, 45

Obama, Barack, 7, 152

Obergefell v. Hodges, 53, *126*

Old Time Gospel Hour, 105

Omar, Ilhan, 64

One Million Moms, 39

opinion leadership, 106–7

party-driven sorting, 15, 142–44, 159–61, *160*

party identification (party ID): definition of, 21–22, 128–29; issue attitudes and, 3, 194n13–194n14; issue-proximity theories and, 137–38; moral issues and, 140–48, *141*, *143*, *145–46*, *181–86*; party messaging, *133*, 133–34; party revision theories and, 37; polarization of, 134–36; policy positions and, 27–28, 125–28, *126*; and public opinion, 129–30; religion and, 118–19, 130–32, *177*, 191n1; revisionist theories of, 136–38; stability of, 5, 138; testing of continuity and change in, 138–48, *139*, *143*, *145–46*, *186*, 193n5, 195n16; theory of moral power and, 12, 138, 140

party platforms. *See* campaign communications

party ties, 21–22. *See also* party identification (party ID)

Pearson-Merkowitz, Shanna, 188n5

Perse, Elizabeth, 41

Pew Research Center, 85–87

Planned Parenthood, 55

policy attitudes. *See* issue/policy attitudes

political identities. *See* party identification (party ID)

political messages. *See* information environment; media communication

political rhetoric, 43

Politico Magazine, 2–3

Poole, Keith, 134

Pope, Jeremy, 192n1

Pope, Olivia, 54

Pope Francis, 106, 110

popular film/TV. *See* entertainment forums (popular film and TV)

Portrait of American Life Study (PALS), 2006–2012, 71, 172–73

progressive anger and disgust: definition of, 10; disgust treatment and, 78–80; messages and, 33; party switching and, 145–48, *146*; socialization and, 31, 78. *See also* moral disgust/anger

Protasiewicz, Janet, 163

Protestant Ethic and the Spirit of Capitalism, The (Weber), 123

Public Broadcasting Service (PBS), 105

public opinion: on moral issue conservatism, 75–78, *77*; on moral issues 1992–2016, *73–74*; on progressive anger and disgust, 78–80

public opinion theories, 7–8. *See also* identity-to-issue theories

Putnam, Robert, 191n2

Reagan, Ronald, 1, 49, 131

religion, 123; campaign websites and, 108; conflict with moral issues and, 11, 16–17, 36–37, 111–13; and the conservative social view, 49, 104–9; definition of, 20; entertainment forums and, 108–9; media and, 107–8; opinion leadership in, 106–7; politics and, 8–9, 11, 123–24, 191n1; religious exit, 11, 112, 114–23, *115*, *117*, 157–59, *158*, 192n9. *See also* religious identity (religious ID); religious "nones"

religious exemption laws, 164. *See also* gay rights

religious identity (religious ID): backlash on, 2, 36–37, 103–4, 157; definition of, 21, 102; identity strength and, 21, 102, 119–23, *120–21*, *179–80*, 189n8; moral issues and, 2, 114, *115*, *175–81*, 191n2, 191n9; religious belonging and, 20; and the standard religious ID to issues model, 103, 114, *115*. *See also* religion religious "nones": definition of, 20; focus on, 21; rise of, 99–102, *100*, 157–59, *158*. *See also* religion

Religious Right, 99–102, 104, 119, 121, 125, 127, 131, 157

Republican Party (GOP): abortion and, 49–51, *50*; culturally conservative voters and, 49, 189n5; gay rights and, *50*, 51; liberalism and, 194n12; moral messaging on campaign websites, *58*, 59; moral sorting and, 159–61, *160*; religion and, 8–9, 130–32

response instability, 6, 23–24. *See also* stability

Roberts, John, 162

Robertson, Pat, 101, 105–6

Roe v. Wade, 41–42, 48–50, 53, 57, 69, 131–32

Rohlinger, Deana, 42

Rosenthal, Abe, 54

Rosenthal, Howard, 134

Ryan, Timothy, 20

Scandal, 54–55

Schiappa, Edward, 43

Schiavo, Terri, 41

Schnell, Frauke, 41

Schwadel, Philip, 89

Seinfeld, 31–32, 188n5

Sermon Central, 47, *61*, 62, 188n3, 188n7

sermons, 47, 60–62, *61*, *67*, 68

700 Club, 106

Sisson, Gretchen, 42, 56–57

Smith, Buster, 157

social categorization, 110

socialization (of moral issues), 30–31

Sojourners, 106

Southern Baptist Convention, 56

stability: discussions of, 13–15; measurement of, 81–84, 189n7; and the micro-macro paradoxes on moral issues, 93–95; of moral issues, 80–84, *82*, 98; of policy attitudes, 5–6; property of, 5. *See also* collective opinion; party identification (party ID); response instability

stable attitudes, 7, 14, 23, 84. *See also* response instability

"stand patters" vs. "switchers," 86, 93–95, *94*, *139*, 140, *175*. *See also* collective opinion

Stenberg v. Carhart, 43

Stewart, Justice Potter, 47

Stokes, Donald, 3, 128

strong attitudes: message reception and, 22–23, 30, 188–89n1; moral issues and, 18; political attitudes as, 22; theory of moral power and, 7, 28–29

Sudbay, Joe, 152

Supreme Court, US, 43, 53, 188n5

Swift, Taylor, 69

Teletubbies, 105

Terkildsen, Nayda, 41

Tesler, Michael, 7

theory of moral power: additional questions for testing about, 155–57; challenges to, 98, 195n4; claims of, 4, 11–13, 18, 28–29, 37–38; core identities and, 28–29, 111–13; vs. folk theories of democracy, 11, 13; group approach and, 9–11; information environment and, 29–30, 111; issue-driven sorting and, 159–61, *160*; party ID and, 127–28, 149; principal findings, 153–55; religion and, 111–17; strong attitudes and, 28–29

Thomas, Clarence, 164

Thompson, Anne, 47

Time, 41

Tinky Winky, 105

Toff, Benjamin, 57

transgender rights, 155, 164, 188n1

Tritt, Travis, 164

Trone, David, 59

Trump, Donald, 1–4, 144–45, 153, 163, 192–93n1

Turney, Shad, 6

US Supreme Court, 43, 53, 188n5

Vanderbilt University, 76

van der Vort, Eric, 78

Wallis, Jim, 106

Walt Disney Company, 33–34, 56

Warren, Rick, 106

Washington Post, 41, 45

weak attitudes, 5, 11, 23–25, 37, 159

Weber, Max, 123

Weiler, Jonathan, 41

INDEX

Wendy's, 56
West Wing, The, 54, 188n6
Weyrich, Paul, 49
Will and Grace, 43, 56

Women and the American Humanist Association, 110
word-emotion lexicon, 48, 63–65

Chicago Studies in American Politics

A SERIES EDITED BY SUSAN HERBST, LAWRENCE R. JACOBS, ADAM J. BERINSKY, AND FRANCES LEE; BENJAMIN I. PAGE, EDITOR EMERITUS

Series titles, continued from front matter:

RADICAL AMERICAN PARTISANSHIP: MAPPING VIOLENT HOSTILITY, ITS CAUSES, AND THE CONSEQUENCES FOR DEMOCRACY *by Nathan P. Kalmoe and Lilliana Mason*

THE OBLIGATION MOSAIC: RACE AND SOCIAL NORMS IN US POLITICAL PARTICIPATION *by Allison P. Anoll*

A TROUBLED BIRTH: THE 1930S AND AMERICAN PUBLIC OPINION *by Susan Herbst*

POWER SHIFTS: CONGRESS AND PRESIDENTIAL REPRESENTATION *by John A. Dearborn*

PRISMS OF THE PEOPLE: POWER AND ORGANIZING IN TWENTY-FIRST-CENTURY AMERICA *by Hahrie Han, Elizabeth McKenna, and Michelle Oyakawa*

DEMOCRACY DECLINED: THE FAILED POLITICS OF CONSUMER FINANCIAL PROTECTION *by Mallory E. SoRelle*

RACE TO THE BOTTOM: HOW RACIAL APPEALS WORK IN AMERICAN POLITICS *by LaFleur Stephens-Dougan*

THE LIMITS OF PARTY: CONGRESS AND LAWMAKING IN A POLARIZED ERA *by James M. Curry and Frances E. Lee*

AMERICA'S INEQUALITY TRAP *by Nathan J. Kelly*

GOOD ENOUGH FOR GOVERNMENT WORK: THE PUBLIC REPUTATION CRISIS IN AMERICA (AND WHAT WE CAN DO TO FIX IT) *by Amy E. Lerman*

WHO WANTS TO RUN? HOW THE DEVALUING OF POLITICAL OFFICE DRIVES POLARIZATION *by Andrew B. Hall*

FROM POLITICS TO THE PEWS: HOW PARTISANSHIP AND THE POLITICAL ENVIRONMENT SHAPE RELIGIOUS IDENTITY *by Michele F. Margolis*

THE INCREASINGLY UNITED STATES: HOW AND WHY AMERICAN POLITICAL BEHAVIOR NATIONALIZED *by Daniel J. Hopkins*

LEGACIES OF LOSING IN AMERICAN POLITICS *by Jeffrey K. Tulis and Nicole Mellow*

LEGISLATIVE STYLE *by William Bernhard and Tracy Sulkin*

WHY PARTIES MATTER: POLITICAL COMPETITION AND DEMOCRACY IN THE AMERICAN SOUTH *by John H. Aldrich and John D. Griffin*

NEITHER LIBERAL NOR CONSERVATIVE: IDEOLOGICAL INNOCENCE IN THE AMERICAN PUBLIC *by Donald R. Kinder and Nathan P. Kalmoe*

STRATEGIC PARTY GOVERNMENT: WHY WINNING TRUMPS IDEOLOGY *by Gregory Koger and Matthew J. Lebo*

POST-RACIAL OR MOST-RACIAL? RACE AND POLITICS IN THE OBAMA ERA *by Michael Tesler*

THE POLITICS OF RESENTMENT: RURAL CONSCIOUSNESS IN WISCONSIN AND THE RISE OF SCOTT WALKER *by Katherine J. Cramer*

LEGISLATING IN THE DARK: INFORMATION AND POWER IN THE HOUSE OF REPRESENTATIVES *by James M. Curry*

WHY WASHINGTON WON'T WORK: POLARIZATION, POLITICAL TRUST, AND THE GOVERNING CRISIS *by Marc J. Hetherington and Thomas J. Rudolph*

WHO GOVERNS? PRESIDENTS, PUBLIC OPINION, AND MANIPULATION *by James N. Druckman and Lawrence R. Jacobs*

TRAPPED IN AMERICA'S SAFETY NET: ONE FAMILY'S STRUGGLE *by Andrea Louise Campbell*

ARRESTING CITIZENSHIP: THE DEMOCRATIC CONSEQUENCES OF AMERICAN CRIME CONTROL *by Amy E. Lerman and Vesla M. Weaver*

HOW THE STATES SHAPED THE NATION: AMERICAN ELECTORAL INSTITUTIONS AND VOTER TURNOUT, 1920–2000 *by Melanie Jean Springer*

WHITE-COLLAR GOVERNMENT: THE HIDDEN ROLE OF CLASS IN ECONOMIC POLICY MAKING *by Nicholas Carnes*

HOW PARTISAN MEDIA POLARIZE AMERICA *by Matthew Levendusky*

CHANGING MINDS OR CHANGING CHANNELS? PARTISAN NEWS IN AN AGE OF CHOICE *by Kevin Arceneaux and Martin Johnson*

THE POLITICS OF BELONGING: RACE, PUBLIC OPINION, AND IMMIGRATION *by Natalie Masuoka and Jane Junn*

TRADING DEMOCRACY FOR JUSTICE: CRIMINAL CONVICTIONS AND THE DECLINE OF NEIGHBORHOOD POLITICAL PARTICIPATION *by Traci Burch*

POLITICAL TONE: HOW LEADERS TALK AND WHY *by Roderick P. Hart, Jay P. Childers, and Colene J. Lind*

LEARNING WHILE GOVERNING: EXPERTISE AND ACCOUNTABILITY IN THE EXECUTIVE BRANCH *by Sean Gailmard and John W. Patty*

THE SOCIAL CITIZEN: PEER NETWORKS AND POLITICAL BEHAVIOR *by Betsy Sinclair*

FOLLOW THE LEADER? HOW VOTERS RESPOND TO POLITICIANS' POLICIES AND PERFORMANCE *by Gabriel S. Lenz*

THE TIMELINE OF PRESIDENTIAL ELECTIONS: HOW CAMPAIGNS DO (AND DO NOT) MATTER *by Robert S. Erikson and Christopher Wlezien*

ELECTING JUDGES: THE SURPRISING EFFECTS OF CAMPAIGNING ON JUDICIAL LEGITIMACY *by James L. Gibson*

DISCIPLINING THE POOR: NEOLIBERAL PATERNALISM AND THE PERSISTENT POWER OF RACE *by Joe Soss, Richard C. Fording, and Sanford F. Schram*

THE SUBMERGED STATE: HOW INVISIBLE GOVERNMENT POLICIES UNDERMINE AMERICAN DEMOCRACY *by Suzanne Mettler*

SELLING FEAR: COUNTERTERRORISM, THE MEDIA, AND PUBLIC OPINION *by Brigitte L. Nacos, Yaeli Bloch-Elkon, and Robert Y. Shapiro*

WHY PARTIES? A SECOND LOOK *by John H. Aldrich*

OBAMA'S RACE: THE 2008 ELECTION AND THE DREAM OF A POST-RACIAL AMERICA *by Michael Tesler and David O. Sears*

NEWS THAT MATTERS: TELEVISION AND AMERICAN OPINION, UPDATED EDITION *by Shanto Iyengar and Donald R. Kinder*

FILIBUSTERING: A POLITICAL HISTORY OF OBSTRUCTION IN THE HOUSE AND SENATE *by Gregory Koger*

US AGAINST THEM: ETHNOCENTRIC FOUNDATIONS OF AMERICAN OPINION *by Donald R. Kinder and Cindy D. Kam*

THE PARTISAN SORT: HOW LIBERALS BECAME DEMOCRATS AND CONSERVATIVES BECAME REPUBLICANS *by Matthew Levendusky*

DEMOCRACY AT RISK: HOW TERRORIST THREATS AFFECT THE PUBLIC *by Jennifer L. Merolla and Elizabeth J. Zechmeister*

IN TIME OF WAR: UNDERSTANDING AMERICAN PUBLIC OPINION FROM WORLD WAR II TO IRAQ *by Adam J. Berinsky*

AGENDAS AND INSTABILITY IN AMERICAN POLITICS, SECOND EDITION *by Frank R. Baumgartner and Bryan D. Jones*

THE PARTY DECIDES: PRESIDENTIAL NOMINATIONS BEFORE AND AFTER REFORM *by Marty Cohen, David Karol, Hans Noel, and John Zaller*

THE PRIVATE ABUSE OF THE PUBLIC INTEREST: MARKET MYTHS AND POLICY MUDDLES *by Lawrence D. Brown and Lawrence R. Jacobs*

SAME SEX, DIFFERENT POLITICS: SUCCESS AND FAILURE IN THE STRUGGLES OVER GAY RIGHTS *by Gary Mucciaroni*